W9-BRD-790

Interior

THE BUSINESS OF DESIGN
PROVEN MARKETING SECRETS TO ATTRACT MORE CLIENTS, MAKE MORE MONEY, HAVE MORE FREEDOM, AND LOVE BEING A DESIGNER!

Vita Vygovska MBA, CWFP

Foreword by **David Shepherd**
President & CEO, Designing Profits, Inc.

Library of Congress Control Number:

ISBN-10   0615390803
ISBN-13   9780615390802

Printed in the United States of America

FOREWORD
by David Shepherd

I'd like to ask you three questions.

First, do you think you could defeat Viswanathan Anand – the current world chess champion – in a game of chess?

No? Well now let's do a little time traveling and imagine that when Mr. Anand was four years old his parents had put a golf club in his hands instead of a chess piece. And assume that, at about the same time, your parents taught you chess, which you then practiced for several hours a day, 300-plus days a year…for decades.

Now who wins the chess match between you and Mr. Anand?

The difference is clearly not talent (that's almost unknowable) but rather the practice of known techniques. Repetition. Perseverance. And most of all, a cult-like dedication to the fundamentals that are proven precursors of success.

My next question is multiple-choice. Which of the following interior designers do you think would be more successful, financially?
A) an enormously talented designer who was completely incompetent at marketing, or:
B) a relentless and fearless marketing machine with only average design talent

I'm going to save my third question for the end, but the professor in me can't resist a quick review. Unless I miss my guess, I've easily convinced you that you could rise to the top of almost any field with enough practice, and that if you want to be successful, much of that practice should be in the realm of marketing.

So imagine my pleasure when I was asked to pen the Foreword for a book that so exquisitely combines these key principles.

In *The Business of Design,* readers are presented with highly focused action items guaranteed to increase their client base and revenue.

5

Some of this advice you've undoubtedly heard before, such as getting involved, networking, word-of-mouth marketing, and using newsletters. But why would any serious businesswoman or businessman ever tire of that which is known to work?

Some of the advice is new, including one of the clearest explanations I've yet read as to the role of Facebook, Twitter, and the like.

And some of the advice is so old that it's completely new again, including innovative and exiting applications of trunk shows, speaking opportunities, and advice on how to get published.

Each of these practical strategies (and I emphasize *practical!*) could grow into a book of its own. But hats off to the authors – all of whom are proven successes in the design world – for resisting that temptation. The genius of this work is that it avoids page-filling bulk in favor of razor-sharp action steps. (Did I mention that they are proven to work?)

If you want to snag only those strategies that you think will have the highest impact on your current situation, you should know that editor Vitalia Vygovska thought of that as well. She provides a helpful system for getting organized and setting your unique priorities.

And if you want more, contact information is provided for each author, and each expert offers a wealth of additional resources to help you succeed.

Now, are you ready for my third and final question? Well, the truth is that your parents didn't put a chess piece in your hand when you were four years old. In other words, if you haven't been practicing these techniques for the past few years, you may feel a sense of regret when you think about where you'd be today if you had. You may have a Homer Simpson moment or two. (*"Doh! I know that! Why did I stop doing that? Why aren't I doing that?"*)

So here's the third question: If you commit to the principles in this book today, how old will you be when the success you crave finally comes your way?

The answer is, the same age you'll be if you don't commit today.

The only difference is your success.

David Shepherd, MBA, is president and CEO of Designing Profits, Inc. His firm produces the annual Business of Design Conference and manages the industry's Best Practices Network (BPN) for interior designers. He is a long-time faculty member of the McCombs School of Business at the University of Texas at Austin and author of <u>Your Business or Your Life: 8 Steps for Getting All You Want out of BOTH,</u> an Amazon best-seller and the source of a seminar attended by over 2,000 interior designers. The 8 Steps are now available in a home study course on DVD. (Find out more at <u>www.designingprofits.com</u>.)*

CONTENTS

INTRODUCTION
by Vitalia Vygovska

My name is Vitalia (Vita) Vygovska, and I'd like to explain how this book came into being.

You see, I saw a real need for this information, easily accessible by and available to all designers worldwide. Why? Because nothing exactly like this exists in our industry. I could find no comprehensive source of marketing information that tells designers exactly what to do and how to do it.

Sure, there are other books on marketing. Sure, there are other books in the design industry. But in my research, there wasn't a single one that goes in as much detail and specifics on marketing as this one. I didn't want to write just another book that simply talks about the importance of marketing – we all know that it's important. I didn't want to give you just another list of marketing activities – we all have enough to do already.

Instead I wanted to write a book that every designer can use as a permanent reference manual – a source that you can refer to on a regular basis, based on the stage of your business at a particular time. And every time you use it, I want you to walk away knowing exactly what to do and how to do it.

I did it for you, because it wasn't available when I needed it for myself.

My Story

I am a wife, a mom, and an entrepreneur. I am the owner of Vitalia Inc., a window treatment firm, and a productivity expert. I've helped countless customers, completed hundreds of installations, attended many seminars, participated in designer showhouses, won awards, made my share of mistakes, and learned from them. Through it all, I developed my own systematic and organized approach for running a productive and profitable design business.

But it wasn't always like that. My path to entrepreneurship began in

9

corporate America. After getting my degree in marketing and fashion merchandising, I went to work for Burlington Coat Factory as a retail buyer. Then I found my passion as a marketing director for Lenox China, where I managed million-dollar P&L's (profit and loss) and ran a marketing department.

And although life was seemingly great, I wanted to be more productive with my time, talents, and energies. I wanted to go out and create my life and future.

So that's exactly what I did in 2005. I started my own business, full of zeal and energy. But zeal and energy can get you only so far. Soon enough, I felt very frustrated with this business and industry in general. I thought to myself: "How hard can it be – I've run multi-million-dollar corporate businesses before." But I found myself feeling constantly worried and even anxious. "What if the design doesn't turn out as it was envisioned? What if something goes wrong – how do I protect myself? How do I market myself? When am I supposed to work ON my business if I can barely keep up working IN my business? Why does it feel so lonely?"

It seemed so unproductive. I worried so much. There were sleepless nights, stress, frustration. I know all of this sounds familiar to you. I know, because I've been there. I felt it. I lived and breathed it. And as I did, I knew in my heart that there had to be a better way – a better way to run a business, a better way to live a life. So I gathered everything I learned through the school of hard knocks, combined it with corporate-America training, added my formal marketing degrees, and relied on my ability to be organized and productive. The result was my own systematized approach to running a successful, profitable, and productive design business.

Now I'm Sharing It with the World

For the purposes of this book, I didn't want you to hear it from just me. So I invited the best experts in our industry to share their secrets about their respective areas. In total, this book includes presentations by 10 experts covering 10 different marketing areas:
1. Traditional networking
2. Referrals and testimonials
3. Speaking
4. Online marketing

5. Social media
6. Outside-of-the-box promotions
7. PR and awards
8. Direct marketing
9. Partnerships
10. Personal branding

From this list alone you can see how comprehensive this book is. Each area of marketing is represented by a different chapter, in which the author walks you through the what, the why, and the how. Each one gives you exact directions, examples, and action points.

Think of all 10 strategies as "slices" of your "marketing pie."

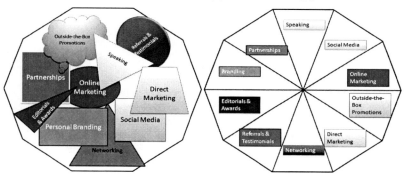

For some of you, this "marketing pie" may be a full-blown, active, and dynamic way that you already run your business. In this case, congratulations! I commend you on a job well done. And yet I still encourage you to read on, because I am sure you will get more ideas and tips to make your marketing even better.

For some of you, this "marketing pie" is more like some half-cooked foreign cuisine with missing ingredients. Please don't get discouraged. First of all, you're in the right place by reading this book. Second of all, take comfort in knowing that not all has to be done at once. Know that this is your reference manual. And this means that even though you may not be making use of all the slices yet, there will be a time that you will. That will be the time to pick up the book again and re-read the section that's become more timely and relevant for you.

The very last chapter is directly from me, and that chapter pulls it all together. There I give you ways to prioritize your tasks and not get overwhelmed. You will walk away feeling that you have a comprehensive

11

plan of action, with distinct and realistic priorities. You will also walk away with a hopeful outlook that you will be able to get it all done.

Best Way to Read This Book

In order to get to this hopeful place, I want you to follow very simple steps as you begin reading.

Step #1: Find a quiet place where you can concentrate. Although the book is an easy read, it is packed with essential information and valuable tips that you will want to remember. It is not a suspense novel that you read on a StairMaster at the gym and forget about as soon as you turn the page. Everything here is practical and actionable. To process it (and more importantly, to assimilate it into your business), you will want to concentrate as you read it.

Step #2: Get out a highlighting pen. Start highlighting anything that you find useful, that made a special impact on you, that you want to refer to later. Use the book as a training manual – your own personal reference bible that you will keep and go back to over and over again.

Step #3: Get out a red pen. Use it when you see an idea that you want to implement in your business. Put an arrow in the margin next to this idea. This arrow is your indication that it is an actionable item. This is something that you would love to see happen for you in your own design business; it's something that you can get behind, and get excited about.

At the end of your read, you will have a LOT of new, great knowledge. This "red arrow" strategy sets you up for success from the very beginning, so that you are ready to spring into action.

Closing Thoughts

What you learn as a result of reading this book will change altogether the way you market your business, and even run it. Be an active reader: Highlight, underline, make notes, put arrows, check out websites, and take advantage of additional resources that authors give you.

But more important, be ready to be an active implementer. When you're finished reading all 10 chapters, be ready to hit the ground running to put into action what you've just learned.

Happy reading! I'll "see" you again at the end of this book.

12

1
TRADITIONAL NETWORKING:
The Power of
Face-to-Face Marketing

by Anna Jacoby
www.annajacobyinteriors.com

In this chapter you'll learn:

How to get yourself noticed by your ideal clients
*The best places to devote your networking
time and resources*
7 key strategies for networking success!

Networking Is NOT Selling

Networking is not about selling. Networking is about building relationships. Since people tend to do business with those they know, like, and trust, the more people you can meet and the more relationships you can build, the more clients you will have. You want to give people multiple opportunities to get to know you. Once they know you, they will do business with you and also refer you to people they know.

There are three major areas on which you should focus your networking efforts:

1. Social groups: where your ideal clients are
2. The business community
3. Your own industry

Networking Where Your Ideal Clients Are

How do you find out where your ideal clients are? First you have to establish who your ideal clients are. Where do they shop? What are they interested in? What are their hobbies?

> ### ◉ Action Item!
>
> Focus your networking efforts in these 3 areas:
> 1. Social groups
> 2. The business community
> 3. Your own industry

What are their ages? What is their income level? Where do they live? Does your ideal client have children? Pets? If you sat down and wrote a description of your ideal client, what would it say? The more specific you can be, the better. For example, my ideal clients are people generally like me: they have children; they are between 40 and 65 years of age; they are interested in decorating and in having a nice home; they are involved in their local community; they are not necessarily high-income, although they do have some disposable income and like to use some of it for home improvement.

To meet your ideal clients, I would suggest becoming involved in social groups, such as book clubs, Bunco clubs, church groups, PTA, community groups, charitable organizations, yoga or exercise classes, and country clubs. I take yoga, for example, and I've gotten to know many of the people in the classes. My yoga instructor recently referred me to a friend of hers who was redecorating her home, and two or three others in the class have hired me as well. These referrals came to me without my even trying. Just by getting involved and meeting people, I was able to grow my client base.

If you have children, becoming involved in school or sports is a great way to meet people and expand your circle. Through my kids, I've gotten to know a lot of people, many who have ultimately utilized my services. Sponsoring my son's baseball team, for example, being a room mom at school, being PTA president – all of these activities gave me opportunities to put myself in front of people, and also gave them opportunities to get to know me. Eventually, when they need your service, they will automatically think of you first because they know you, like you, and trust you.

Networking within the Business Community

To grow your business, I strongly recommend joining business-related organizations like your local Chamber of Commerce. There are many organizations you can consider joining. Some examples include American Business Women's Association (ABWA), Realtor associations, and leads groups like Business Networking International (BNI) and Le Tip.

Joining these kinds of groups enables you to expand your circle and your potential client base by meeting many new people, and also to get to know other business owners – they might have resources that you or your clients need. They will be able to refer you to their clients, and you will be able to reciprocate and refer them to your clients.

Great Tip!

Join groups such as Chamber of Commerce, ABWA, Realtor associations, BNI, or Le Tip.

Leads groups are designed specifically for generating and trading sales leads and referrals between group members. Generally only one type of business is allowed in each group. For example, a leads group will allow one Realtor, one interior designer, one insurance salesperson, and so forth. This is to help build loyalty

15

among the members. Most meet on a weekly basis, while some meet less often, such as every two weeks, or once per month. Group members have the opportunity to introduce themselves at each meeting and talk for a few minutes about their business. There is also usually a topic of discussion or a guest speaker as part of the meeting.

Once again, it all goes back to the idea that people do business with those they know, like, and trust. And the more you're involved in these kinds of groups, the greater your results will be.

Networking within Your Own Industry

The third place to focus your networking energy is within your own industry. Join groups like IRIS (Interior Redesign Industry Specialists), or IDS (Interior Design Society), or NARI (National Association of the Remodeling Industry), just to name a few. By joining industry-related groups, you will find camaraderie and support, as well as many learning opportunities.

Belonging to an industry-related networking group can actually yield a good number of clients for you. This is because different group members specialize in different services, and as they get to know you, they will refer you for jobs that are beyond their scope of services. For example, I recently got an email from someone who was looking for a vacant-home stager. Because of my involvement in our local IRIS chapter, I was able to refer her to a colleague who specializes in vacant-home staging. Some specialize in window treatments, while others focus on color consultations. So when a designer needs assistance with a particular type of service, they will call you.

Great Tip!

Joining an industry-related networking group can bring you clients!

Within these industry-related groups, you can get to know flooring people, tile installers, painters – all of those people can be a potential source of clients for you. And they can also be great service providers and resources for you and your clients.

Strategies for Networking Success

1. Join one group per category, and get involved!

You could spend your whole life going from group to group to group. So I would recommend joining one group per category: one social group, one business-related group, and one industry-related group. Start there and see if you can add another group later. Select a group where you can really get involved. It doesn't do much good just to be a member, sitting around waiting for something to happen. The more you put into it, the more you will get out of it. At a minimum, you should plan on attending as many of the meetings and events as possible.

Let's look at the Chamber of Commerce as an example. Each month, there are several Chamber mixers and ribbon cuttings that their members can attend. For best results, you should plan attend at least one or two per month, and more if you have time. Industry-related groups like IRIS or IDS usually have monthly chapter meetings. Social groups may have meetings or events once a month. Again, to maximize your chances for success, plan to attend as many of these meetings and events as you possibly can.

An important part of attending the meetings and being a good group member is to give, give, and give. Yes, you are there to receive leads and meet new people. But you are also there to give. Give your time, give information, give free advice, and give leads and referrals to your fellow group members. The more you give, the more you will receive in return. So if someone comes to you and says, "Hey, I have a question: I just painted this color and it's not quite right; what do you think?" Just help them. Give away a bit of free advice. It's only going to enhance your reputation.

Choose a group that you really believe in and can really sink your teeth into. For example, there may be a charitable organization that you feel passionate about. Become a board member; volunteer to chair a committee; organize an event. Not only are you doing a wonderful thing for the community, but you are also getting your name and face out there.

Great Tip!

For best results, schedule your networking time and make it a priority!

2. Make networking time a priority by scheduling your events.

Networking events should be high on your marketing priority list. In my situation, for example, I know that once a month I have an IRIS chapter meeting. That goes on my calendar, and unless something horrendous happens, I'm always there. I attend a Chamber of Commerce leads group that meets two Thursdays per month. Those meetings are also on my calendar. If you can schedule your networking appointments, I think there is a higher likelihood that you'll go.

You should be marketing yourself and your business each and every day. Networking is obviously one important aspect of marketing, but clearly you will not have time to go to meetings and events every day. My recommendation would be to plan to attend two or more meetings per month.

> **Important!**
>
> Networking is about building relationships.

Remember that networking is about building relationships. If you look at it that way, then there are many ways for you to fill your calendar with networking activities.

Here's what a sample week might look like:

Monday: Attend networking leads group.

Tuesday: Visit a store in your area and introduce yourself to the owner or manager. Visit regularly to become familiar with the merchandise and also to develop relationships with the employees and the owner. Eventually, you can ask to leave business cards there or even give a presentation at their store.

Wednesday: Follow up with somebody you met at Monday's meeting. Call them to learn more about their business; send them some information that they might be interested in.

Thursday: Attend your book club meeting and have fun socializing with the group.

Friday: Meet a related service provider (such as a window treatment specialist, or faux finisher, or Realtor) for lunch or coffee to talk about how you can refer clients to each other.

Don't expect instant results from your networking efforts. It really does take six months to a year before you'll start seeing some good results. Networking can be a little bit intimidating for some people, so if you have an event on your calendar, it's more likely that you'll go. Push yourself a little bit and just do it.

3. At the event: Master the art of small talk.

So you've decided to go to your first networking event – what do you do now? Well, first of all, congratulations for getting out there and going! You should have a goal in mind for each event. For example, you know you won't be able to talk with everyone in the room, but you can set a goal that you'll meet and connect with two or three new people each time you go.

If you are feeling a little bit intimidated – let's say you don't know a single soul – go over to the food table and serve yourself a small plate. Food can be a great conversation starter. You can say something like: "Have you tried these crab cakes? These are really delicious. Have you ever tried the crab cakes at such-and-such restaurant? I had some great crab cakes there last week." The food table can give you an opportunity to get a conversation started.

> ## ◎ Caution!
>
> At networking events, keep your conversation light, with topics such as food, hobbies, children, pets, vacations, weather. Stay away from controversial topics like politics and religion.

Keep your conversation light, with topics such as food, hobbies, children, pets, vacations, and weather. Stay away from controversial topics like politics and religion. You can also ask them about their affiliation with the organization: How long have you been a member of this organization? What do you like best about this group? What other events do you like to go to?

If you see a person you know, feel free to approach him or her to say hello and chat. But resist the urge to go hang out with your friends. Remember that the whole point is to meet new people!

If you don't know anyone at all, try this tactic: Approach a friendly-looking person, introduce yourself, engage in a short conversation, and say, "This is my first time here and I don't know anyone here. Can you help me by introducing me to someone you know?" That person will be happy to help you, I'm sure.

4. Transitioning from "small talk" to business talk

At some point, you will need to transition from small talk about your pets and kids to the business at hand. Ultimately you are there to promote your business and increase your client base. If you're involved in a conversation with somebody, what I tend to do rather than start talking about my business is ask them about theirs. And if they're polite at all, they'll return the favor and ask me about my business.

Develop a compelling statement, sometimes called a 30-second introduction. So when someone asks, "What do you do?" you reply with something interesting and compelling, rather than simply "I'm an interior decorator." What I suggest is to describe what you do in a problem/solution kind of format. For example, instead of saying "I'm an interior decorator," talk to them about a problem that a lot of your clients have and describe how your service is the solution.

> ### 🌀 Great Tip!
>
> When talking business, describe what you do in terms of a problem and solution. YOU are the solution to your clients' decorating problems!

Example: "Have you ever felt overwhelmed picking paint colors for your home? I just worked with somebody the other day who had 10 shades of yellow on her wall, and she didn't know which one to pick. That's where I come in. I take the mystery out of it. In an hour I can help you pick all the paint colors you need for your entire home."

Isn't that more interesting? Speaking in terms of problem/solution gives them something they can relate to. You know what their problem is and you have a solution for it.

Another example: "Did you know that hiring an interior designer can actually save people money on their remodeling projects? My clients avoid making costly mistakes because I guide them in selecting the perfect materials that fit their style and budget. And I have access to below-retail shopping resources."

So when the conversation turns toward business, make sure you can discuss what your ideal client's problem is and how you are the solution to their problem.

5. Business card etiquette.

Always carry plenty of business cards with you. You never want to be caught in a situation where someone has asked you for a card and you have to say you just ran out. That is a missed opportunity. On the other hand, do not go to a networking event thinking that all you're going to do is hand out all your business cards. People will not look at you very favorably if you do that. It's very pitchy, and no one likes to be pitched to at a networking event. Remember, that networking is not about selling but rather about building relationships. Avoid being "sales-y."

Instead, offer your business card at the end of a conversation. Ask them for theirs, and offer yours as well. And, of course, if you're talking with somebody and they're really interested in you and your business, then they will ask you for a card.

Keep your business cards in a separate container within your purse or briefcase, and always make sure they are neat and free of smudges and wrinkles.

6. Dress for success.

Wear a name tag. I would suggest getting a professionally made name tag and not only wearing it at the networking event, but wearing it everywhere you go: to the grocery store, to pick up your kid at soccer practice, and of course to client appointments and business meetings. Wearing a name tag is just one more way to engage in a conversation with somebody. You'd be amazed at how many times people will ask you about your business while you're standing in line at the grocery store. Since you never know where your next client might come from, why not try to meet as many people as possible?

> **☉ Great Tip!**
>
> Wear a name tag! It's a great conversation starter.

When I first started my business, I had a mentor. She was a real estate agent who had been in business for quite a long time, and she was a mother too. I remember her telling me, "Even if you have no clients today, get dressed, dress professionally, put on your name tag, and go out and do something. Go shopping, go out, and be among people." She said that nobody needs to know that you didn't just get out of an appointment with a client. She said when you go pick up your son at soccer, look professional. Wear your name tag. Nobody needs to know that you didn't just come from a meeting. You have to act the part. The more you act the part, the more you start becoming what you want to be. It's a self-fulfilling prophecy. Dress for who your ideal client is. If your target clients are very affluent, you need to look like they do. My tag line is "Real Rooms for Real

21

People," so I tend to dress more casually, yet professionally. I like to dress in colorful clothes, because I deal in color all the time.

One client asked me whether having a polo shirt made with her company's information on it would be a good idea.

I do think it is a good idea to wear a company polo shirt when you are working. For example, in my business I do a lot of furniture arranging and a lot of window measuring. So wearing a polo shirt with my company name would be really appropriate for that kind of situation. However, if you're going to a mixer or other type of networking event, especially the first few times you go, I would dress up more than that. I wouldn't make the polo shirt be the first impression people have about you. If you've gone to several events already and you're dressed up and then the third or fourth time you wear your polo shirt, I don't see any problem with that. Think about the impression you're trying to convey, and dress appropriately.

Dress for the job or client you want, not the job you have.

7. Following up after the event

You've gone to these events; you've gotten to know all these people. Now what do you do?

> 🔊 **Important!**
>
> Follow up, follow up, follow up with people you meet at networking events.

Make sure and follow up with them the next day. Send them an email or, better yet, send a hand-written note. For example: "It was really nice to meet you last night at the Chamber mixer. I really enjoyed talking to you about your business...."

Include one of your business cards, and let them know that you look forward to seeing them at the next event. Be genuine in your note. Make reference to something you talked about with them at the event. For example, if you talked to them about the 10 shades of yellow on their walls, you can remind them about that conversation by saying "I'd love to help you pick the perfect shade of yellow for your living room. Please feel free to give me a call."

Also, let them know that you would like to add them to your mailing list, and ask for their permission. It is important for you to build your database so that you can continue to market to them on a regular basis.

Some decorators send postcards, or e-newsletters, or occasional deco-rating tip sheets.

To add a personal touch, send them an article or some information about something you talked about at the event. For example, let's imag-ine that you talked to them about going on vacation to Italy. Send them an article about a museum or restaurant you recommend visiting. "I just read this great article, and I thought you might be interested." Send it to them because it's a very friendly gesture, and it makes you memorable. It shows that you're thinking of them.

In Summary: 3 Action Points

1. Join at least one group per category: one social group, one business-related group, and one industry-related group. Be se-lective about the groups you join, and join only the groups where you can really get involved.

2. Schedule your networking events. Putting them on your calendar will make them a high priority.

3. Follow up with the people you meet. Continue to build and nurture the relationships you start.

Networking is an important part of your marketing strategy. Keep ac-tive, spend the time, and get involved. I guarantee that you will experi-ence great results.

ABOUT THE AUTHOR

Anna Jacoby has been interested in interior design since childhood. "It all started with my first dollhouse," she said. "I had four as I was growing up. I was constantly rearranging the furniture and redecorating the rooms." She also recalls giving her own room a new look many times over the years by rearranging furniture and trying out new accessories and colors. From there she moved on to decorating her own home and helping friends with theirs.

In 2000, Anna Jacoby launched her interior redesign and staging business, Anna Jacoby Interiors. Since then, she has helped hundreds of clients decorate, redesign, or prepare their homes for sale. From 2003 to 2008, she wrote a bi-weekly column called "Real Life Rooms," which appeared in five San Francisco Bay Area newspapers, and her own remodeled kitchen was featured in two national decorating magazines in 2006 and 2007. Her business was featured in U.S. *Business Review* in November 2007 and in "Career Path" in July 2008.

Besides working with design clients, Anna also teaches IRIS-Certified redesign and staging courses, and offers marketing and business coaching. She became a Certified Guerrilla Marketing Coach in 2009. Anna currently serves as the Executive Director of IRIS.

On a personal note, she is married to her high school sweetheart, and is the proud mom of two teenagers. Her hobbies are yoga, reading, and spending time with family and friends.

2
MAXIMIZE YOUR BUSINESS
WITH REFERRALS
AND TESTIMONIALS

by Kelly Galea
www.thedesignbizcoach.com

In this chapter you'll learn:

** Tools to target and attract more of your ideal
design clients
* Simple strategies to dramatically increase
referrals and repeat business
* Cultivating loyalty to create abundance*

Why We Tend to Forget about Referral and Testimonial Marketing

There can be a bit of a fear factor around referral and testimonial marketing, as we may feel intimidated about asking our clients for this kind of feedback. What tends to happen is we get so wrapped up in our projects. When we first start a project, we're excited and having a great time with our client; then we become so involved in what we're doing that we aren't doing regular check-ins with the client. Nothing formal is necessarily required; it can be as simple as asking, "How are things going?" or "How are you feeling about this?" If we stay engaged with our clients by asking for feedback, it's very easy then to ask for referrals or testimonials as it becomes a natural flow of things.

Great Tip!

Make sure you have referral and testimonial systems. Having systems helps you feel like this is a natural process. You'll know what to do (and what not to do!) and when to do it.

You may find yourself wondering how to build your design business through referrals and testimonials. What is it that you should ask your clients, or what should you say to them? That's what we're going to cover with these two heavy hitters from your design-biz tool kit so you can target and attract more ideal design clients.

Your Target Market and Ideal Client

It all starts by identifying your target market and ideal client. If you don't have a clear definition of your target market, you will never be able to network effectively or spend your marketing budget appropriately, and that includes referral and testimonial marketing.

The more defined your target market and ideal clients are, the more referable you become. Think about who it is you want to meet and also where you'll meet them.

Getting Quality Referrals

Many of us want more referrals and know that referrals are a big part of our marketing strategy. We also realize that people want to do business with and refer business to those we know, like, and trust. We know from being referred and providing referrals ourselves that those who come through a referral are more likely to give referrals. We like referring those who are like us to those we know, like, and trust!

Despite knowing these things, in many cases we're reluctant to ask for referrals because it makes us feel a bit needy or maybe a little pushy and "sales-y." I want to challenge you for a moment and ask you to think about times people have asked you to provide a referral or asked you for a testimonial. Most likely you've been thrilled to do so. And you probably thought it was nice of them to ask you, and perhaps felt a little flattered when they valued your opinion.

 **Great Tip!**

Overcome a fearful mindset by approaching referrals from a point of service. You're not asking for business; you're striving to be of service to your clients, their friends, and colleagues.

Know that in most cases, this is how people are feeling when *you* ask *them*! They're actually very grateful and happy to do that for you, so it's time to get over that fear. I'll share some scripts, messages, and tips that will help you through this transition.

Begin by approaching referrals from a place of being of service to others. The founder of BNI (Business Networking International), Ivan Misner, defines referrals as the opportunity to do business with someone who is in the market to buy your product or service.

There is someone who needs the services you're offering; that's why you're looking for the referral. That's also why people want to provide you a referral – they feel you can be of service to someone they know. As Michael Port (who wrote *Book Yourself Solid* and *Beyond Booked Solid*) says, "If you feel called to share a message, it's because there are people in the world who are waiting to hear it."

Yes, your ideal design clients are out there, they need your services, and they're waiting to hear from you.

This shifts you and puts you in that better place. That's why you origi-

27

nally went into this business – you're very passionate about what you do. You're creative, you want to help people with their spaces (whether you're doing residential or commercial design), you're beautifying spaces, making them more functional and inhabitable. That is how you're of service. It comes easy to a lot of us, but our clients don't know how to do these things – that's why they need you!

Spending Marketing Money Wisely

For those of you who aren't quite convinced about the value of referral marketing, let's explore where you might feel the pain a little more: with your time and money. By doing referral marketing, you're spending your marketing budget and dollars more wisely. How so? Here's the thing – you've spent the money to get your current clients, so why wouldn't you focus on referral marketing, where you get a bigger return on your investment? Let's look at the real value of a referral. Here's a formula I learned about from David Frey. The value of a referral equals the lifetime value of a client multiplied by the average number of referrals received per month (that result in sales) multiplied by 12.

Important!

Spend about 40% of your current marketing budget on current clients.

So what's a referral worth to you? Do you see the value here? Want some more good news? It doesn't cost a lot to pursue those referrals.

Obviously you want to do some things to reach out to your clients throughout the year as part of your normal marketing budget. We're going to go through lots of ideas and techniques for ways you can keep reaching out. First let's look at a budgeting strategy and how you can maximize your marketing dollars.

When it comes to budgeting and where to spend your marketing dollars, look at spending about 40% of your current budget on current clients. Have systems in place to reach out to and keep in touch with those current clients. That could be your email newsletter system, or sending out greeting cards, special postcards, or birthday cards to your contacts so you're keeping yourself top-of-mind with them.

Then you want to spend about 40% on strategic alliances and developing those partnerships. The remaining 20% would be for ads, pay-per-click, and some of the more traditional marketing methods.

28

Educating Your Clients

When you think about your clients and the people you know (and maybe even you!), many are wired to give referrals but some aren't wired that way at all. A lot of people just don't think about it, so you really need to ask. It starts with educating your clients. You'll get better-quality referrals if you do a better job of asking for them.

Sometimes we experience that fear, and think that if someone is hesitant, it means no, they're shooting us down. Oftentimes someone's hesitation is nothing more than them taking a moment to think about what you've said. Maybe they're scanning through their memory banks to see if there's somebody appropriate to refer you to.

Also realize that people are very protective of their relationships, so make it easy for them to provide a referral by asking for an introduction. It could be as simple as asking for an introduction by email. It doesn't need to be a formal face-to-face meeting or a request asking someone to call someone else. A call providing an introduction is much better, but it could be done by email as well. If you're still feeling some of that hesitation and thinking they're giving you a bit of pushback, here are a few tips to overcome the hesitation or an awkward moment.

* Let your client know not to keep you a secret or not to keep you or the services you offer a secret.
* Let you client know that you're never too busy to be a resource to them and to their referrals.

When to Ask for Referrals and Testimonials

Beware!

Are you busy? Do you constantly tell everyone how busy you are? If people think you are busy, they may feel you're too busy for them and so won't reach out to you. Just let them know that you're never too busy for your ideal clients.

Let's look at the different situations where you might ask for referrals. The first is when you're in a business group, where giving leads and sharing referrals is part of the whole program. In business networking situations, you're growing your sphere of influence; mixing with a large and diverse group of people who will continually refer business to you and you to them.

29

Too often in these networking environments, people will give you a name of someone who may or may not need your services. Having just a name and a phone number really isn't a referral; it's more of a general lead. So what makes a good-quality referral? When the prospect knows about you and is waiting for your call.

Here are some tips on self-introductions in a business networking setting. Let's say your name is Jennifer Jones and you own Jones Interiors. When it's your turn to stand up and introduce yourself, say "Hi, my name is Jennifer Jones, owner of Jones Interiors. I help homeowners in XYZ community with remodels and redesigns. Right now, I'm working with lots of empty nesters who were ready to refresh and update their homes once the kids have headed off to college. Please take a moment to think of all the couples you know who have recently sent the last of their kids to college, and who live in XYZ community. Those are the people I want to meet!"

Depending on how your networking meeting is structured, you may even have a chance to ask them to take a moment to jot down names of people they know who are like that and forward those to you.

Action Item!

Help your referral sources paint a detailed picture of your ideal client, so it's easier for them to know exactly who you are looking for.

It's the best way to get quality referrals because the more specific, the better. We're visual people. When you read the example above, you were picturing people like this, maybe thinking, "I know people like that." Your referral sources will be doing the same. You really want to get that specific and help frame your ideal client in their minds.

Now everyone is picturing their neighbors and people who fit these descriptions, so it's time to collect those names. After you collect the names, have a chat with each person who gave you a list of referrals. Ask them to call their friend and ask them if it's okay for you to call. That way, when you do call and follow up, it will be a warm lead and not a cold sales call. This puts you again in a better mental place because they are expecting your call.

The key here is to have your contact warm up the prospect for you. When you hear, "My sister-in-law absolutely hates painting her house and selecting colors. I think she could use your design services," gently push back on your contact and say, "That's great! Can you do me a favor and ask her if its okay for me to give her a call? Just shoot me an email or text or give me a ring and let me know if that's all right." The next day, you can certainly email your contact or text them or call them to remind them to warm up the referral for you. Here's what to write or say: "Hi, Susan. It was great talking with you yesterday. Thanks for telling me about your sister-in-law. Did you have a chance to talk with her about my services? I'd like to give her a call but I want to be sure she knows who I am before I do."

In addition to warming up the prospect, this technique also helps reduce the amount of time you spend chasing down bad leads who often have absolutely zero interest in using your services.

Great Tip!

Be sure to work with "warm" prospects!

What if Susan gets busy with her life, never calls her sister-in-law, and forgets to give you her number? Have you potentially lost that referral? Say "If you'd like to give me her number, I'll be happy to call her. Is it okay if I use your name and let her know you referred me?"

Expanding Your Network

If your current business networking activities aren't producing results, look for ways to expand your network:

- Make sure you can be found on the Internet.
- Participate in both online and offline groups and discussions.
- Cross-promote with vendors, service providers, installers, and professionals who have the same ideal client as you. Some examples include travel agents, professional organizers, concierge services, personal assistants, personal chefs, people who sell luxury vehicles, personal trainers, pet trainers, florists, and au pairs.
- Leverage your email signature and all of your client touch points, such as your business card, brochure, and website.
- Utilize tell-a-friend and refer-a-friend links or buttons (in emails and online) or printed referral cards or slips (mail and in person).

You can also get good referrals from your personal network using a slightly different approach. What question do people ask you every day?

"How are you?"

31

If you're like just about everyone else, your answer is usually, "I'm fine." That's a dead-end street. Next time, use this as an opportunity to talk about your business, and in a way that doesn't feel sleazy or slimy. We often assume in our personal networks that our friends know what we do. But many times, they really don't. Even if they know you're a designer, if they haven't worked with a designer, they don't really know what being a designer means and what it is you do. If they're not in your ideal client base, they may think things like, "I could never afford you," "I don't want to know what you do," and "I'm not going to tell any of my friends about you."

So this is a way to break down those barriers and help everyone understand what it is that you do and specifically how you help and how you're of service. Here's the formula (you can use this in a business environment as well, but it's really effective in a personal networking environment):

Beware!

We often assume in our personal networks that our friends know what we do. But many times, they really don't. It's our job to educate them.

You can say, "I'm great! I'm working with a new client who (describe your client). I'm helping him by (fill in what you're doing to help that client). I really like working with people like that because (say why)." If you're acquainted with the terms "unique selling proposition" or "personal benefit statement," this may seem familiar.

Need an example? Here's something an interior designer might say:

"I'm great. I'm working with a client who decided to renovate her home rather than move. I'm helping her plan the space to make the most of the existing footprint. We're moving walls, doors, and windows to create the home office she's always wanted. I really like this type of project because I know that with my help, she's going to get a great return on her investment when she eventually does sell her home. Do you know anyone thinking about renovating rather than moving? If you do, send them my way. I'll be happy to talk with them to see if it makes more sense to remodel rather than look for a new home."

You're sharing something that's interesting, and even though it's in a personal setting, they'll be thinking, "Wow, I didn't know you did that. I thought you just did the design. I didn't know you could help people

32

renovate their homes." And you're thinking, "Well, of course we can do that!" But again, people out there aren't thinking of us as much as we think they are, and they don't necessarily know what it is that we do.

Need another example? Here's something a designer or decorator specializing in color consultations could say. "I'm great. I just introduced a package where I'm offering color consultations online. I can work with people around the world because we handle everything by phone and email. It's an easy way to get started working with a designer or decorator. My clients just love it! I like being able to help them make what's so often a difficult decision when they just want to make quick and inexpensive changes in their living space. It makes me feel like I'm really solving a big problem for them. Do you know anyone interested in updating their space with color? If you do, send them my way. Be sure they tell me they know you and I'll take extra special care of them."

> **◖Action Point!**
>
> How do you answer the question: How are you? Be sure to do it in a way that leads people to understand what you do and how you can help them.

The important thing here is be ready to change the subject as soon as the conversation is finished. If the person you're talking to seems interested, offer to follow up with them and then do that. But if you are at purely social event don't spend too much time talking about work.

> **◖ Great Tip!**
>
> Are you staring at a stack of business cards on your desk? Are your client files in disarray? If you're overwhelmed by the thought of organizing your contacts, get help! Work with an assistant or intern.

Having Systems in Place

Have systems in place to reach out, stay in touch, show you care, and continually add value so that referrals almost fall right into place. Here's an acronym for SYSTEM that I like, courtesy of David Frey: *System* stands for Save YourSelf Time, Energy, and Money. Sounds good to me!

How do we put a system in place to generate referrals? Start by organizing and updating your contacts. Go through and identify your current clients, your past clients, the vendors, installers, and service providers you work with, and your business networking contacts and personal contacts.

Classify your contacts. Think about who your referrals or testimonials are coming from. Those are the people who are likely to be key influencers and the best people to continue to reach out to and stay in touch with because they're the ones sending you business.

Setting Expectations

Keep in mind that the only way you have been able to obtain your goals has been by helping clients obtain theirs. Again, it's about that mindset and knowing you're being of service so you can set expectations with people about referrals as early as the moment you hand someone your business card. For example, your business card may state that you are by referral only or by appointment.

Important!

It's about the mindset and knowing you're being of service! Set expectations upfront.

You can mention that you have a referral-only design practice. When you're working with your client, remark that they were introduced to you, and since they were provided an introduction, they can now provide an introduction to others who may also benefit from your services. This is how people want to meet you – through referrals. You can comment about how everyone you talk with gives you three names and that's how you came to meet them.

Set expectations up front. Something we did with our design firm and had great success with was what we called "Our Commitment." We enumerated the things that we would do, not necessarily specific to the design project but more from a business practice perspective. We included the way we would work with our client and stated what our commitment was. At the end of that commitment document, we included a statement where we asked that in return for our design and professional services, guarantee, and commitment, our client refer three clients to us over the course of their design project.

We would sign that commitment sheet and ask our clients to sign it, too, and we each had a copy. It was great way to set expectations because our clients understood that we were coming from a place of doing the best design work and providing the best service we could. And in exchange for that, would they be willing to refer us to some clients like them?

34

We also included the statements in our letter of agreement or contract with our clients. Every document they received from us included it as well. Something we didn't do that I would do now is to include the referral statement in all email signatures, too.

You have flexibility here. Do what you feel is right and authentic for you. Plant those seeds throughout the process so it's not like you're waiting until the end of your project and saying "Oh, hey! By the way, I could use a referral."

Here's an example from a friend who is a property manager. She had this great blurb in a letter she sent out:

"A referral is introducing someone you care about to someone you respect. My business continues to grow and thrive because of referrals from clients, friends, associates, and others just like you. Who is the next family member, friend, coworker, or neighbor you believe could use my help that you feel comfortable introducing me to? Please don't keep me or my business a secret."

Great Tip!

Be more aware of different examples of the ways people ask you for referrals. Model after what others are doing if something really resonates with you.

What I like about that example is that it feels very natural. Her business is doing well and thriving because of the referrals of people that she is working with. She's also making a point of including those "that you feel comfortable introducing me to," acknowledging that there might be a little discomfort there, but that it's okay; she's here, and don't keep her a secret.

After you've landed a new project, it's always helpful to send out a referral letter to your client a few days later. It could be as basic as a short note that says, "Thank you for the confidence you've placed in me. It's important that you know that regardless of how busy I may be, I'll always have the time to connect with anyone you think will benefit from my expertise."

Then let them know that you'll keep them in the loop and that you'll also let them know if their referral is not an ideal client for you. You're probably wondering how to do that and let them down easy, because they might feel insulted. What you could do is tell them that you'll be happy to talk to the person but you'll meet with them only

35

after you've had that initial call and determined whether there's really a fit.

Doesn't that sound extremely reasonable? Would anybody ever push back on that? It makes sense. You will follow up with the person I referred you to, and if there's a fit and you want to work together, that's great and you'll let me know.

We're spending so much time on referrals because if you have a process and do this right, the testimonials flow very naturally. And it's easy to ask for them. When you're in the midst of your design project, you'll want to make sure that you're doing follow-up calls and doing what we call "relationship check-ins."

This is actually something my husband and I did when we first started dating. We had a date night that we honored every month (still do!) and we would do a check-in. Just a quick "How are we doing?" We didn't want to let anything miniscule escalate and get out of control. I think having something in place like that with your clients is just fabulous, and it can be very simple.

Great Tip!

Your referral system should include your voice mail. In your outbound message, include this verbiage, "If you were referred to me, let me know who we need to thank."

It doesn't have to be a formal, drawn-out thing. If you're meeting with a client, let them know that as part of your discussion, you just want to do a quick check-in. You could do this face-to-face or by phone.

You might say something like, "It's been a month; how are we doing?" Or "On a scale from 1 to 10, where do you feel we are?" And if they're not giving you a 10, ask what it is you need to do to get a 10.

This kind of check-in with your client keeps it from becoming an adversarial relationship. It keeps problems from escalating out of control very early on, and it's simple. It's a nice, easy conversation to have, and they'll be thinking how no one else they've worked with has ever asked them for this kind of feedback.

Anytime you are meeting with your client face-to-face, then absolutely you want to do this check-in. If it will be weeks or months before your next meeting, put something in your tickler file to remind you to make a phone call to them or to send them an email.

You need to reach out somehow. You will know, based on your client's preferred communication method, what that needs to be. Make sure you've asked them in your client intake process how they want to receive updates and how they want to do check-ins.

Go Givers

Are you a "go giver"? I highly recommend Bob Burg's book *Endless Referrals*, and especially his books *The Go Giver* and *Go Givers Sell More*, so that you can learn more about this whole philosophy. Make a point of asking your clients about things they're working on in case you can refer business to them, or be a resource to them in some way. Ask your client a lot of questions so that you can know whether someone you're talking with is a good prospect them. Go give!

It's about being that center of influence in creating connections for others and for yourself, and introducing people and suggesting ways that they can work together and look for leads for one another.

> **Important!**
>
> It's important to position yourself in front of your customer as the center of influence.

It's important to position yourself in front of your customer as the center of influence. Be that person who's sharing helpful information (sharing tips and ideas in your newsletter and blog, providing referrals to other professionals), someone who knows a lot of people and resources, who has pull in the community and is the hub of introductions. This leads right into an example I actually received from a Realtor I worked with years ago when I bought my current home.

This was a letter that included the following:
"Let me take just a moment of your time to introduce a complimentary service I provide for all my clients. I call it my Client Appreciation Program. It's part of my recent commitment to run my business exclusively by referral.

Every month I'll be sending you something you may find valuable, e.g., an article on current affairs or other information that I believe you will find useful. I make a constant effort to improve the level of service I provide to you because, in my business, the most profound assets I possess are your respect and trust.

37

I'll contact you soon to see if I can be of any help or meet any of your needs."

What I really like about this example is he's setting himself up as that center of influence but also making it clear he has a commitment to run his business by referral.

Mindset Tip!

It's not being needy or pushy. It's saying that you know you've provided value. Your clients know that you provided value. This gives you the confidence to ask for a referral.

This example feels like a great welcome letter, too. If you're doing an email newsletter and somebody has signed up for it, then including something like this in an introductory or welcome letter will go a long way in setting positive expectations with your clients.

Staying in Touch

All of these are ways that you can reach out, but they're also ways you can stay in touch.

When you stay in touch with your clients and your potential referral sources, it is so much easier to ask for a referral. In essence, you've given yourself permission to do it because you've maintained that contact with them. Plus, you've been of service and have provided so much value to them already. You've provided excellent service, you're coming from that place of service to others, and this also puts you in a place of confidence and strength.

It's not being needy or pushy. It's saying that you know you've provided value. Your clients know that you provided value. And now you both know that the other one knows that. I know that you know that I know that I provided value!

Expressing Gratitude

When it comes to referrals, what's rewarded is repeated, so be sure to express your gratitude. This could be as simple as a thank you note. It might be a card you send out. It could be a token gift such as a book, frame, magazine subscription, floral arrangement, or a bottle of wine. It could also be a client appreciation event, only for those clients who have provided you with referrals throughout the year.

Many times it just depends on the nature of your relationship with who is referring you. On the other hand, you may have an agreement in place, such as one you may have with a vendor or service provider where you're offering a percentage of the project.

By the way, I have no problem with offering a percentage of a project to the referrer. Why is that? What if you had to hire a salesperson to go out and get that project? You would pay a lot more than that percentage your referrer is asking for!

Testimonials

If you're seeking to convince someone to give you a try, nothing beats testimonials. When it comes to your ideal design clients, the best testimonials would be from someone that your prospect knows personally.

The second best would be from one of their competitors, if your focus is commercial clients. In the case of residential clients, this would be testimonials coming from neighbors (if there is some "keeping up with the Joneses" going on) or their in-laws!

> ## Great Tip!
>
> If you don't want to request testimonials yourself, ask someone else to reach out to your clients, such as a business partner, an assistant, or a friend who just happens to be your biggest proponent and supporter.

How do you solicit excellent testimonials that will be effective in helping you to attract your ideal design clients? Again, you start by going through your client list and contacts. Think about who you could call or send a request to in order to get a testimonial.

Here's something I did in our design firm. I had a business partner at that time and there was no way he was going to call people up and ask for testimonials that we could share on our website and in our marketing materials. So I contacted our clients and told them I was arranging a little surprise for my business partner. He had a business anniversary coming up and I wanted to do something really nice for him, so I was requesting testimonials that I could share with him. Everyone I asked to do this thought it was a fun idea and was so excited and happy to help.

As with referrals, set your expectations up front with clients that when you're providing a fabulous design service, your clients will then provide not only referrals, but also testimonials. The two topics go well together because they really do work so hand in hand with one another.

If you set up your systems for referrals appropriately and you're reminding clients that your primary source of growth is referrals, and maybe they came to you as a result of a testimonial they read, remind them of that and ask them for those testimonials.

You can also use tools like LinkedIn to request a recommendation. If you do, be sure to customize the note you send to your connections. Don't just use the standard LinkedIn request. If you're using technology and tools to gather testimonials, this is an easy one because people in that social media environment are used to sharing recommendations and referrals that way.

Focus on Results

Your clients are buying results, so make sure your testimonials are mentioning the specific results that clients have realized working with you. Think about what you would like your clients to say about their experience in working with you. Picture meeting with your client, hear your conversation in your mind, where they are saying all these fabulous things, and then reframe those statements as questions.

> ### ◗ **Great Tip!**
>
> Your clients are buying results, so make sure your testimonials are mentioning the specific results that clients have realized working with you.

You're sort of mirroring back to them what you would like them to say. There's nothing subversive about this! Many times our clients don't know what to say, so we need to give them a little hand. When they were first seeking your design services, what problem did they want solved? Or what were they trying to improve?

Another tip: Refer to your client intake questionnaire for the specific service your client originally requested of you. Reframe that request as a question to elicit additional details.

Let's say your client came to you to remodel their kitchen to improve the work flow. You can ask them about that. For example, how would you describe the difference improvements to the work flow have made?

Another option is to ask generic questions like, "What did you think of our design services? After using our design services, what changed for you?" That's where you really learn a lot about the pain points you didn't know they had. Sharing this, the pain points that led them to seek out your services, the experience of working with you, and the difference it made would be excellent testimonial material. This is because other people are looking at that and saying, "That's me. I have those same issues and I want some help."

You can also send your clients surveys. Many email marketing systems like Constant Contact have a survey tool and include standard templates you can use if you're struggling with the types of questions to ask. There are also tools like SurveyMonkey and Zoomerang.

> 🔹 **Important!**
>
> Make it EASY for your clients to give you testimonials!

You can certainly offer an incentive to your clients for completing a survey or providing feedback. Give them a special bonus, such as a copy of a book you've written or one written by the HGTV designer they're always mentioning. Even something as simple as a gift card to Starbucks would work.

Again, look at your client intake process. What is the problem that your client wanted solved? What are their concerns?

This tells you about their expectations and criteria for success, so you can use those statements to come up with questions or to guide their testimonial.

You really do want to make it easy for your clients. Whether it's sending a request for a LinkedIn recommendation or sending a link to a survey or feedback form, those are ways to make it easy. For some clients, you may just have to write their testimonial for them.

A lot of times people are stumbling and don't know where to start and what to say, so provide them something, give them a sample, give them a selection. You may want to come up with three standard testimonial templates that you have ready to share. As your clients go through the sample(s), it will occur to them how they want to say it in their own words.

If you've requested a testimonial from a customer and she just hasn't replied, it's appropriate to go back and remind her. If you live nearby, offer to stop by and pick it up. If you've emailed them something, maybe they just don't have time to get to their email. Maybe they don't feel like putting it in a letter and going to the post office with it. It depends on your client's preferred communication methods, and it's about making it easier for them. Certainly do follow up with them and ask.

If you know your client well, have been doing your check-ins, and have a great relationship with them, but you notice that they're not coming through with a testimonial, you might just check to see whether they prefer not to provide a testimonial. You're acknowledging if they are feeling uncomfortable about it at all, that you don't want to push them…but maybe you need to go back and ask if they were completely satisfied with your service. Find out what might be holding them back.

I know it might be difficult to do. It's uncomfortable. But you want to know from their perspective what they think went right and what went wrong. Of course, if something went wrong, you want to fix it so it doesn't happen with another client.

We had an example of this situation in our design firm, where one of our most problematic clients became one of our biggest supporters because of how we handled what seemed to be an impossible situation. We sat them down and told them we really wanted to understand what happened and get their thoughts about how to fix it. We asked what would have made a difference for them because we intended to change our process and our system so we wouldn't end up with other clients in this same situation.

Great Tip!
Often, facing an uncomfortable situation head-on will turn your problematic client into a big supporter.

By being proactive about what you will do about it, you've acknowledged your client's concerns and accepted responsibility in a way that shows you are serious about fixing what's broken so it does not happen again.

Another excellent example of being proactive and requesting this type of feedback comes from a friend who was a mortgage broker. After she would meet with her clients, she would send them an email that said, "I'd love it if you'd take a moment to *give me your feedback*. It's so important to know firsthand what went right and (even more important) to hear from you if you're not 100% satisfied. I'll share your thoughts on the *testimonial page* of my site, so if you'd rather keep it just between us, let me know. I also want to remind you that referrals are really the highest compliment and best vote of confidence you can give. Keep your eyes open for people who are thinking of <describe service>. I deliver the same level of service to all my clients. If you've got someone in mind right now, *CLICK HERE* to send me a referral."

The beauty of this example is the use of links (all the phrases *italicized* in the above example) to make it easy for her clients to respond right away. The first link, "give me your feedback," led to a form on her site with standard questions, almost like a survey where they could provide input on what they had just experienced. She also linked to her testimonial page so they could see examples of other client testimonials. Finally, she's mentioned the importance of referrals and has provided a link to enable her clients to send her a referral right then and there.

In Summary: 3 Action Steps

◉ Important!

1. This is all about relationship building, and consistency is key. Put together a simple plan identifying the number of clients or contacts you'll reach out to tomorrow, this week, and this month. Start building that referral network, and start gathering client testimonials. It doesn't have to be a big and insurmountable task. Breaking it down in a simple plan makes it very easy to accomplish. If you reach out to only 1 person each day, at the end of the week you'll have 5, and within the month you'll have 20.

Referrals and testimonials, just like anything else in marketing, are a relationship-building process. Be consistent and persistent.

2. Realize that this is a process. Don't wait until the end of your project to ask for referrals or testimonials; do it continually throughout the project. Look at your process and the ways your business interacts with your clients. What will you do and where will you add these specific steps? Earlier I gave an example of how we included a commitment statement with our proposal. We added it to our letter of agreement. We provided weekly progress updates if the project was large. With each invoice we would include our statement about referrals. Thinking about your own process and all the times you're interacting with your clients, where could you add referral and testimonial lingo? Consider examples I've given you, and look at where you'll include something similar in your own process.

3. Testimonials and referrals really do go hand in hand. By checking in and continually measuring your results, doing check-ins with your clients, you're going to get testimonials right away without asking in a formal, uncomfortable way. You'll also be making it much, much easier to ask for referrals. Repeating these small things over and over is what will lead to your success.

I encourage you to do just one thing every day – whether it's making a phone call, sending a thank you note, sending out birthday cards, or sending letters of introduction – starting with those "A-list" clients you've identified as your primary influencers. I also want to recognize that what you've read here may not be new to you; maybe you've been thinking that you've already seen it, heard it, or know it; so my question to you is: Are you implementing it?

I always like to end with a quote to provide additional inspiration. This one is from Charles Schultz, and I just love it:

"Life is like a ten-speed bike. Most of us have gears we never use."

Get out there and start using your referral and testimonial gears!

Here's to living your designer life!

ABOUT THE AUTHOR

 **Kelly Galea**, "the Design Biz Coach," is a strategic marketing and efficiency consultant, author, and coach. She helps design entrepreneurs and business owners like you boost their bottom line with simple and proven strategies and systems.

Kelly's mission as the Design Biz Coach is to inspire and provide guidance to design business owners, providing strategies and tools to take their business to the next level. Sharing all the knowledge she loves to seek out, focusing on what she does best – integrating business and marketing systems, processes, and technology, distilling it to what is relevant and essential to her clients – so they can focus on what they do best as creative entrepreneurs and design professionals.

Start designing the business of your dreams now by going to **www.thedesignbizcoach.com**.

3
USE SPEAKING OPPORTUNITIES TO GET MORE CLIENTS

by Mary Larsen
www.GrowYourDesignBiz.com

In this chapter you'll learn:

*3 things that you MUST cover every time you have a
speaking engagement*
** The TOP 2 venues for speaking on what you love – and
they are not what you think!*
* Easy ideas for putting together your speaking topics
* The best way to grow your "list" from speaking
* Why giving away your "secrets" gets you clients!
* And much, much more

One of the things that you will hear time and time again when you pursue your marketing is, "I need to get more clients – what can I do?"

And you go out there and maybe you do a Google search that says "How do I get clients?" or "What kind of things can I do to market my business?" And almost without fail, somewhere in there, you're going to come across this point: People work with people that they *know, like, and trust.*

And one way to get someone to *know, like, and trust* you is to speak to them.

Everyone has heard of a first impression – so how do you get that first impression? It's when you engage in a conversation. So when I talk about speaking for clients, I'm talking about all types of speaking.

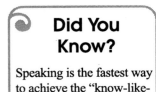

ⓐ Did You Know?

Speaking is the fastest way to achieve the "know-like-and-trust" factor!

It's as simple as saying hello to your cashier at your grocery store – that could lead you into a discussion about your business – all the way up into doing the formal kind of talks and speaking, where you've got an audience and they've come to see you specifically.

So it's that *know, like, and trust* factor that you are trying to achieve. And speaking is the fastest way to make it happen.

Getting Over the Fear of Talking

I've actually consulted with people one-on-one who have said to me, "Oh, I find what you do so inspirational and I love what you say about speaking, but there's no chance on earth I'm ever getting up in front of a group, and there is nothing that you can do to change that."

There is a great quote from Jerry Seinfeld that demonstrates the point:
According to most studies, people's number one fear is public speaking. Number two is death. Death is number two. Does that sound

right? This means to the average person, if you go to a funeral, you're better off in the casket than doing the eulogy.
The best advice I like to give to help people who have such a big fear is to try to remember that when it comes to speaking, the best way to approach it is as if you are speaking to a friend. Just imagine that your best friend called you up on the phone and asked you a design question. You would have no problem answering it and speaking about it for some time. You probably do this every day already.

When doing more formal speaking to attract clients, you can think of that, too, as if you're speaking to friends, answering their design questions, and helping them with their design challenges. Mentally you have to bring a public talk closer to home, and just think of it as a conversation with a friend.

Great Tip!

Mentally, bring a public talk "closer to home," and think of it as a conversation with a friend.

Another piece of advice to help designers get over the fear of public speaking is to bring in a moderator. A moderator is someone who you can have a conversation with, who can ask you questions, and lead you to the next topic of your talk. This way you are not alone in the front of the audience, you feel supported during your talk, and you get to take little breaks while the moderator does his or her part.

3 Things to Cover in Your Talk

The first thing to cover in your talk is why. *Why are you qualified* to get in front of this group? What you have to do is qualify yourself. Why are you the person who is okay to be speaking about this in front of this group of people?

Number two is *why does your audience care?* What you are talking about should be something that they care about. And remember we spoke earlier about that it could be something very casual as a conversation that maybe you're having sitting next to your child's friend's mother at a volleyball game.

It could be you're sitting side-by-side and something comes up about work and now you're having a conversation with her. That's not formal, but even in that conversation when you're talking about the work that you do, why would that person care? Why does that person care that

49

you're an interior designer?

Well, on a high level, they might care because you're going to help them make their home feel like their favorite place on earth. Or you're going to be able to make them have less stress in their lives, by helping them have a more beautiful surrounding.

> ## Recap
> 1. Why you're qualified
> 2. Why the audience cares about your topic
> 3. How long your talk will last

Or not even more beautiful surroundings, the home could be a more functional one – but we all know that the beautiful will come in with the functional. Why they care has a lot to do with what it is specifically that you're talking about.

So it could be why you're an interior designer, or it could go all the way to the top – for example, "Top 7 Favorite Trends for 2010." And why would they care what the latest trends are?

Well, they care about that for the same reason they would care about fashion: Because they want to know what's in, they want to make sure that they're on top of things, they want to make sure that they're in the know, they want to make sure that they are keeping up. So all of those things turn into why a person might care.

Lastly – and this might surprise you – it's *how long your talk is going to last*. People get antsy when you don't set their expectations. You have to let your audience know what to expect. Are you talking for 20 minutes, or an hour and 20 minutes? You know how long it's going to last and basically what's going to happen, so share that.

What to Talk About

To find a topic, the best and easiest thing to do is to think back about what a client may have recently asked you. What has a client recently asked you that you had to answer? And then flip that around and say to yourself, Is this something other people might be interested in, too? If this client didn't know it, is this perhaps the information that I need to share with other people?

Another idea is to think about what other people are talking about. And by that I mean, What are the magazines talking about? The decorating industry is huge, and there are lots of publications that talk about decorating tips, things you can bring into your home and do yourself. Can they spark an idea in you? Pay attention to what's around you, and think about applying it to your signature talk.

Another place of inspiration is design channels on TV. There are many design shows – and they never get old. Make it a point to watch them to see what topics are being discussed and what questions are being asked. Can they spark an idea in you?

One of the topics that always works is color. Without fail, year after year you can be talking about color. Every season you can be talking about color. It changes all the time, and there's nothing better than being on the forefront of that and being able to share that with your audience.

> ## ◉ Great Tip!
>
> Turn to design channels on TV and design magazines for inspiration on the topic of your talk.

For example, speak on The next 5 hot trends in paint color. How to pick the right color for every room in the house. How the right color can enhance your life. What your favorite color says about you. Which colors go together. This list can go on and on.

It's important to make your talk informative and entertaining. People want to have a good time. They just want to walk away feeling like it was worth their time. If you've promised them seven design tips and you deliver that, then they got what they wanted. They'll be happy.

A lot of times we get so hung up on our own fears of speaking that we forget that people come to us to hear the information. So really it's not about us, it's about the information that we give to the people who come to listen to us.

The second important point here is to deliver on the information that you promised. So if in your advertisement (flyer, website, etc.) you have promised five top trends – you have to remember to talk about all five trends. As long as you deliver on the information that you promised, that's all you can ask of yourself, and that's all the audience can ask of you as well.

Where to Speak: Venue 1

It might surprise you that one of the best places for designers to have small speaking engagements is literally in their clients' homes or in their friends' homes. Think how much more relaxing that already is. So if you're not a natural-born speaker, now you're suddenly not on a stage, you're just in your friend's living room. So we've already taken the pressure down tremendously.

To get into a home, you would just call up a friend or a client and say that you want to share your seven design trends that are happening right now. Would she be willing to host a small get-together? It's just that simple – it doesn't have to be complicated.

And suddenly that's just not the pressure that it was when you had to stand up on a big stage. And there's a bonus here: that *know, like, and trust* factor that we talked about at the beginning of the chapter, because the person hosting the party is your friend.

Great Tip!

Use your friends' or clients' homes as great speaking venues – especially if you're just starting out.

It'a a great introduction for you to have a client or a friend who is saying on your behalf, "Hey, guys, I want everyone to get together. We're going to have a great night out, and my really good friend is just going to share the latest tips in decorating. You're going to love her talk. It'll give you great ideas – nothing to buy – and she's going to talk for a few minutes."

There's already a tremendous amount of know, like, and trust going on there because the people being invited already know, like, and trust this person who's doing the inviting. And if she's saying you're good, chances are high that the party is going to be pretty good. Then you're so much further along that path to the *know, like, and trust*.

It's really interesting that from the friend events, where a friend or a client hosts, without fail I get a client. I don't know that there are many marketing things that you can say without fail you're going to get a client. I know that this has worked for me; but I'm not guaranteeing that if you host an event, you'll get a client. But I'd be a little surprised if you don't, even if it takes a couple of reminder notes. Because, of course, these things have to be followed up and you've got to keep in touch.

Where to Speak: Venue 2

If you're not going to be in a client's home, if you're not going to be in a friend's home, my next favorite place is to partner up with a store. Choose a store that has the same kind of clients that you do but doesn't necessarily offer the same things that you offer.

My favorite partner in my town is a rug store. It's a fabulous rug store, and they do everything from machine-made to handmade. I approached the owner of this store and said that I thought we could get something going for the both of us by hosting an event.

My first event was a teaching class on how to do a floor plan for your living room. We got 12 people attending this class – it was a class you had to pay for – and of those 12 people, not one of them had ever taken a step into his store before.

From this arrangement, the rug store owner got 12 people in his store that he had never heard of before, and I met 12 people who had never necessarily heard of me before. That kind of joint partnership can just really be tremendous, because of the support that each of you can bring.

Where to Speak: Other Ideas

Clients' or friends' home and a store are my two favorite speaking venues, but there are lots more. Here is a few additional ideas:
- women's groups
- professional groups
- church functions
- silent auctions at schools
- country clubs
- day spas
- beauty salons

 **Great Tip!**

Partner with a retail location that caters to the same clientele you do.

Pick the venue where you think that you will shine, and also those that seem the easiest for you – pick the one that you feel is low-hanging fruit for you. If you think that you have a friend and who will just be delighted to host something for you, then just go that route – pick the easiest route you can find. If going after a paint store or rug store seems like a really hard job and seems like an uphill battle, then don't take that route. Take the route that you think is the easiest for you to implement immediately. Think in terms of immediate implementation.

How to Approach a Potential Partner

One thing that I will say for anyone who's ever considered this is that if you approach someone and they immediately don't jump on hosting an event in their store, do not try to convince them otherwise. If it is not immediately apparent to the person you're talking to that joining forces would be to both people's advantage, my advice is that it's not worth it to try to convince them, because they'll never really be on board. Whatever their resistance is, it's going to show up as resistance throughout the whole thing.

> **◉ Action Item!**
>
> Approach partnering as a win-win opportunity that will help both businesses get new clients.

There's no reason to fight an uphill battle. There are plenty of other opportunities out there in other stores and with other potential partners. And it's so much easier to work with someone who understands and who really gets it.

So, having said that, let's talk about how to approach a potential partner. What it comes down to is just getting up the courage to ask the question. Similar to Woody Allen's famous saying that 90% of life is just showing up, your getting the courage to ask the question is going to be that 90%. And what's left is 10% of them just saying "Oh, yes, let's talk about how to make that work."

All you have to do is say, "I have a win-win marketing idea that will help you bring more clients into the store." Wait for their response. If they show interest, then you go into the description of the event you have in mind.

You would say, "I'd like to partner with you by hosting an event in your store. I'd like it to be special and nice. I will introduce it to my list of people – people who have perhaps never been to your store. You can introduce it to the people on your list, so that they are inclined to come again, because they will love the topic that I will be sharing with them. We can both benefit from this cross-promotion."

The reason special events work so well in a store is because it gives people a special reason to come back to the store that's otherwise always there. It gives people a sense of purpose and a sense of urgency. When you have a special event, people have to take notice: "If I don't do this, I will miss it; if I don't commit to this, it will be gone. It's very different than the store just being open 9 to 5 and I can go anytime." So that's one of the biggest reasons that a store would be looking for a special event.

How to Approach a Country Club

A country club can be a fabulous place to arrange speaking opportunities.

The first step is to check out their schedules to find out whether they are doing something similar already. Are there already events that they're hosting for their members? The answer is very likely yes. So you need to ask for a list of what those events are, to see how a design presentation can fit. What kind of things are already being talked about? What kind of things already get attendance and get interest from the members? That's how you want to fit your work in.

> ### 💿 Great Tip!
>
> Ask for a schedule of events to see how your design presentation fits with what the club is already doing. Most important, approach from the standpoint of being of value to them.

So for example, let's say you go to a country club and it turns out that every month they host something for their members – and let's make this difficult, let's just say that every month it's something really dry like how to do your taxes, and then the next month it's something else that doesn't thrill us to tears. Well this is actually a great time to be looking at that list because you could approach them now. You could say, "It looks like you do a lot of things for members, and you get really great attendance; well, let's shake things up a little bit – let's do something a little bit more fun."

"Let's talk about how to turn their beautiful home into a place they love; how to take their amazing views of the golf course and frame them with beautiful window treatments; how to accentuate the view they already have by using simple interior design tricks and tips."

Now let's say instead that they are not doing any programs for their members. You can still approach them and position yourself as a true asset for them and their members. You could say, "I'm a member at this club; I've been coming here for several years. You've got this beautiful place, and I just think you might have a lot of members who'd be inter-

55

ested in hearing about my topic. Here are just a couple of examples: 7 best ways to get your home ready for the holidays. 5 decorator tips that they can't live without."

It's important to remember that this is not supposed to be super-hard. None of it is rocket science. It's all about getting up the courage to approach the marketing director and say, "Hi, my name is Mary. I'd like to be of value to your members."

If this seems like a big move, you can break it down even further. First day you can drive up to the country club and you can drive away. The second day you can drive up to it, get out of your car, walk up to the door, and walk back to the car. Next day, you can take it a step further. Give yourself permission to do it in baby steps if needed.

How to Monetize a Speaking Engagement

> **◉ Important!**
>
> The key to monetizing your speaking engagements is in growing your list!

The key to monetizing your speaking engagements is in growing your list. Your list is the main asset of your business, and all of your marketing activities – speaking included – should be targeted and positioned to grow your list. In conjunction with growing your list, your parallel priority is to set up a mechanism to follow up and communicate with your list.

When I do my speaking engagements, I could deliver my talk and then just wait. I could wait for anyone who was interested enough to email me or just reach out to me on my website. So I could wait, or I could do what I suggest to every designer who wants to grow her business, which is to have a mechanism in place for following up.

That way, everything you do in your business leads to the next step. It never ends with a final step on a project, installation, appointment, or a phone conversation. All of those touch points lead to the next step. It should never end when you think it's going to end. It doesn't end at the end of a phone call, it doesn't end at the end of the speech at your friend's house. Never think Okay, I gave the speech at the country club and I'm done now. It's always about what are you going to do next, what follow-up steps you are going to take next.

Your talk is actually just the beginning of a long relationship with a potential client. The best way to continue that relationship is through persistent follow-up. And the best way to do persistent follow-up is with an email newsletter.

> ## 🖋 Important!
> Create a no-pressure situation where the attendees *want* to give you their information.

So how do you get these people who came to hear you speak to sign up for your newsletter? Hands down, it's to use a free give-away, a drawing or a door prize.

It is one thing to say, "Hey, everybody, I have a newsletter. I would love to send it to you, so please fill out your information." You may get some people who would probably do that for you. It's a whole other thing to say, "I'd just like to do a quick 'thank you' drawing for everyone who came out tonight. The door prize tonight is _____." (Ideas for a door prize could be: a favorite pillow, favorite fabric, a pair of key tassels that you absolutely love that could work in anybody's home, or your favorite little accessory.) When you position it as a valuable prize, almost everybody will enter their name.

You pass the bag around and everybody drops in their business card (if some don't have a business card, you can distribute index cards and ask them to print their name, address, phone, and email address). When you give away the gift, you can say, "I'm going to follow up with you guys, and hopefully we'll be able to work on a project in the future. If the time isn't now, that's no problem either. Thank you so much for coming."

Or better yet, you say, "If you enjoyed what you heard tonight, you'll love my newsletter on best decorating tips for your home. And if you get it and it's not what you need, just hit unsubscribe at the bottom." It is a no-pressure situation. You are letting them know what's going on, that you are growing your list, and that you would love to stay connected with them.

The reason that speaking engagements are such a great marketing vehicle is because, like few other activities, they foster that know-like-and-trust factor. Your listeners have taken their time to come see you, hear you, and get to know you. They know you are real, personable, human – just like them. Now when you follow up with them, you are that much closer to being their "go-to" designer when they need your services.

Just remember that the main purpose of any speaking engagement is to build your list so that afterwards you can follow up with your listeners. Don't start your talk with the expectation of getting a client right at the event. You might, of course, which is always nice. I've had people come to me right after I spoke and said that they've been meaning to decorate their living room forever, but didn't know any good designers, and wouldn't it be wonderful if I came out to help them. So, yes, I have gotten clients right on the spot.

> ## ◉ Remember!
>
> The main purpose of a speaking engagement is to build your list, so that you can build a relationship with your listeners afterwards.

But my expectation for the potential of a speaking engagement far outreaches just one client at an event. My expectation is that through my follow-up vehicles, I will be continually in the email boxes of hundreds of my potential clients, who will eventually get to know, like, and trust me so much that they will want to hire me for a design project, purchase one of my products, or book me for another speaking event.

Why Giving Away Your Secrets Gets You Clients

"I don't want to give away all my secrets – the clients won't hire me afterwards if I tell them everything" – this is one of the strongest objections I hear on a daily basis. I understand your concern! How do you not "give away the farm" and at the same time, give them the taste of what you're capable of? You are afraid that if you share too much, the clients won't need your services.

My biggest piece of advice: Let go of this fear! It is just not possible for them to know everything that you know. Think about how many clients you've helped; how many projects you've completed; how much experience you've garnered; how many mistakes you've made; how much education you've received; how much industry information you've absorbed; how many people you know; how many situations you've faced.

You dispense countless advice every single time you're with the client. You could stand in front of them for a lifetime, before exhausting everything that you do. Your talents are immense; your tips and tricks are numerous. Sharing even half of what you know will never give them the amount of knowledge and confidence to do it alone.

Be generous with your information, because your generosity toward your clients will attract their generosity toward you. Share your best little secrets that nobody knows so that your listeners can try to replicate them in their homes; make it special, and tell them that it's something that you do every single time you work with a client.

As an example, I'll give you one of mine. So I'm at a friend's house and I'm talking about best design tips. And I say that one of the things that I do is when I'm arranging accessories, I reduce everything to a shape. I'm not looking at a thing as that thing: I'm not looking at it as a book, or as a plate, or as a vase, but instead a shape. I reduce everything to shapes.

◉ Important!

When you're open with your information, it makes the listeners think: "If her free information is that good, her other stuff must be really great!"

When I work with accessories, I put them together in the most appealing way so that the room has balance, harmony, scale, and proportion. As I do that, I might find out that there's something missing. And when that thing is missing, it's a shape I'm looking for, it's not a thing. So you don't have to go out shopping saying that what you need is a blue vase because suddenly the only thing that you can think of is a blue vase. If you use a shape instead, you know that you need something that's roughly 5 inches wide and anywhere between 10 and 15 inches tall, and it could be this range of colors.

Well suddenly, a lot more things fit that than a vase. And it opens up a whole new world of possibilities. So the next time that you're accessorizing a shelf, don't think about the thing – think about the shape. That's one of my favorite design tips, and I share that with people all the time. It's not readily available; it's just something that I've developed.

We, as designers, have a million of those kinds of secrets. We use them every day and often we don't realize they are secrets because it's so innate to us. But when you share that kind of stuff and have the whole room nodding their heads yes, going "Wow, I could do that," you suddenly realize that it's not innate to other people. Of course, often what happens is that those people who thought they could do it on their own really can't, and end up calling you anyway.

59

If we as designers are generous with our information during our speaking engagements, then the audience is that much more likely to come back to us for more information. Because we have a lot to share – we have so much to offer. People who come to hear us want to learn best design practices; they have best intentions of doing it themselves, but in the end, if they are our customer, they will be calling us to get it done for them.

How to Promote the Event

Here are my favorite simple ways to promote your speaking event.

Action Item!

Take your time to create a plan of action – then simply follow your plan.

1. Create "save a date" cards and mail them out to your list of guests. This idea works particularly well if the event is being held in your friend's home and you have a list of people to invite. Once the invitations have gone out, make sure to schedule enough time to do good old phone follow-up.

2. Use your e-zine to build the momentum about the event. Be sure to start far enough in advance so that you can send several email promotions without hammering your audience over the head. My recommendation is start 8 weeks ahead. If your event is at a retail location (like my example of a rug store), be sure to supply the owner with pre-written messages so that he can easily copy and paste them into the emails to his client database.

3. Use social media to talk about your event, what you'll be presenting, and what kind of information they will learn as a result of attending. In addition to regular posts, you can also do a special invitation.

4. If the event is held at retail location, posting flyers around the store will let people know that they are welcome to attend. Check out neighboring stores – grocery stores, nail salons, pharmacies – to see whether you can put up a flyer there, too.

5. Use local Chamber of Commerce event calendars to spread the word.

6. Ask whether local networking organizations have newsletters (email or printed), and see whether you can buy ads there.

7. Use local bulletin boards in your place of worship, the fitness club, and your kids' schools.

How to Handle Revenue Generated from a Speaking Engagement

Chances are really high that the client or the store has never done this kind of event before, so if you tell them how it works, they'll nod their heads and say Okay. So you get a lot fewer questions when you tell the person the process and explain how it works.

It is important to note that it should not be your goal to make money from the actual event. Instead, the event is your introduction to the people – it's the beginning of the know-like-and-trust relationship, not necessarily a revenue-producing activity.

Having said that, I would encourage you to charge for your event. I actually like to charge for events because I like to have a commitment from people. People who pay to attend are much more committed to dropping everything and making your event a priority, versus someone who doesn't have a financial stake in it. This especially applies to the training events, like my event at the rug store was, for which I charged $125 for two days.

> ## 🕮 Remember!
>
> The main reason you're doing a speaking engagement is to start a relationship with a prospect, not to get paid for doing a one-time event.

Any additional business that comes as a result of the event is that person's business. I don't see that any revenue needs to be split between the two parties putting on the event.

Please remember that the main reason you're doing the event in the first place is to start a relationship with a prospective customer. Once you get that customer on your list, and once you follow up with her, that's where the relationship gets built. And that's where down the road she hires you as a designer, and you can do a whole room full of furniture or several rooms' worth of window treatments.

I have a great story about that. The very first time that I ever held one of these classes, one of the attendees actually came only one of the two nights. Something came up and she wasn't able to come on the second night. Of course, I followed up with her, and for whatever reason, I just didn't know her. It turns out I was supposed to know her because she owned a marketing company in the next town over and she was really well known.

She added herself to my newsletter list, and every once in awhile she'd respond to one of my newsletters with a quick note: "I've been meaning to get in touch with you but I've been so busy." I wouldn't be surprised if it took us as much as two years with her being on my newsletter list before we really started working together.

Two years later, she hired me to work on two of the rooms in her home, and it turned out that her home was this fabulous historic home. So now I suddenly had an opportunity to work in this historic home, and it was a wonderful experience. And you know how this works: You work with your clients, they see your work, they burst into tears, start hugging you, you become part of their family, and the next thing you know, they host an event for you. Well, that's exactly what happened with this customer: She went from coming to only one night of class to two years later becoming my client, and ultimately hosting my book signing.

Mechanics of the Actual Event

How you handle the nitty-gritty of the event itself has a lot to do with the venue.

Beware!

Sometimes it may take years to see a prospect face-to-face. Don't be discouraged. Important thing is to continue to foster the relationship.

If it's at your friend's or customer's home, it will probably have a more informal feel. You will probably be the one bringing in the food and the drinks, greeting people, mingling actively, and getting to know the crowd. Your actual presentation is casual. Your props can easily be passed around. Your visuals don't have to be large-scaled, since it will be easy to view them in the smaller crowd.

If your talk is at a larger venue, consider putting together a PowerPoint presentation so that everyone can see your visuals. You may want to have a larger flip chart if you need to write things down or draw.

I've done it both ways: without props and with props, where I'm literally pointing at things and holding them up. I almost always bring in the fabric and trim books, because who doesn't like to come up and

62

touch and feel them? I also always make sure to thank the host of the event and recognize him or her for taking care of me.

Think of your own comfort level, think of what you would like. If someone invited you over to hear what a designer was talking about, what would you want to see?

In Summary: 3 Action Points

1. I want you to think of a friend or a client who loves to throw a party. We all know somebody who loves to entertain. The easiest way to start thinking about that is who throws the Christmas party every single year, and then you can kind of backtrack from there. If you know somebody who throws a Christmas party every year, they're throwing some other kind of party, too, I can almost guarantee it. So think of that friend and pick up the phone and say, "Hey, I just learned about this new idea and I need your help."

2. The other thing that you could do (even as early as tomorrow) is to walk down your downtown street, stop at a store that you either already shop in or you just think is the cutest thing on earth. And walk in and say, "What would you think if we had an event here, if it was a marketing event that helped both you and me?"

3. The last thing would be to think of the last question a client asked you, and turn it into three tips so that you can get over the fear of what on earth would I talk about. So just think of the last question a client asked, and think of three quick answers that you would have for that. That's what you talk about.

ABOUT THE AUTHOR

Mary Larsen is the founder of Grow
YourDesignBiz.com and YourDesignBizBlog.
com and author of *How to Open and Operate a
Financially Successful Redesign, Redecorating,
and Home Staging Business* (www.designand-
stagingbizbook.com)

A widely recognized expert in the field of design, drapery design,
redesign, and home staging, Mary's work has been featured on ABC's
"Extreme Home Makeover – Home Edition," and she speaks at conferences throughout the nation. If you need a speaker or teleseminar or
webinar for your professional group, contact Mary and learn more at
Mary@marylarsendesigns.com and GrowYourDesignBiz.com.

Mary offers her "Designing Your Success" Mastermind group coaching
program and one-on-one consultations to those in the design field so
they can make more money in their business. She also offers newsletters for designers to use as their own, and many other business-building
programs.

4
ONLINE MARKETING:
Getting More Clients & Referrals in Today's Marketplace Using Simple Online Techniques

by Nika Stewart

www.nikastewart.com

In this chapter you'll learn:

What your website must include to attract ideal customers – and what it shouldn't (the answer may surprise you!)
The biggest mistakes designers are making online, and how to avoid them
2 simple ways to use email to boost sales
Where to find the resources for creating a professional and effective online newsletter campaign
How to quickly build your list of email newsletter subscribers

What Should a Good Website Include?

Website is what people usually think when talking about *online marketing*. They think of "a website." And I wish it weren't true, but we actually still have to talk about it – that designers need websites. It is such a given, but unfortunately we have to tell some designers, "You need to get a website!"

Most of the clients I work with do have a website because they're really serious about business. And if you are serious, you, of course, want to get a website. That's how people are finding service professionals nowadays. It's just the way that people work. They look online. But even if you do have one, there are things that make you more visible – make it easier for people to find you when they're looking for what you offer.

Unfortunately, most of the sites that I see from interior designers and people in the design profession – stagers, organizers, re-designers, window treatment professionals – are nice-looking but not informative. We're all artists and we're designers and we love everything looking good and being beautiful, so that's what we think our website should be – all of our beautiful photographs of our design work.

Beware!

Your website should not only be beautiful – it should be enlightening, filled with text, descriptions, and information.

And while we do need to show off what we can do, pictures do not allow people to find you. So you need a lot of text. And designers usually are not text people; they really are visual people. Instead of reading words, we want to look at beautiful pictures and be inspired and hope that other people are inspired.

But when people are seeking, for example, a designer in Freehold, New Jersey, they might type in "Designer Freehold New Jersey." They're not going to find you if you don't have "Designer Freehold New Jersey" written in your site a dozen times. And usually that's kind of an "aha" for a lot people when they're putting up their website. You may think that you probably need to put your address somewhere in there, *but you need to have that a lot.*

Google and all of the search engines – they like words. That's how they find you – from your words. So you absolutely have to have the key words that people are searching for. And how do you know what they are? Well, you can do a little research. There's actually a keyword search tool in Google, and can put in "designer in your area" and it'll give you some hints of words that people are typing in more often.

Then it will give you dozens of suggestions of words that people are looking for. And something that I found interesting is that people are not always writing *designer*, which is what I thought people were typing in when they were looking for a designer. People are instead typing in *design company, design firm, or design business*. So make sure those words are in your site because your site will come up in the search engines high up – closer to the top of page one – if you have the most popular keywords in your site.

It's pretty much across the web; it's what people all over the world are typing in. But you can also type in your area and it'll give you suggestions of things that are similar to what you're typing in. You have to get a little creative and look at it, but it's pretty intuitive. You'll look at it and realize that if there are many thousands of people typing in this word, it's very likely that people in your area are doing it also.

⊘ Great Tip!

Brainstorm several words by which people can find you on the web. Then make sure to have these words implanted in your website.

You also want to include information about yourself. So often, we think that when we go into business, we want to put company information on our website and in our advertising and marketing materials. But people want to know *you*, especially in this business: It's a one-on-one service. You're working personally with your client, and it's such a personal service. I'm not going to work with a company just because the pictures look nice.

I want to know *who you are* and to see whether I connect with you and like you. People only work with people that they know, they like, and they trust. How can you get these strangers to know you, like you, and trust you if you don't reveal yourself on your website? So talk about yourself, talk about even things that have nothing to do with business. About your love of flowers, about your pets, about your children. This is what connects with people. In my bio, you may learn that I sing in a

67

band and I act in murder mystery shows…

> ## Great Tip!
>
> Make sure to have your name on every page of your website!

A lot of us are scared to reveal a lot about ourselves. It is possible that people won't like me because of what I wrote, and that's okay.

That's okay, because those are not my clients. We wouldn't have connected. It would have been a waste of time had they called me and I'd gone over for a consultation. We wouldn't have connected. If they think that singing in a rock band is, I don't know, amoral, I don't – I mean really. If they don't like that, let them know about that before they even call me.

So essentially the website becomes almost a pre-qualifying tool.

People will find you based on the keywords. Think about yourself, too. If you're looking for something, what do you do? You usually go to one of the big search engines, like Yahoo or Google. So you type in a few words that kind of describe what you're looking for, and you usually get the sites that are the most relevant. So a business that has most of those words on its site will comes up at the top, and you want to be one of those people who come up high in the search engine results.

Make sure your name is in the website, not just your company name. If people use The Window Dresser to do their windows, and they want to recommend you to their friends, they probably remember working with YOU. So someone might say, "I recommend Vita; she was terrific." Not "I recommend the name of your company." That's less memorable to people because they get to know YOU, so their friends may look you up on the web.

Plus even when someone refers you, people want to know more about you, so they type your name into Google. Make sure your name is on your website, and not only on the home page but a lot all over. This is actually a great test to see how easy you are to find. Everyone reading this should go into Google and put their name into Google. Put your name in the search box with quotes around it and see how many things come up. Most of my clients, when I start working with them, will get nothing. That's not a serious business.

If I'm thinking of working with you, someone recommended you, I type your name, and nothing comes up, then I think to myself: "Oh,

she's either so new that she doesn't have a web presence, or she's really
not that serious about this. She's not building herself, her business,
online." Make sure you're online. Make sure you have a web presence.

Purchasing Your Own Name as a Domain Name

It doesn't have to be the one – the URL – that you use for your business, but you should have it even if it's just for the reason that *no one else has it*. You want to own that, and you could even forward it to go to your company website. So if someone types it in – you know, I don't remember the name of her company. I'll type "her name" dot com – and let that go to your company website as well.

What if your name is really common? Well then, first of all, you should be the one who has that website; but at this point, if your name is very common, it's very unlikely you can get it. So perhaps put in – well what do you people know you as? If people don't know you as Vitalia, but they know you as Vita, get that name. Put your middle initial in, or your middle name.

> ### 🔵 Great Tip!
>
> Buy your name as a domain name. If it is no longer available, buy the next closest thing.

Get something as close as you can to your first and last name. Yes, it's best to have the name that everyone knows you as, but if that is very common and you can't get it, you have to, at this point, come up with something that is as close as you can. You know, it's harder now; 15 years ago we would have all just run on and got our name. Luckily Nika Stewart wasn't taken all those years ago when I got it, but you know, "NIKA" actually was already taken.

Additionally, spotlight your contact information – this is something I see missing so many times. We all realize that we have to put our contact information on our website, but it isn't prominent, and it's not *right there*. When I land on your website, I want to know how to contact you – without even having to scroll, or look at a different link, or even to click to contact you. Is your phone number or email address *right there at the very top*?

It's so true that our lives – all of our lives – are so busy and stressful and overwhelming that if you make me do *one tiny second or ounce of extra work*, I'm just not going to do it. So make it easy for your

69

prospects when they land on your site to be able to contact you immediately. And along with that, make sure you have a sign-up box to capture people's names and email addresses so that you can market to them and contact them again. People often will look at a website but not be ready to pick up the phone and call you at that second.

Great Tip!

Have a sign-up box for your free gift (and your newsletter) at the top of every page of your website.

They may even say to themselves, "Oh, I like this gal. I think I'll contact her when I'm ready" – and then just completely forget. But if you ask for their name and email address to give them something for free, like a free report or a newsletter, which is my favorite thing (I'm sure we'll talk about that), you now will remind them over and over again.

So when they are ready to purchase from you, *you're* the one they think of. You're the one that keeps contacting them.

My website is NikaStewart.com. That is my name. Very clear and easy to remember.

And it's very important to have the sign-up box for your e-zine or your free report, which we'll talk more about. It should be at the top of your home page at the very least, but if you have it on every page, that's much better. Because you never know how people are going to find you. They may Google something, and Google may send them to one of the pages on your site – but not necessarily to your home page. So however they get to you, you want them to be able to put in their name and email address so that you capture that. And now it's your responsibility to market to them over and over again.

Mistakes That Designers Make Online

I think one of the mistakes that's very big with interior designers – and those of us in this creative profession – is that we're waiting for everything to be perfect before we put it out there. We want things to be beautiful, and everyone can relate to that.

It's the perfection paralysis.

Designers I work with have said, "I want to launch an email newsletter. I've been thinking about it for 3½ years, but I just don't have, you know, it just doesn't look right yet." Well, for 3½ years you could have had it out there and gotten a lot of business and been tweaking it as you go. *Good enough is good enough.* That is my favorite motto. Not in the quality of your work, though: When you serve people, you want to be as close to perfect as you can be in the services that you give to people.

But in your marketing, just get it out there. Seriously. If you've been thinking about putting out a blog, but you don't like how it looks, or you don't think your articles are good enough, you'll still get people to find you if you put it out there. And look at it next week and change it and make it better. Look at it every other week and add to it and improve upon it, but at least it's out there.

> # Beware!
>
> Stop waiting to be perfect! You never will. Start doing, and course-correct as you go along.

Stop waiting, because if you do wait for things to be perfect, you'll actually be waiting for a very long time. Because nothing is ever perfect. Come on. Even your design work. You can always look at pictures and say, *What could I have added to this that would have made it even better?* Keep tweaking your web stuff as you go along, but get it out there.

There's always more that you wish could be better. But at some point, you're getting so much business that you forget about caring about that. Seriously – that's what happened to me. I am definitely one of those "let me just make this perfect" people. I'll spend too much time looking for a better clipart picture to put there because it's not pretty enough.

Or, let me wait until my photographer can take better photos. You know what? Send it now; do a different one next week. Change your website; add to it; and, like I said to myself, *I'll do that*, and then at some point – I still like to improve upon things, but I started getting so busy that I stopped caring so much. Because look…it's working, it's giving people value, it's getting out there. It's not perfect, but it's doing its job. So do it.

I think that's probably the biggest challenge I see – that people are just not getting it out there. And there are a lot of mistakes also with email marketing, and I don't know if you want to talk about that now, but that's usually where I see a lot of mistakes, also. And that's my favorite way to market online – through email and email newsletters.

E-Zines

E-zines, or email newsletters, are what tripled my design business originally, and they're what made me such an evangelist for newsletters. It became my favorite marketing tool, and I think it's because it really helps to build and solidify relationships with your customers, your clients, and their friends, your prospects. People get to know you, like you, and trust you – like we were talking about.

> ## ◉ Important!
>
> An e-zine is a great way to build and solidify your relationship with your customers. It's also a way to establish your expert status.

It's a way to communicate with the people and build your expert status, and people start getting excited about hearing from you on a weekly or bi-weekly or monthly basis. At one point I said, I need to teach designers how to do this because it's so powerful a marketing tool. It's kind of funny. Now when people hear that I'm coming to speak, they all say, "Oh, is Nika going to speak about newsletters?"

I don't only speak about newsletters, but I guess it's what I became known for because I'm such a big proponent of it. Because I put out a program to teach designers the step-by-step process, and we can go through that. But so many designers were out there still saying yes, now I know the steps, but I still don't think it's going to be perfect enough, and I'm not a good writer.

So I said to them, I want to take another obstacle away from you, so let me write the articles for you. So I wrote a few years' worth of articles, and I have those available for designers. Then there were many designers who said, "You know what? I still don't want to do it. Can you just do it for me?" So I started a program where *I do it for them*. I mean, you can't *not* do a newsletter. Either learn how to do it yourself – and we'll go over some of the steps right now – or have your assistant do it for you. You can get articles and just copy and paste. Just do it. No matter how it's done, make sure you're doing it.

So what do you do? Gosh, the first thing you need to know is that it's a lot easier than you think if you haven't done it yet. You don't do it from your own email account. That's one of the mistakes I've seen is that people will start a newsletter – they'll do it on a word document to perhaps make it into a PDF. And they'll attach it to an email and try to send it out to all their clients.

72

And that is wrong on so many levels, and I don't think we have time to go into all the reasons why that doesn't work, but it doesn't work. And it's a lot harder, and it adds a lot of work and stress to doing your newsletter, which should be simple. So you need to get an email service provider; you need to sign up online. There are some free ones out there. You can Google it and look around, but my favorite one still is Decorator Contact, which is actually my affiliate link to Constant Contact, and you can sign up for a free account to test it out. I believe it is a 60-day trial, and they give you all the templates.

I find it easy, but tell me what you think. Someone took over doing the sending out of my newsletter – a VA (virtual assistant) of mine – and she moved to another program, which I like also, which is IContact. But I still find Constant Contact to be simpler if you're getting started because you don't have to know codes, you don't have to know html – all that stuff, which, if you don't know what that is – good! You don't have to learn what it is.

You just pick a pretty template, put in your pictures, paste in an article, and you're done. They take care of your address list. So all the legal stuff goes out, like you need to make sure in every newsletter that you give people at the bottom an option of unsubscribing. That's just, legally, what you need to do in any email newsletter. So Constant Contact takes care of that for you, and you don't have to worry.

They do make it easy. And once you spend a couple of hours setting it up, you don't have to do that every time you send out a newsletter, because once you create the template that you like, you just use that same template. You don't have to reinvent it every time.

> **Beware!**
>
> Don't send your e-zine from your personal email account!

When you're picking the template:

Constant Contact, and I'm sure all of the other email service provider services out there, have many templates, and some of them are really beautiful. Let me warn you, designers, that you're going to want to pick the most beautiful, complicated one there is because it's so pretty to look at. When they show you the little thumbnail, it's really pretty.

If you see it all on one page on your web or if you see it in *print*, it's really pretty. **But it doesn't work in email**. You want to pick a very simple, one-column newsletter template. And the reason is – this is kind of interesting if you think about it – if you look at a piece of paper, your eyes can go all over the whole paper. You can have a three-column newsletter with pictures and articles and loads of things, and your eyes can just, you know, look around and look where you want, finish an article, go to another column, look at something else.

With email, we're conditioned to scroll *down* as we're reading. So you want to have one column where people read and keep going down, down, down to read more. If people have to finish an article, and then scroll back up and to the right to read the next article, well you've just added something else for them to do. They're probably not going to. It's too complicated in an email to do that – to have to scroll in different directions to get to different parts of it. It doesn't show up all at once. You want to have a very simple, single-column template. So I hope I was passionate enough.

> ⟲ **Important!**
>
> Keep it simple! Pick a one-column template so that the reader can easily scroll down.

Keep it simple. It doesn't have to be boring, of course! You want to add your brand, your colors, your logo at the top.

About content...

The most important thing – you want something valuable for people, and you also want to be consistent. So send an article, or even just a paragraph. (By the way, don't worry – you don't have to write an *article* every week. You don't even have to do this every week. You could do it every other week, or once a month – as long as you're **consistent**.) And it could be something as simple as a great inspirational idea you just came up with; it doesn't have to be a long article. And write conversationally, as well.

So you want to give them something valuable. That's your feature, your main article.

You want to have a note from yourself so that people do get to know you personally. And you reveal as much as you want about yourself. Don't go crazy and reveal things that should be kept secret. But let people know about you, what's going on in your life, things that will connect with people. Like, Hey, I took my daughter to New York to be with her cousins this week and she had a great time. Hope you're having a great holiday week, too. Here is your main article about such and such...

I think when people hear that you should share personal information, they get scared. But when I say it, I don't mean share *private* information. There are things that you don't share with strangers. And these people – you want to talk as if they're your friends, because they are. They are your potential clients, if not already your clients.

These are people you would want to have lunch with, hopefully. I mean those are the people you want to attract to you to be your customers. So you chat about – like, if I said I just picked up my daughter from her cousin's house, that's not sharing something so personal and private that I wouldn't want the world to know.

You know, someone might say, "Oh how cute, she has a little daughter, I do too." And people even write me on Twitter and on emails and Facebook. They write to me things about their life, too. We're connecting. "Oh, my daughter is the same age… what school does she go to, etc."

> **Great Tip!**
>
> Share personal information. Don't share private information.

That's how you get clients – by building relationships like that. Not by saying "Dear so and so, here is how I can help you decorate your house." That's not what I want to hear from you. I want to know if I know you, like you, and trust you. And, yes, I want to see that you're an expert in decorating. But I don't care if you're an expert if I don't like you.

I just don't care.

Nobody cares how much you know unless they like you, so give them the opportunity to like you.

I think it Mother Teresa who said: People don't care how much you know until they know how much you care. And that's kind of along the same lines. So they feel that you care if you're chatting about yourself and it relates to them, too.

Another mistake I see designers do is, either they put in so much valuable information – and nothing about themselves and how people can contact them to get more services from them – or they put in only promotional information.

So you definitely need a call to action. After I read your great story about what's going on in your life and this great tip on how to move my furniture around to create a more cozy atmosphere, I now want to know *what to do next*. So tell me how I can contact you to make an appointment, or to get a free report, or to have a phone consultation. You know, tell me what to do next, and make it easy for me to know what to do next and how to contact you.

Great Tip!

Have a call to action!

So that has to be in there, make sure. And you want that "promotional part" to be about 20% to 25% of the newsletter.

Not much more! That's a big mistake that people do in every business with newsletters. People don't want to be reading advertisements, so you don't want to just be sending out promotional material. And so people go the opposite way and put no promotional material. And then – I'm not contacting you. I don't know how.

So now, who do you send this to? Well you start with all of your past clients. Everyone you've ever worked with, anyone you've ever done any business with or for – if they have done business with you, they can go on your newsletter list. So you start with them. And you actually add your friends and family. (You do ask their permission.) But it's amazing how many referrals you get from friends and family.

Don't think – well, I'm not going to send it to my mom and my best friend. They're not using me. But you know what? Even your mom and your best friend – who you think know everything that you do, something that they read may spark their memory that someone they know said something about needing someone like that. And, oh gosh, so and so might – let me forward this email to them. And you get business that way. And they also think, you know – my friends could use this newsletter. And so it builds that way. You want it to forward, you want to remind people to forward it to their friends and tell them to sign up.

As for your subscription list: In the marketing world, it's called *the list*, which is so impersonal. The size of your list, of your community of subscribers, is important. You want that to be large, but that's not as important as the *quality*.

In the marketing industry, I have always had what is probably considered by most of the big guys a tiny, tiny list. But it is so niche. Only people who are qualified leads or people who really want to hear what I have to offer – they're the only people signing up. I don't try to get on a list and get a few hundred people to sign up for my newsletter, if they aren't perfectly suited to what I have to offer.

So with my tiny list of just a few thousand, I get really good results, I have to say. I used to think, Oh I have such a tiny list. And then I would hear what the big guys get as far as percentages or rate of return and all this. And I do better than them, because I get by with a better-quality list. So I've discovered that quality is a lot more important than quantity. Regarding your subscribers, *who* you have and *how many* you have are both important.

Building a List

I think one of my favorite ways to get really qualified people, subscribers on my list, is by sharing my knowledge, really sharing an article with someone else. Like, "Vita, can I give you an article to put out in your newsletter?"

Call to Action!

Ask another business owner with a similar (but not competing) clientele to feature your article in their e-zine.

Let's say you're tired this week and you don't want to send out, you don't want to write a whole new article. I'll give you one.

So if you'd like an article, I'll give it to you. Just put my name and website at the bottom. And almost every time I've done that – shared it with the right person who has a community of subscribers who are very similar to my target audience – I may get 100 extra people signing up because they read my article.

They liked it and they clicked on my site and signed up for my newsletter.

So what would be some of the partners who designers can consider to swap articles with? Well, Realtors are terrific. Actually, first think of who your target audience is. You have to know that, and be very clear on that. And then think of who else has that same target. And it isn't always people in the design industry.

And that's kind of great because these other people you want to partner with are not competitors in any way. So it's not like you're saying to a local designer, hey, let's swap articles. Well, then you're taking my

77

clients and I'm taking your clients.

You don't really want to be doing that, probably, although that's not always a bad idea. But think about CPAs, lawyers, Realtors definitely, because they're working with new homeowners, people in other parts of the industry.

> **● Great Tip!**
>
> A great way to distribute your content is to share your articles through article marketing websites!

If you're a window treatment expert, work with a color expert, or a Feng Shui expert, or an organizer. Find other people who are local and have a local subscription base that is very similar to the target you want.

And you can get very clever, also.

Other examples are retail locations, like a rug store, a flooring store, or a paint store. Of course, they need to have a newsletter that goes out so that you can give them your article.

As I'm saying that, there's a way to put your article out there on the web without even giving it to a specific person. It's called article marketing. You just take some things that you've written, and you put them on article marketing sites, and they go out to the world. So anyone who finds your article would then click on your link and sign up for your newsletter.

It's not as targeted because it's out there on the web, rather than specifically to a target audience that's ideal. But it is another way to build your list.

One of the biggest ones is eZineArticles.com. I have someone who now does my online marketing, but that's the first one I signed up with. And they're probably the best – best attended, best visited. You get it free. And I'll just give you one fun idea that I just recently heard of, and I shared it with my community. I've heard some great results from this. It's putting out a box for entries to win something – like when Mary Kay puts a box in a salon where you enter to win a free makeover or something like that. The prize could instead be a free week at a gym, or something like that. The visitors put their names and email addresses or phone numbers on slips of paper and puts them in the box to enter.

If you can come up with something fabulous to give away, like a free

78

pillow, or a free one-hour color consultation, then put a sign-up box in a local retail shop where they have your target customers coming in. Someone I know did this and got about 500 new sign-ups.

And they're all ideal. I mean, these people all want what she has to offer because her prize was something that she offers. They all wanted this prize, so they all want what she has. So that's a fun thing to do.

Of course the retail store, or wherever you're setting out the box, has to give you permission. But you know, if you can give a local store something, they're going to let you put a little box on their front table.

> ## ⬤Action Item!
>
> Build your list by partnering with a local business and doing a raffle for a free consultation (or pillow, or window treatment).

How could they say no to that, especially if you're going to give something to them. Sometimes you say to the owner, hey, I'll give you a free window treatment, or something. I mean you don't want to give away the store. But you give them something that they want, if they do this for you. Make it so that *only* members of this salon or this gym get this. So their customers feel they're getting the VIP treatment, and it's good for the gym or the salon to have that out there.

How to Encourage People Who Are Hesitant to Give Out Their Email Address

That's a great question because it is becoming more and more difficult. About 10 years ago, if you had on your website "sign up for my newsletter" or "get on my mailing list," people would just put their name and email address in.

Now you really have to sell to give away this free newsletter. You really have to be good at selling. And in person, it's kind of easy. You just let people know that this is really valuable. If you don't like it, just unsubscribe, you tell them.

Reassure them that there's an unsubscribe link in every newsletter that goes out there. Don't worry about it. I promise you it's going to be great. You're going to love it. But if you hate it, you click unsubscribe. You never hear from me again.

According to studies done on this, most people are much more likely to give you their name and email address on your website or wherever if you have something really compelling that people will get *instantly*. So rather than "sign up for my newsletter," it has to be much more compelling than that, even if it is just a newsletter they're getting. And you can see some samples of this on my site. I have some bullet points: "This is what you get…"

> ### ⊙ **Great Tip!**
>
> People are more willing to share their information with you if they can get something instantly in return.

You get specials that are only available to designers on this subscription list. You get tips from six-figure designers, you get all of these things that people are excited about and they want. So you have to give them reasons to want to get your newsletter.

But even more compelling is to say put your email address here and I will immediately, within a minute, or instantly, send you my free report on the five most costly mistakes that homeowners make when starting a new design project, and how you can avoid them.

Or something like that. Some free report that they get instantly. People seem to be much more likely to say, Oh, I want that. They think, I'll give them my email address if I can get that valuable report.

And then they're on your newsletter list.

E-Zine vs. Blog

Regarding newsletters and blogs, I'm not a blog expert, but I do some blogging. There are certainly more qualified blog experts. However, I can tell you what's working for me.

You shouldn't rule out blogging. However, for me, posting an article on a blog is sort of passive. I post it there and then I hope that people find it.

I can take that same article and put it in my newsletter, and send it out to thousands of people and they get it in their email box. Now of course, they have to open it and read it, but they get it. You know it comes directly to their computer, rather than me just hoping they get it.

That being said, when people are searching, people who aren't on your email newsletter list are not going to find you from posting in a newsletter; that's an email. Search engines don't pick up the emails – they only pick up what's on the Web.

Blogs are great because search engines like continuously updated things. And your website is pretty static: Once you create it, you usually don't update it that often. But blogs are updated every time you post – you update it. And search engines love that. So if you're writing articles that have a lot of good key words in them, then people are going to find you.

There are certainly more search engine optimization techniques that we're not getting into now, but just writing new things gets you coming up higher in the search results.

When you're posting, you have to use good key words. If you write a story about "I saw a pretty bird outside and it was on an oak tree," then people typing in *those* words are going to find you. Not that you shouldn't write stories.

> **⊙ Great Tip!**
>
> How often should you update your blog? Studies show that 3 times a week is ideal.

But if you're posting often, make sure that in your stories, in your articles, in your thoughts that you're posting, that there are some good key words in there so that if people type in *designer or window treatment expert,* that those words are in there. Then people will find you.

And how often do you think we should update our blogs? Studies show that three times a week is ideal.

Here's what's interesting. I am not a blog expert, and I'm not perfect at my blogs. So that is not my forte. However, when I post more often, I get more traffic to my website.

And I'm not talking about posting articles. I'm talking about posting a few sentences. So if you can tweet (not everyone loves to tweet. I do, but…), you can write a few sentences. Like, "today I met with a client and we worked on his home office and he chose blue over green and blah, blah, blah."

That's it. You're done. You go to sleep. That's a post. Or, "I loved working with this client because I like how he moved the desk around to here, and picking furniture is a lot of fun. And this is what I learned today at the furniture store…."

81

That's all you have to write – some thoughts, not an article. And it doesn't have to be like literature, good literature. And it doesn't have to be grammatically correct. It's just your thoughts. I mean, that's really what a blog is supposed to be.

It's a web log. It's a journal, an online journal. So you post a few sentences about your clients, (not using their names; you're not giving away other people's private secrets). It's about the inspiration that you want to give to people.

💡 Great Tip!

A blog post is nothing more than a few sentences expressing your thoughts. Not an article. So keep it simple. And do it often.

And then you're using good key words. And it's easy because it really is a little journal. When you think it's hard, just remember – when you're doing it the hard way, it's actually less effective.

So just post a few sentences.

How do you feel about pictures, actually, on the blog? Well, people do like pictures. If you're talking about design, people like to see the illustration of what you're talking about. But search engines, like we were saying, don't pick up on the pictures.

So if you're doing this to get more traffic, don't worry about the pictures. What I hear from designers is – *I'm spending hours and hours on this post because I'm looking for the perfect picture.*

Well, you know what? Do that later if you want. First put the post up. Get it up. Click "post." Post now!

How does having a blog actually attract clients to us?

Well, like a newsletter and like writing articles in any way, a blog does a few things. If you're writing conversationally and you're just posting your thoughts and ideas and tips, then people are getting to know you and like you.

And they'll certainly *trust* you because you're building your expert status. Writers are considered experts in the areas that they write about. And now you're a writer when you post a blog, when you launch a blog. You are now a writer. Even if you don't think you're a good writer or a writer at all. When you write down your ideas and your thoughts, you are a writer. So you are now an instant expert. And you, of course, are an expert in the field that you're in.

That's why you decided to go into it. But you need everyone else to see you and believe you and trust you as the expert. And a blog does that for you. It helps you gain expert status.

Because it's also interactive, people can post comments. Not everyone does. But people feel like it's an interaction and they feel like they're in a conversation with you rather than you lecturing to them. So again they're getting to know you as a person and hearing your thoughts, and building that relationship with you. And they can comment and you can comment back. That's how you build relationships and get clients to like you.

You're getting search engine optimization. More people are finding you because of the blog. Now this brings up an interesting point. Make sure you have the sign-up for your email newsletter on your blog as well. Because people may come back and read, or even just read once and forget to come back, but at least they gave you their email address.

So now you're marketing to them. Getting people on your email newsletter subscription list is so important. Even if you posted a blog that had some good key words and got people there, they may never come back to your blog.

> **◎ Action Item!**
>
> Make sure to have an e-zine sign-up box on your blog!

But you got them there and they entered their email address. That's just so vitally important.

And it's not necessarily to get a client instantaneously. Yes, ultimately, of course, you want to. But your most important job in marketing online is to have that person "raise their hand and sign up for your newsletter," or for your ezine.

I wanted to make sure that everyone understood that all of their promotional efforts online (and offline, but since we're talking about online now) have to be focused on bringing that potential customer onto their list.

Once you have them on the list, then you can communicate with them

83

and build that relationship with them through the content-rich information that you give them. And that information is your article or a paragraph or a picture and your personal note.

Your first objective is to start a relationship. And how you start that relationship is…you invite them into your newsletter community, and they get to know you.

Important!

The main objective of all of your marketing efforts is to get people on your list, so that you can start and build a relationship with them.

I've heard people describe it as asking someone to marry you on the first date. People don't find your website and call you up and hand you a $50,000 check for a design job. That's not how it works. They need to get to know you, and see if they trust you. That's what the newsletter and the blogs do for people. So get them on your list so that you will be able to show them how great you are.

Facebook vs. Blogs

The search engines really love the social networks. They love Twitter and Facebook and LinkedIn – those are like the three biggies. And people find you through these.

You probably should do this – I have a Google alert with my name in quotes. So every day I'll get an email alert from Google saying…if someone typed in Nika Stewart, this is what they'd find. Every day I'll get a bunch of those, and always there are a bunch of ones from social networks.

So if people are looking for me, they see all of my – mine and my connections' – posts and updates. That's another great search engine trick. It's not really a trick, but it's how you get higher in the search engines – by having connections on the social networks and posting a lot, and by conversing with people.

But the only difference is, it isn't yours. If you have a profile page on a social network, you don't own it. Your blog, on the other hand, you have complete control over – the look of it and the content and how much and how long and how often.

The social networks are kind of in charge. But they're very important.

84

You know they work. So use them.

I love the idea of starting to put something on – say starting a comment on Facebook and then off of that comment, directing folks to your blog. And it works really well. And then from there people will probably want to opt into your newsletter or comment on your blog, and start a conversation. Or go back to Facebook or Twitter and comment and chat with you.

I knew that this was working, but I didn't know how well it was working until I started really looking, tracking where my customers were coming from. I get a lot of hits on my website from Facebook and Twitter, and these people are turning into customers.

So, don't discount that method.

You don't say to your connections, "Here's my site, click on it, and then call me and buy my stuff." It's "come look at my free stuff." Because I'm likely to click if I want to look at free stuff. And then if I like you, I'll sign up for your newsletter. Then if I like that, I call you to buy stuff from you.

 **Great Tip!**

The most generous entrepreneurs are the wealthiest.

And even though that stuff is free, it still needs to be very valuable so that people are willing to raise their hand and say Hmm, if her free stuff is this good, her paid stuff must be really good. Or, She must be really confident in her skills and her abilities that she is willing to give away so much for free.

The most generous entrepreneurs I know are the wealthiest. So don't worry about giving too much away. And we're not talking about giving away your time and energy in designs, but it's okay to share knowledge, to show off what an expert you are.

And then people will want to work with you.

Free Things to Give Away (to Get People to Sign Up for Your Newsletter)

Of course it depends on who your target is, because not every audience will want the same thing. So first think about what your audience's biggest challenge is and find a way to answer it.

Your free report or your free audio…you could have a free report that's just a text document made into a PDF that people get, or you can record a 20-minute audio and send them a link to listen to it online.

It could be a checklist, or five mistakes to avoid when you start remodeling.

The one thing you can not worry about is that you're giving away the store. You're just giving them the basics.

> **Great Tip!**
> Give away the "what" and "why." For the detailed "how," they'll have to purchase your services.

You don't have to teach them in a whole book how to avoid the five biggest mistakes, but you give them the "what" and the "why." And then in order to have the very specific hand-holding of "how" to do it (or you do it for them), they of course have to purchase your services.

But you're giving them a taste. It's like an appetizer or a sample tray coming around. You give them a little taste and then they want to buy the entrée. That's kind of what you have to think about in your free stuff.

If you look at the menu, like "Here's the stuff; what do you want to buy?" Well, I have no idea. I may not want to buy anything, but if you give me a little taste of it, oh, now I'm craving it.

But that's really what you want your free report or your audio to be.

In Summary: 3 Action Points

1. Good enough is good enough. (Like you may have felt that it was weight lifted off of you when I said your blog doesn't have to be long perfect articles – that is kind of my philosophy of business.) And stop worrying about perfectionism, about everything being perfect. You shouldn't strive for perfection; you should strive for excellence.

If you wait for things to be perfect, you never get a chance to be excellent, because nothing ever gets out there. So my biggest suggestion is – whatever you've been thinking about working on for a while, you have to get it out there.

2. Make a decision. You can get it out a lot quicker than you think. If you don't have a website out, you can have one out by next week, if you just decide it's going to be out. You will find a way. You can even get your newsletter out by tomorrow. You can start a blog right now, tonight. Whatever you've been thinking about, stop thinking about it. Just do it.

3. Create an email signature. One small thing having to do with emails and online marketing can actually be done *this instant* if you're by your computer. Make sure you have a great email signature. That's just something that goes out in every email you send out. It's a link to your website or a link to sign up for your free report, or audio, or newsletter. And a little description of what you do. So many times designers will write back to me within a week of me telling them to do this, and say "I just got a new job from my email signature."

Think about all the emails you send out, and how they get forwarded around. Your email goes out to lots of people who you think may know what you do, but they may not, or their friends may not.

And they go, "Oh, look what she does. Let me click on her site. I've been looking for a great window treatment professional, and here she is." So write a good email signature with a link to your site right now.

ABOUT THE AUTHOR

Some describe **Nika Stewart** as a talented, quirky, edgy designer, while others regard her as a cutting-edge marketing guru. And while both descriptions are accurate, they do not capture her true essence.

Nika is a lifestyle entrepreneur: A professional who has seamlessly integrated her profession into her life. She loves designing, loves marketing, and loves her network of colleagues, clients, and collaborators. Nika's passion comes through in all of her endeavors and projects – and that is her true value.

Nika has won prestigious design competitions, lectured as a faculty member of national design organizations, created highly acclaimed marketing systems, and partnered with industry leaders to create groundbreaking programs. But did you also know that Nika is the cantor on the Jewish High Holidays at her local temple? Or that she is the loving mother to four-year-old Ellie? Or that on the weekends she enjoys belting out tunes as the lead singer in a rock band (when she's not portraying villains and heroines on tour with a national murder-mystery acting company)?

Nika enjoys sharing her techniques and strategies on achieving career and life happiness with her clients. She has coaching programs, business products, and marketing systems that help entrepreneurs shape their businesses to complement their lifestyles. Nika is a multifaceted, approachable, and creative entrepreneur who is always eager to tackle new challenges, make new contacts, and expand her horizons. So, while you may know Nika as a designer or a marketer or a rock singer, there is a lot more to her than meets the eye!

To get a copy of Nika's most popular program, *Email Newsletters for Designers*, or to look at all of her *powerful programs for boosting your success*, visit <ins>www.NikaStewart.com</ins>.

5

SOCIAL MEDIA FOR DESIGNERS: Explode Your Visibility, Enhance Your Credibility, Build Profits

by Melissa Galt

www.melissagalt.com

In this chapter you'll learn:

*3 tested time-saver shortcuts to harness
the power of social media*
*5 easy essentials to social networking success in
an hour a day*
*How to capture your competition's leads
without them even knowing It*
*How to take your online connections
to real-time profits*

My Background

I will give you the CliffsNotes version because otherwise we would
be here all day. I actually started out in hospitality purchasing, which
meant that if you ate it, drank it, wrote with it, or slept on it, I bought
it. I have a degree in restaurant administration from Cornell University.
My mom passed when I was 24 years old, and it took me about 5 years
to get the big lesson, which was that life is too short to be miserable,
and while I was very good in that career, I was extremely unhappy doing it.

> ### 🔵 Great Tip!
>
> Sometimes it takes
> years to get your life's
> lesson. But when you
> do, the time to act on it
> is now.

The great part of my career in hospitality
purchasing was that every eight months, I
moved among cities, states, and hotel prop-
erties, and I got to reorganize the purchasing department. So my joy was organizing
store rooms and freezers and food selections. It was kind of like space planning.
So after my mom had passed and 5 years
had gone by and I was really unhappy,
I decided to go back to school and get a
degree in design.

But at the same time, because I had already been in the working world
and I had to support myself, I had to get a full-time job. So I was in design school and I was also working full-time. I got a job at a local firm
that did architecture and sold steel-case furniture. From there I moved
on to managing a fabric store. I jumped to Atlanta, and I worked for a
big-box retailer for about 18 months.

About 18 months is the limit for me to work for any other person. I tend
to be very headstrong and stubborn, and that is exactly what happened
with that job. I planned a vacation and I went into my boss and I said
I'm planning to be gone this date and that date, and she said You don't
have the time coming. I said Yes I do. We argued briefly, and I walked
out. I took the vacation. I came home. I had a vacation paycheck, and it

90

was the last paycheck I ever saw.

I started my own business six months premature to my planned startup, which was very scary because I did not have a client in the world. I was not allowed to poach from the company I had worked for – that would have been a major no-no. And I had to work a hot, sweaty dish machine and supervise a catering kitchen on nights and weekends to make ends meet. It wasn't pretty.

I was $70,000 in debt, living in a cramped apartment with a big old car payment and a whole lot of bills. Like most of us with the idea of "build it and they will come," there was one big flaw in my Field of Dreams vision – well, aside from the fact that Kevin Costner has not shown up…

> **Beware!**
>
> If the prospects and clients aren't beating a path to your door, the reason is the lack of marketing.

The problem is that prospects and clients weren't beating a path to my door, and the reason was because I wasn't marketing. That was a big lesson to learn. This was back in 1994, so it was the fledgeling stages of the internet, and we didn't have webinars. We barely had conference calls. So I attended a lot of live events, got a lot of good information, and took what worked and tossed the rest. The advantage I had was that what worked for me was different than what most designers use. And subsequently my results were often 5 times that of my colleagues. I went from being $70,000 in the hole to being six figures and debt-free within three years.

Today you could probably do it faster with the internet. It just depends on whether you know what you are doing. The first way I started marketing was by teaching. I didn't teach ordinary students; instead I taught busy homeowners and professionals about decorating. I taught as many as three to four classes at any given period of time, at night, at Emory University and at Oglethorpe University's Performing Arts Center, both in Atlanta.

And it was phenomenal because what happened was like an early social media experience, because they would have me for six weeks – and in six weeks they would get a chance to know me, like me, and trust me. And that meant that at the end of six weeks, they could make a determination that if they were a DIY'er, terrific. They would call me in for a consultation or two. But many of them would determine that they couldn't possibly do it themselves, it was a lot more complicated than they thought, and I would be invited to work with them.

It also gave me phenomenal exposure because my name, my heritage, my talent was all over the catalogs, and this was back in the day when a print catalog meant something. (Today it doesn't mean as much.) Today I would have to be in their online network. I actually stayed with Emory for a decade. I stayed with Oglethorpe for the duration of their program, which was three years.

C.R.E.A.T.E.

That unconventional teaching was kind of my early foray into social media, and that is the equation that I recommend people use today. I call it C.R.E.A.T.E. It stands for Connect, Relate, Educate, interAct, Touch, Excite, and close. There is no *sell*. There is no pitching, and that is the part that we, as designers, don't want to do anyway. We don't want to sell somebody something. Ewe, gross! We want them to hire us because we're taste makers, we're style setters. And this is what social media allows us to do so much more easily and so much better, and that's why it is such a great fit for designers.

> **⬤ Important!**
>
> C.R.E.A.T.E stands for:
> Connect
> Relate
> Educate
> interAct
> Touch
> Excite
> close

So in everything you do, and in all the strategies that you will be hearing throughout this book, everything goes back to building that KLT factor. Not necessarily to getting the sale right away, not necessarily to getting the customer right away, but to building that relationship, to doing the most important thing that you can do while marketing: building the *know, like, and trust* factor.

The easiest thing to compare this to, and I certainly have a lot of experience in this avenue, is dating. I am still online-dating. But when you think about it, you are courting a prospect, and when they "marry" you, they become the client that you want. But in order to marry them and profit from the relationship, you have to court them. Imagine if you had a first date with your husband and on the very first date he proposed. You would be flabbergasted and amazed.

Unfortunately that is what too many creatives are doing in business.

They have one point of contact and suddenly they are proposing, and the prospect freaks out because they haven't been courted. There is no know-like-trust. So if you get stuck, just remember the dating algorithm.

Courting goes on indefinitely. Even after you've made the first sale, you're making the second, the third, the fourth. Lifetime demand is what you are going for. Doing one-shot jobs is exhausting. I did it in the beginning. As a solo entrepreneur, I used to juggle as many as 30 to 40 projects with just one intern on board.

Did You Know?

Fun definitions of social media today:
Twitter is a cocktail party.
Facebook is a backyard barbeque.
LinkedIn is a networking event.

I was a crazy person! I don't recommend it. And when I got really smart, I took a hard look at my market and I realized that the 80/20 rule had kicked in. I dumped the 80% that weren't producing and I kept the other 20, and they are still my clients today.

Social Media, As We Know It Today

I will give you the fun definitions and then I will give you the technical definitions. Here are the fun definitions, as I know them. Twitter is an online cocktail party, Facebook is a backyard barbeque, and LinkedIn is just a plain old formal networking event. And when you look at those networks in that way, it is going to make it a lot easier to understand the type and style of interaction required.

When you are at a cocktail party, you're flitting about, you are having very short conversations with people, and you're not diving deep. That is Twitter. At a backyard barbeque (Facebook), you are with friends and family, you are hanging out. You're going to go deeper. You're going to share a bit more; you're going to spend a bit more time. And with LinkedIn, you're going to keep it professional. Your visits or interactions don't have to be as frequent as at the barbeque or cocktail party, but you are going to be sharing a lot more of your expertise, and that really makes a difference.

Now the technical definition of social media, as I know it, is that it represents a profound and permanent shift in global communications and how consumers buy goods and services. Traditional news was static and reportive; now news is interactive and we, the people, impact it on an ongoing basis. No longer do we go and look for products and news. Instead they go and look for us and find us, which is why you've got to go out and find your prospects and your clients.

So in social media, the question really comes down to this: Are you out there finding your clients, or are you letting the competition get to them first?

Whether you like it or not, social media is here to stay. And if you are to grow your business, if you are to market your business and get more clients, this is just another piece of your marketing pie that you have to participate in. It is an inner circle part of your plan. It is not your entire plan, but it is an absolutely not to be missed essential component.

How to Find a Prospective Client Using Social Media

> ● **Important!**
>
> You have to know your target market well enough to write them a personal letter discussing their values, priorities, pains, and pleasures.

There is one challenge that has to be addressed first: Who is your target? I ask designers this all the time. And the answer I get back consistently is "well they're somewhere in the age range of 20 to 60 and they've got disposable income to spend on decorating." That just makes me cringe because that is not a target, that is a population.

You've got to know your target market. You've got to know them well enough that you can write them a personal letter discussing their values, their priorities, their pains, their pleasures, their kids. You've got to know them that well. They've got to be in an age range spanning no more than five years. I know you're creative. If you want to have 3 targets, that's fine. But limit it to 3, and don't do 23 or 53 targets.

And you have to be able to answer questions about their lifestyle, what their educational background is, what their home value is, what their favorite restaurant is, and whether they cook at home a lot. You've got to know whether they are a boutique buyer or whether they're a mall-hopper. There are just a lot of questions you have to be able to answer – because if you don't have a clear target, you're going to get on social media and get absolutely buried, and I don't want to see that happen to anybody.

Let's say that the target market is a female who is 45 years old. She happens to have an executive position in a company. She likes to play tennis. She likes to play golf. She dines out at least once a week, maybe twice, with her family. She's got two kids and she is married. She lives in a single-family home, a home that's half a million dollars. She makes six figures at her job, and she lives in the suburbs of Philadelphia, as an example.

So, you are going to be doing this differently, depending on which network you are on. But first of all, a lot in the above example would be keyword search terms. Tennis, Golf, those are keyword search terms. If you knew certain restaurants and you can find them online, it would be good for you to go and take a look at who is following them and who they are following in the social networking media.

Obviously, not Pizza Hut. That is not going to work very well. With her income level, chances are that she is going to be on LinkedIn. That is going to be a no-brainer. LinkedIn has the highest ratio of six-figure earners, as opposed to any of the other networks. They also have the highest ratio of corporate people. There are members of the Fortune 500; every single Fortune 500 company has members on LinkedIn. And I think it's 70% of C-level executives, which means CEOs, CFOs, COOs, and folks like that. So she would definitely be targeted on LinkedIn.

As for Facebook, she is probably there but she is more relaxed. She might be a little bit more difficult to find. You need to find her on groups through Facebook. You need to know a bit about whether she has children and how old are they, because that is going to be another good way to search her.

So let's say she has two kids; one is a teenager in high school and is about 16 years old, and the other one is say around 10 years old. How would knowledge of the kids' ages be helpful to designers on Facebook?

> **Did You Know?**
> LinkedIn has the highest ratio of six-figure earners, as opposed to any of the other networks.

You've got to know about those age ranges, and what the kids are into,

95

because a lot of times the parents will follow what the kids are into on social networking media – brands, particularly.

I would bet that there are number of schools or school bands that have Facebook pages.

School bands – any extracurricular-type activities that you can imagine that maybe she's got her kids involved in – those are good opportunities to explore more of that target market.

When you know your target market really well, you should be able to imagine having a conversation with her, and part of the conversation would be Okay, Judy, you know when you're on Twitter, what are you going to claim as your 10 identifying words – either 5 or 10 – Twibes (groups on Twitter) might be 10, and Twitter's WeFollow might be 5 descriptors.

◉ Action Item!

Use hash tags (#), which are descriptive terms, to find groups with which your customers identified – mom, working mom, soccer mom, etc.

For example, if I put in what are called hash tags, which are descriptive terms for me, mine are interior designer, social media, blogger, and I think I've got foodie in there. I don't think bungee jumper was available, or I would have put that. Traveler, things like that.

So when you know your target market that well, chances are good she's going to put in mom or working mom, and you might want to take a look at both of those hash tags and see how big of a market each of those has. Because what we follow shows you all the people who have raised their hand and said That's me.

The other big advantage with this is there is Twittergrader.com and when you visit that site, you can search your city and your surrounding area for people on Twitter. You can do the same thing on LinkedIn. LinkedIn has a search by geographic area, and so does Facebook. So you may want to keep it geographically restrictive. Personally, I love long-distance projects instead – there is nothing better, because I only have to deal with the people for a much more limited time.

And with long-distance projects, the work is very intense for the two to three days you're there, but then the rest of the time you're not being called on every night. Well, gee, can you swing by the house? No, I can't, I have a life. That makes a big difference, and that's why I love long-distance projects. I'm a little unusual. A lot of other design professionals don't love them. But if you don't love them, figure out your perimeter areas and do searches on those, for people who are in specific networks, for people who are already online, and go check them out.

Don't just connect to them randomly, though: Go check them out. You see what they are doing, see what business they might be involved in, see what causes they might be associated with. Look up your local charities online.

> ⬤ **Important!**
>
> When connecting with prospects, be sure to make those connections personal.

Most of the nonprofits now have social media preferences. And you can gauge them – for example, Junior League is always more the high-end crowd, so if you were to look that one up, you would come out with more high-end clients from that. But there is a big difference between a Junior Leaguer who is young and starting out with a family, and an empty-nester Junior Leaguer. Chances are good that you need to be focused on one or the other and not both.

Social Media Time Savers

WeFollow.com, Twittergrader.com …

There is TweetDeck.com, which is my favorite interface. If you're just climbing on board to Twitter and you're not on Tweet Deck, get Tweet Deck – it's a free download. I have to tell you that it saved my Twitter experience. I hated Twitter up until that point. I thought it was just the most awful bunch of rubbish.

Tweet Deck makes a big difference. Also check out SocialOomph.com, formerly known as TweetLater. Gravatar.com (Globally Recognized Avatars) is where you put in your favorite headshot, and that will populate on any other network that is tied into Gravatar so you don't have to upload your photo.

Also check out Ping.fm. You can tie all of your networks into Ping very simply, very easily. And then you can put in a status update, hit the ping button, and it will go to Facebook, to Twitter, to LinkedIn, to all those places you want it to go at the push of a button. You don't have to go to each network if you don't want to.

If I were to pick one to start with, I would recommend that it be Tweet Deck, because it supports both Facebook and LinkedIn, and a lot of times I will interact on Facebook on Tweet Deck because then I don't have to go out to Facebook and I don't have to go out to LinkedIn.

For those readers who are a little bit more experienced, and let's say you do use Tweet Deck, then SocialOomph would be the next shortcut I'd recommend you start implementing.

●Action Item!

Familiarize yourself with these shortcuts:
WeFollow.com
TwitterGrader.com
SocialOomph.com
TweetDeck.com

SocialOomph allows you to program Twitter updates, you can program Facebook posts, you can program blog posts…there is an enormous amount of functionality with that. And you just want to be careful that you don't buy a version until you've experienced the free version, because the free version is really loaded.

How do you pursue your target market on social media and start interacting with them without seeming to stalk them?

First of all, you don't want to go on as your business. Go on as yourself. Because when you go on as your business, that is when they would feel stalked. If they are talking about decorating and you jump into the middle of a conversation and you're a design professional, they think you are going to be pitching at them, they think you're going to be soliciting their business. If you go in as Susie Smith, that is non-threatening. Later they can find out that you're a design professional, but they don't need to know that up front.

Always use a realistic avatar of yourself. Do not use your pet, your children, a rug, a lamp, a chair and interior shot: You can't see it in a tiny thumbnail. Please get brave, have a friend or family member snap a headshot of you smiling – smiling counts…let's see some teeth. And please don't get on these networks if you're not going to share a picture of yourself.

Understand that most people will not connect with a logo, or a pet, or a rug. I had to tweet that to somebody today. They sent me a comment and they had a rug as their avatar. I wrote them back and I said Gee, I would just so love to connect with you, but I can't converse with a rug.

But many people do that. You can do searches, you can search inside Twitter. You can search for current conversations involving the phrase *interior design* or involving the word *decorating*. I know it makes people's skin crawl, but honestly that is what consumers say. So put yourself in the mind of a consumer. What kind of words would a consumer use when they are having a discussion about their home?

They would use remodel, they would use decorate, they would use décor, decorating, design, designing, although those last two could get you in trouble because you could run across graphic designers and web designers. So if you can keep interior in it, that should help. And consumers are probably not going to be using hash tags on them. The pros will, but the consumers won't.

How to find the customers using these keywords? You do the search inside Tweet Deck. There is a place at the top, kind of upper left-ish, as a magnifying glass. You click on that and it will ask for your search term, and you can either put hash tag and a word, or you can put just the word.

> ◉ **Great Tip!**
>
> Put yourself in the mind of a consumer and use the search words they would use.

So you just put plain old "interior design" or "decorating." And any conversation that is on Twitter at that moment with those words in it will come up in a column for you to look at, and that way you can skim through that list to see if there is anything you can contribute to. And you just jump in and you give your two cents' worth. It's not hard to do.

What to Talk About

Now by the same token, you don't want to limit this to design. The things you want to talk about are both social and professional. It's *social* media for a reason. This isn't personal. This isn't about what you ate for breakfast. We don't want the intimate details of your life and your family dramas. Please hang on to those; we don't want them.

What we want are news and views talked about within the industry.

99

Talk about the trends. Talk to us about the latest thing you saw at the shop around the corner that you really liked and thought was totally cool. Send us a twit pic of it. It is super-easy on Tweet Deck to share pictures. Facebook loves pictures. Facebook is the largest repository of images globally. Globally! LinkedIn is not as heavy on images as the others are.

They want you to share your experience and your expertise. You're a professional. You've been in the field for at least a couple of years, some of you 20 years. Share what you know. It sounds second nature to you, but it is not to a consumer. There is an enormous industry about how to care for furnishings, accents, accessories, that silk pillow, that wool upholstery fabric.

As for rave reviews, if you've had somebody rave to you that "You've just transformed my whole life with my new living room," then share it. It makes perfect sense. Even better is when they share it for you. Get your clients online.

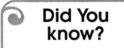

Did You know?

Facebook is the largest repository of pictures globally! Be sure to post pictures of your work on Facebook.

Also share events and openings. When you've got a storefront, a design storefront, you've got events and openings to share. And share hobbies and interests. You want to be a well-rounded human being. If you are in doubt, go look at my profile. You will find that I am not all business. I've got in there skydiver, foodie, bungee jumper.

You've got to be a well-rounded individual. So also do some searches on some of your hobbies. If you're into cooking, search cooking. If you're into travel, search travel. But be well-rounded because the whole point of social media is about being a whole person, not just the business side. Social 80%, and 20% business.

And the important thing is that you realize the frequency at which these streams move. With Twitter, in order to be heard, you need to be repeating the same thing either five or six times over the course of a day or over the course of three or four days multiple times. It moves really fast. Facebook, I would say the same thing a couple of times a day, if it's business. If it's personal, you are not going to say the same thing twice; you don't need to. But on the business side, again, balancing it 80/20 is really important.

100

We get to go to Kbiz, we get to go to the ICFF show, we get to go to the European shows in the U.S. and Milan and Germany. Consumers don't get to see those. So share about what is going on in the industry. There are definitely very successful design professionals who have made a whole living out of green online, and what that is doing. You're experience and your expertise are valuable.

You definitely want to dish on the nuggets of gold that to you are second nature but that aren't to the consumer. When I schedule out, I schedule a lot of nuggets about marketing and about social media. I've actually created entire lists of tips on design and decorating. I have a "209 Home Improvement and Decorating Tips" booklet that I created, and I'll pull material from that when I want to tweet out and when I want to create Facebook posts about decorating.

Now Twitter is very different than Facebook in that you can do all that scheduling out and people are comfortable with it. Facebook wants more interactivity, so on Facebook, you want to include your portfolio and share your pictures from your work. That is incredibly important.

> **◉ Action Item!**
>
> Think about design tips that are second nature to you. Share them via social media – they are not so second nature to the consumers.

Tips about things that people can do in the home – whether it is five ways to organize your closet, what's the best height for a lampshade, why do you want to use a pink lightbulb – little things like that that are things that consumers love that, even though they're second nature to you. If you're stuck, go watch HDTV. They have now started putting tips on almost every show, and that makes it very easy to think of similar tips.

Care and resources: Most of us get care and resources from our vendors, but we're not telling anybody about it. Tell customers how to maintain that beautiful drapery. Tell them about being able to put UV film on windows and how that can protect silk. Tell them what linen will do and that if they want a tailored interior, they probably don't want to go the linen route because it is going to become shabby chic and crinkle on them. Share little tips like that.

Obviously you want to share any events or openings that you have. It is really important that you keep them in the loop. Most of us have so much going on, and we forget that the people around do not know what

101

we are doing. And this is your chance to trumpet it from the highest mountain and include everybody in it. Know that there are going to be people who will interact with you, and there are going to be other people who are just going to be voyeurs who are just going to sit there and watch. There are several different followers on these networks, and some of them are watchers, some of them are interactors, and some of them are re-tweeters.

Re-tweeters is what I call them because they don't interact except to re-tweet, which is kind of strange to me, but because they spread their word, I'm not worried about it. If you've just cooked up an incredible batch of brownies and it's a new recipe, share it. These social networks were designed for that. This is like that proverbial fence between the two houses, and you're leaning across sharing what is going on. But this is the virtual fence, and this is where instead of having that conversation with somebody live-time, you are having it virtually and it is going out to hundreds of thousands of people.

How to Leverage 30 Minutes' Worth of Work to Get Presence on Social Media

> ### 🔖 Action Item!
>
> Come up with as many tips as possible in one sitting. Then schedule them at one time to go out in a daily basis.

Once when I had to speak at an expo, I didn't have anything to sell, so I had no way to make money because I wasn't being paid for speaking. I decided I wanted to make money, so in 48 hours, I drafted a little booklet that I then had printed up at Office Depot. It had the 209 tips in it. And they were for home improvement that would change your life. Then I spent half an hour to take those very same tips and put them through Twitter.

If you can take some time, if you are on a deadline or if you can schedule some time with yourself, write down various tips on how to remodel, how to choose the right color, how to choose the right fabric, how to choose the right furniture. There are so many topics that you can pick out of everything you do on a daily basis – just write down as many tips about that as humanly possible. Simply write them down on paper and then you can preschedule them. And those posts can go out automatically without you having anything to do with it anymore.

Now the only place that I would be really cautious about doing that is LinkedIn – I wouldn't do that there. LinkedIn is more interested in the professional knowledge in the industry and what is going on. LinkedIn is more news and views than quick tips. But that is okay because LinkedIn doesn't require the level of interaction that Facebook and Twitter do.

How to Capture Your Competition's Leads without Them Even Knowing It

This is ridiculously easy, especially so on Facebook and Twitter, because the networks are open source (it's a little trickier on LinkedIn). What that means is that you can go to anyone's profile unless they have made it private, which is rare. I don't come across many of those.

Assuming it's public, and mine certainly is, you can go to theirs and look at who they are following and look at who is following them. In the case of Facebook, look at who they've friended, and you can friend the very same people. You can follow the same people.

You can literally go into their followers on Twitter and click down the entire list. Now I don't know that you would want to click down the entire list, because they've probably got some personal friends in there, but let's say you've got somebody in your same part of town, your same neck of the woods, that is an interesting shortcut to explore, particularly if you were doing a similar style of design and your target market really is that similar. Get a jump on it, get a leg up.

Did You Know?

Facebook and Twitter allow you to see who follows whom. If you want to, you can easily follow the same people that your competition does.

Now just because you get those people and you follow them doesn't mean they'll follow you back, and it doesn't ensure that you're going to have a good relationship with them. You've still got to relate and interact with them. Remember: It's connect, relate, educate, interact, touch, excite, and close. When you start skipping steps, you are going to skip profit, and that would be unfortunate. But you have this enormous ability.

I don't know of any other opportunity in time that I've experienced where I could look up a competitor and see who they are dealing with, see who they are talking to, see who is following them, and see who they are reaching out to. How cool is that?

And again you may find that there are some really neat opportunities for synergy with other people in related fields. What about the furniture store down the street that is struggling a bit right now, but you know that some of your clients have bought things there, so that means that some of their other clientele would be good clients for you. Well, find them on one of the networks. Dive deep and see who is there, and I bet you anything you will come up with gold.

This is really easy. We all as business owners know that our biggest asset as a business is our clients – it is our client list. And historically, companies have guarded their client list with everything they've got, and it used to be the most private thing, the most guarded thing they could possibly have. And social media has completely broken down those barriers, broken down those gates. Everything that your competitors are doing you can now see online. And the customers that they have in their database, you can see online. So essentially, their databases that used to be private are no longer private. They're public now, and you can have access to them. And to gain access to those clients is just as easy as sending in a friend request on Facebook or reaching out and following them on Twitter or reaching out and connecting with them on LinkedIn. It's just that easy.

Important!

Client databases are your (and your competition's) biggest asset. Social media have made this biggest asset available to any savvy business person willing to do the work.

The key is also to make those invites personal. Please don't use the generic invites on Facebook and LinkedIn particularly – please don't do that. I get 30 to 50 generic invites a day, and I am ignoring the vast majority of them. Anybody who sends me a personal invite rises to the top of the list immediately because it is so rare and yet it takes only 10 seconds to do. It is incredibly easy, yet nobody does it. So do what nobody else is doing, and make it personal.

Personal Page vs. Fan Page on Facebook

For your business you need a fan page. Hands down, no questions asked: You must have a fan page for your business. It must be well-titled. Which means that if you have Josephine's Interiors, that is not enough. And especially if the word *interior* or *design* is not in your company name, you're going to have to put it somewhere in that titling. The titling is tricky because once you hit the button "publish," that fan page is up and live and you cannot change that title. And if Facebook says you can change it, it'll probably take an act of God, I wouldn't want to go through that process.

Your fan page actually will feed to your main friend stream. That is the beautiful part. If you want to have another page up on Facebook, it can be more private. I never started mine as a private page. My goal on Facebook was to always have a business presence. And since I started three or four years ago, way before fan pages ever came about, the people who have largely connected to me on there are business contacts, associates, and so forth, and also clients. So what I do now with my fan pages is I invite, on a regular basis, all of those people who are not already fans to become my fans. And you probably have something similar where you have a mix. You can invite them one at a time to your fan page. You don't have to invite your family to be your fans, but you can invite those clients who might have friended you awhile ago, before fan pages came out.

Now if you're new and just getting started on Facebook, I would create a minor profile, and then I would create your fan page going forward and focus your activities on your fan page. Your fan page is all-important. It is one of the hubs of your business. Your first hub is your website. It doesn't

> ## Action Item!
> You must have a fan-page for your business. Create one today!

have to be a website; it can be a blog site. But with your fan page, you're feeding your blog to your fan page. You've got your opt-in on your fan page. And you're regularly – daily – updating, interacting, and inviting activity on your fan page.

It is okay to have a personal page, and it should focus on your friends and family. But if you are on social media to create more business for yourself, then you must have a fan page. It may be more comfortable for you (as it is for me) to call it a "business profile page," or a "business professional profile," because *fan* sounds kind of funny. But that is what Facebook called them. The interesting thing is, you can have as many fan pages as you want. So if you've got multiple businesses, you can have multiple fan pages. This is not an encouragement to go out

105

and design multiple fan pages – one is enough. But yes, you absolutely must have a fan page – it's critically important.

The biggest benefit of a fan page (vs. personal) is that you can message all of your fans at one time, kind of like a broadcast email. And you cannot do that through friends; you'd have to do it in small batches, and that would be perceived as spamming. And you would probably be shut down.

The other beautiful part about it is that there is not a limit to fans. There is a limit of 5,000 friends, though. I just bumped my limit, so now I can't accept any more friends. I have to go back through and dump people, which is a very tedious process. So what I am doing now is redirecting everyone to my fan page. It just makes sense. It is facebook.com/prosperbydesign instead of Melissa Galt. Melissa Galt is my profile. But I want everybody over at the fan page because I am going to start restricting my activity on my profile and I am going to put all of my efforts into my fan page.

On my fan page, for example, I can put an opt-in feature. You can do an e-zine opt in. I have an eBook. My eBook explains seven surefire steps to marketing that will make you money. And I have the opt-in on there; I ask for your name and email address. You get the book, I get the contact, and then you're on my list.

> **Important!**
>
> Just like you have an opt-in box on every page of your website, you can have an opt-in box on your fan-page.

And the neat part about it is that every time you update your fan page, it goes into your main feed anyway. So there is no reason for you to really carry on both, unless you want to have that private personal one and you want to have the business one.

How to Invite Friends to Be Fans

Take a look right underneath your picture on the fan page – and if you notice, I said your picture. I didn't say logo, I didn't say picture of the front door of your design studio; this is still about Brand You. You are the most important piece. Now if you've got a team, a smiling picture of a team is wonderful. But I am not a believer in logos. And I know a couple of big name designers have them; they've gotten established that way and that is fine. If you're not established, don't try it.

106

But underneath that picture are several options. One of them says *suggest fans*, and you click on it and it brings up all of your friends. And you can literally just click on one picture at a time and whoever you don't want to be a fan because they're personal and it's family or whatever, you don't click them. And for everyone else, it will show up as an invite to be a fan of yours. And you may have to invite some people several times before they'll click through.

The first time we opened up my fan page, I think I had probably 3,000 friends and I immediately landed 900 fans.

Boom, really simple. The thing about Facebook is that you don't know who has gone inactive. There could be 1,000 of those people who could be inactive now. And I won't know unless I manually go in each one of their profiles and check when they've actually updated, and that is just more work than I am willing to do. So there is some dead wood out there. Happens on Twitter all the time. 70% of the people who climb on Twitter fall off within three weeks.

It's sad and it's scary and it doesn't have to happen; the networking can be exhausting and can be overwhelming. When I first climbed on, I had a horrible experience. Two weeks later I was screaming bloody murder, I wanted off; but then I figured out how to do it, because I went and paid for some serious training and mentoring. And today you don't have to do that; there are shortcuts. But back in the dark ages, two years ago, there weren't.

The first thing that everyone reading should do in order for it not to become a nightmare is to go ahead and download the free Tweet Deck because it makes it that much easier for them to manage all those interactions and messages popping up on Twitter.

> ## Beware!
>
> You may need to invite some people several times to be a fan before they click through. Be persistent!

You have to have a profile on Twitter to make that work. You also have to have a profile on Facebook – otherwise it won't work – but you know it is not that hard to do. The beautiful part of Twitter to me is that it took me 5 minutes to set it up. Facebook took me about three hours because I answered all the questions thoroughly. It said what kind of movies do you like, and I listed 25 movies.

The key in this is that you want to take action. Step up on one network at a time, get active, make a difference, see results. Give yourself 30 days; don't rush it. Most people are on Facebook to start with, so I would start on Facebook, although my personal favorite is Twitter. I would start on Facebook, and then I would add Twitter and then I would add LinkedIn.

For those you who are going to hate this in general and you don't have kids and you just want to get straight to the networking, then jump on LinkedIn. If you're serving DIYers, if you're doing low-end or mid-end, LinkedIn isn't going to be where your market is.

Balancing Daily Activities That Immediately Bring Us Money with Social Media Activities That Will Bring Us Money Eventually

Great Tip!

Create a success routine, where social media is consistently present. The most important word here is *routine*.

Well I guess part of the key is that I don't know what you are doing right now for your marketing, but I bet there are some pretty big gaping holes in it, and that is where you want to plug social media in. You want to create what I call a *success routine*. It depends on what your day looks like.

I happen to be an early riser. I log on, and the first thing I do is not check my email, but instead talk to my networks. And I usually will spend as much as an hour at the front end the day doing that. Then when I jump on Twitter a couple times during the day, it is just for maybe 10 minutes. If I have time at the end of the day, I will climb back on and update again. I don't always have that. Maybe two or three days a week I will have that end-of-day time.

Some people stay on the network seven days a week; some don't. Sometimes I do and sometimes I don't. If I do it on weekends, it's far less business for me and it is more about connecting and having fun.

You've got to create a routine that works for you. I usually start out with Twitter, and then I move to Facebook and then on to LinkedIn. That is what works for me. And it is about having goals on each network and finding a way to move people from the network to voice-to-voice and then ultimately face-to-face. When you move them to voice-to-voice, you're not asking them to buy from you. You're just saying, I noticed you were struggling with this design challenge; would you like to have a short conversation?

Make sure they understand that you're not going to pitch them, but you want to find out more about what the challenge is. Ask them to email you a photo. You would be happy to give them a few tips. But don't be spending an hour doing it, because that would just defeat the purpose.

You're not here to give them free design, but it is kind of like doing a virtual home tour. Taking a couple of minutes to do this will reinforce your credibility and create a sense of reciprocity, and the reciprocity is where they want to give back to you. You'll rise to the top of who they most desire to work with when they are at that point.

It's just as if somebody is talking about needing a great Italian restaurant and you happen to know a really great one in your neck of the woods, and you recommend it. The way I became a lifetime demand for my clients is because I am a go-to resource in my market for far more than design.

> **◉ Great Tip!**
>
> Social media gives you an opportunity to reinforce your credibility and create a sense of reciprocity.

I'm a resource for caterers, and I'm a resource for event planners. I am resource for restaurants, boutiques, doctors, lawyers, financial advisors – I am their go-to lifestyle source. And when you become a go-to lifestyle source, you always come to mind easily. Every time they have a design need, I'm there, I'm it. There is no one else; there is no competition. I've never bid a project, and I never will. It's quite simple: I'm it or else I'm not for you.

Create the routine that works for you. And that goes to answer the question, How do you balance your daily activities with the demands of social media, which can get quite time-consuming? It is a really important point, and you have to figure out a way that works best for you. You have to find the time during the day and during the week where posting on social media and interacting on social media works with your schedule.

But the most important word in this phrase, *create the routine that works for you,* is *routine.* It has to become a routine. You can't hop on

109

Twitter and Facebook today, tomorrow, for a week and then say Oh the heck with it, it is too time-consuming, I am not going to do it. You'll never see any results that way. You have to invest at least 30 days of routine activity in order to see any kind of tangible results.

So I encourage all of you to invest 30 days, and make it into a routine, and that routine needs to work for you.

You need to be consistent and persistent. You need to be congruent on every network: the same picture in every place, so that your visibility is blanketing the net. That makes a huge difference. If you look at this as the bran cereal that we might eat every morning to stay regular, well, to keep your marketing plan regular and successful, social media is the bran in your marketing plan when it is consistent and persistent. When it is sporadic…well, we all know what happens when we don't take our bran. It may be too vivid of an image for you, but you'll never forget the comparison.

In Summary: 3 Action Points

You've got to step up on at least one network. If you are already up on one, then step up on a second one, or go back to that first one and finish your profile. Be complete when you do this; don't do 50%. Step up, be complete, get active. Jump in…the conversation is fine! If someone offends you, then block them or unfriend them. But keep it going – that is incredibly important.

◉ Action Item!

Invest at least 30 days into a routine activity before you start seeing tangible results.

The only way you will see results is by being consistent and persistent. So you're stepping up or you're completing or you're doing both and you're getting active. Just sitting there watching the conversation go by is not going to get you anywhere. Being a voyeur is not how you win in life. Sitting on the sidelines isn't going to cut it.

Then when you start to see results and you start to gain traction, which you will, step up on a second network. But you've got to step up on that one or complete the one you already have. Probably at least 60% of designers have incomplete profiles on networks. Please don't do that: It is really doing you a huge disservice. But your visibility and your credibility are all important in building your profitability, and that is what social media does.

110

ABOUT THE AUTHOR

 As a successful interior designer and entrepreneur for over 15 years, **Melissa Galt** knows about marketing, mindset, and motivation. She has taught busy professionals and homeowners the ins and outs of design, branding, and marketing globally. Melissa shows her clients how to design their lives and careers from the inside out, and shows her colleagues in creative professions how to use systems for success to reclaim their time and energy and to stop leaving money and opportunity on the table.

Inspired by the runaway success of her great-grandfather, Frank Lloyd Wright, known to many as America's most famous architect, Melissa understands how to build your brand and take you from being a best-kept secret to well known and well paid now. The Profit Designer™ and Success Architect™, Melissa works extensively with the trade and home furnishings industry to leverage the latest in relationship marketing tools and tricks to drive business to new heights, while living each day truly engaged, connected, tuned in, and turned on. Learn more at www.melissagalt.com. Or connect with Melissa online:
www.twitter.com/prosperbydesign
www.facebook.com/prosperbydesign
www.linkedin.com/in/melissagalt

6
OUT-OF-THE-BOX
PROMOTIONAL EFFORTS

by Margo DeGange
www.MargoDeGange.com

In this chapter you'll learn how to:

Build and lead a loyal tribe that follows only YOU!
Engage your community with exciting trunk shows
Create a simple but powerful real estate program to build local celebrity status
Capitalize on designer showcases and home shows
Catch high-quality clients through coaching (2 money-making models that can stand alone or drive additional product sales)
Be yourself and have a blast doing it!

Build a Tribe, Lead Them, Have Loads of Fun, and Create Your Success!

I'm pretty passionate. I'm a *passionate mentor*. I'm a mentor to design professionals and I also help other entrepreneurs to start and super-charge their businesses. I am going to try to share with you through my energy and through my words that I really want you to become a passionate mentor too. I want you to become a passionate professional to *your local tribe*.

> **Out-of-the-Box Thinking**:
>
> We must think tribal in our businesses today in order to be firmly planted with our customers and prospects!

I'm going to help you to create a tribe and lead them. I'm first going to talk with you about what a tribe is and how you actually create and lead a tribe. Then I'm going to talk with you about some specific activities you can do to accomplish just that. So that's our basic agenda for discussing the topic of *Out-of-the-Box Promotional Efforts*.

What It Means to Go TRIBAL

You have probably heard a lot of leaders and speakers use the term "*know-like-trust*," referring to the fact that your potential customers and clients need to know you, like who you are, and have a sense of trust in you in order to do business with you.

Building a tribe is basically building on the "know-like-trust" factor and taking it to a new level – a holistic level if you will. So instead of me saying I want my prospects and customers to know me, like me, and know that they can trust me, I say "I want to build and lead a tribe."

I'm going TRIBAL! Something has really changed. What's different today is the way we have to do business in order to be firmly planted with our customers and prospects. We have to do things a little differently today.

114

I don't know if you've ever heard the phrase "There is nothing new under the sun." Well, there really is not. Things kind of come and go in waves. Things come onto the scene and then they leave, and then things come back around again. No matter what ideas come and go, people are still always going to be people, and what people want deep-down stays pretty much the same. What changes is not what we want in general or what we want to do as people. What changes are the avenues we use to do the things that we want to do.

Today the avenues have changed, and because the avenues have changed, the balance of power and influence have changed as well, and in a big way. This is the day of the tribe because it's a day of community and meaningful connections. We have really always been people who want connection and community, but in today's new-media environment, we now have the tools to make those connections happen. Like never before, people are flocking to these tools with a strong desire to use them to build communities because they resonate with who we are at our very core. We are social people!

What People Want Today

People today want to use their voices and they want to be heard. They also want to be a part of something bigger than themselves, but at the same time they want to hold onto their sense of personal power. In terms of business, the old era of the "big company" is gone. You know the one – it's the image of the big, important guy (the boss) who's sitting behind the big desk in his big private office. He's the guy who doesn't talk to his employees and doesn't really mix and mingle with his customers. He's the guy who's hiding behind his big TV ads and pushing sales, sales, sales, without connecting to the people he is selling to, and trying to use that as a viable business model. Well, that's not going to work anymore. The image of the big, overly important, impersonal businessman is just not one we like anymore.

People today want personal, meaningful, and authentic associations, and in fact, in today's social media climate, that's all that's going to work. The "sell lots of stuff" focus is done. It is the day of community, social interaction, and the tribe. You should no longer simply have customers. Today, you should be leading a tribe.

> ### 🌐 Out-of-the-Box Thinking:
>
> A tribe is a group of like-minded people with a leader and members who rally around a compelling story or idea.

115

What Exactly Is a Tribe?

Basically a tribe is a group of people who have a common purpose that they share. The tribe has a leader. The leader guides them, the leader informs them, the leader definitely respects them, and the leader heralds change.

> **⟲ Out-of-the-Box Thinking:**
>
> If you want to create and lead a valuable and lasting tribe, you MUST lead with passion!

Today, people WANT to be a part of a tribe, and a lot of people are seeking tribes out. That's what the social networks are all about. Really, though, tribes have always been in existence. Communities such as Weight Watchers and New York Yankees fans are certainly tribes, but the online tools of today allow tribe members to connect with one another like never before.

Today if you are a Weight Watcher or a die-hard Yankees fan, you can get online and talk about your interests with people from all over the world.

There are several "ingredients" that go into the making of a tribe. A good solid tribe has a leader, followers, and interaction. The interaction goes in many directions. We'll touch on that in just a bit.

What Do Tribe Members Want?

What tribe members are especially looking for is somebody to lead them. They are looking for innovation and new ideas, and someone who can bring those elements onto the scene for them. That's where you come in as a decorating professional, and in a very powerful way. Once you form a tribe around the subject of interior decorating or interior design, you can continually infuse into it innovation, new ideas, and topics that get the tribe talking. Your initiative gets the tribe members connecting and interacting.

This is so important, because tribes are not only about common topics of interest and gaining new ideas around these topic areas. Tribes are all about social interchange. For a tribe to even exist it not only has to have a leader, but it also has to have members. You will come to realize more and more that tribe members don't want to just interact with you but they want to interact with each other.

116

How Does a Decorator Become a Tribe Leader?

In the past, as a decorating professional, you were most likely just interacting with your customers when you went to their homes. You would see them, chat, help them with their design projects, and leave. But now, because of how most of our customers interact socially and because of the tools and channels they use to do that, you have the incredible opportunity to interact not only with your customers, but with their networks as well. Their networks also interact with one another. People today are talking to one another in amazing numbers and with amazing speed. If you know someone and you are tied to them through social networks, your influence can reach thousands quickly. In a local community setting, this can be leveraged to give your business an amazing advantage. BUT, here is the most important point about building and leading a tribe: You have to have something worth talking about – something worth sharing – something people want to infuse into their social networks! You have to have a story, and it must be compelling.

> ## Out-of-the-Box Thinking:
>
> Tribal interaction and communication goes in many directions. Good news and exciting ideas travels fast within and outside of the tribe.

What Makes a Tribe Work?

The key to creating a valuable and lasting tribe is for you to lead with passion. You're going to have an opportunity to share your story with your tribe members. It's essentially your story that the tribe members are going to rally around – it's the theme by which you get everybody talking to one another. Your story is what you are all about. Your story in a sense is your mission, or even your brand. Your story is what you are passionate about. Your story is what drives you, and your story is contagious. It will spread through the tribe and begin to drive your tribe members, too, and those who resonate with it will become passionate members of your tribe. They'll also share their passion with people outside of the tribe, building curiosity.

Your tribe members can talk to your other tribe members. That is where tribe-building really comes into play. Your tribe will consist of many of your customers and past customers as well as people who simply want to connect with your mission or story. Your customers can really help ignite the tribe. All of your customers have something very solid in common – YOU have been their design consultant. They have worked with you and they have felt your mission and your story, and they have seen it in action. This is reason enough for them to talk, and if you make the opportunity for this interaction easy and fun, you will soon have a tribe that rallies around you, your thoughts, your expertise, your insights, your knowledge, your story, and what you bring NEW to the conversation. You can encourage your tribe members to talk to one another. This can become a strong and amazing force to solidify you as the decorating professional to call on and connect with. There is one golden rule, though: You MUST be sincere in all of your efforts. You have to really care about your tribe members and do all that you do from a place of authenticity. If you are truly passionate about what you are doing, this will be easy.

Could Having a Tribe Work against Us?

> ● **Out-of-the-Box Thinking:**
>
> A passionate leader can't help but draw people to the tribe.

A lot of business owners DON'T want their customers to interact with each other. They fear it. They fear that if there is any bad news, it can spread like wildfire. That's the myth! The reality is, social interaction provides a golden opportunity for word to get out about how wonderful you are and how great your products and services are, too.

It's true, sometimes problems come up with customers. It is a natural part of doing business. The good news is, customers expect you to be human, and they are not looking for perfection. What they do want is a professional who will stand firmly behind the products and services they sell. They want you to be committed to helping them solve problems. They want you to address and overcome any unforeseen obstacles and challenges that may arise during the decorating and design process. If you skillfully fix mistakes and find solutions, you will be heralded as someone who really cares, and that's absolutely a good thing!

What Message Do I Communicate to the Tribe?

You're going to have an opportunity to share your story with your tribe members. Within your tribe, there is interaction and communication that goes in several directions. It's not just you talking to your tribe – telling your story. Your tribe members are communicating back to you as well, and your tribe members are going to have opportunity through you as a leader to communicate with one another.

You are going to create a decorating tribe and infuse it with your message! You may be the very first person (or the one who does it the best) in your local community to create a decorating tribe. You are going to rally your troops (your members) by engaging them with interesting ideas, concepts, events, and content that they can share with others – that they WANT to share with others because they feel compelled to do so. This goes back to the passion you have and the way you communicate your passion with your tribe members. By the way you lead, you can encourage them to share face-to-face (in person) as well as through their online social networks.

A Tribal Example outside of Decorating

If it is hard for you to get the concept of a decorating tribe, let's think for a moment about an example of tribe-building outside of the interior design arena. I get up every morning at around 4:30 AM and go to a fitness boot camp. I get there about 5:20 AM and work out until about 6:30 AM with a fantastic group of women and an amazing coach – Coach Cliff – who leads us. We women take our cues from the coach, and we really connect with him and with each other. The coach has done a terrific job of building and leading the tribe. He is with us each and every morning, helping us to focus, pushing us, and encouraging us, too. We know he is passionate because he walks his talk and he is in amazing shape, and he keeps us in the loop of what's happening in the local fitness world.

> **Out-of-the-Box Thinking:**
>
> Your tribe can thrive with the use of social media outlets, but there is nothing better than personal communication and interactivity.

We tribe members are working out together each morning, and encouraging each other, and talking to each other here and there with a "good job" or a "you go." Every now and then someone cracks a joke or a funny one-liner and we all laugh, but we are still working, sweating, and pushing ourselves at the same time. Because the workouts are very challenging, once in a while someone complains about how hard something is and in response, the other tribe members cheer that person on

119

and we all try to encourage them and help them to re-focus. Everybody is patting each other on the back. We all feel as though we are needed and an important part of the tribe. It takes all of us for it to be the way it is. Without any of us, it just wouldn't be the same. Without the leader – Coach Cliff – it probably would not exist.

In addition, on a regular basis, the coach is sending out nutrition information online and is facilitating online social interaction by asking people to share recipe ideas and helpful tips for the tribe. He also does little online surveys and he creates mini events that get us all involved, like a 50's day, and a monthly meet up at the local coffee shop to hand out awards and positive affirmations. Once a month we also take a picture that shows off our fitness progress. I currently have many great photographs of my boot camp friends on my refrigerator (from our monthly group pictures), and I think of these tribe members on an almost daily basis!

> **Out-of-the-Box Thinking:**
>
> As a leader, you infuse your tribe with ideas and activity. YOU can get the conversation going and let it take off.

There are many things this coach does to keep the tribe not only connected with each other, but feeling appreciated and accountable to one another, too. Because the group is counting on us, none of us wants to miss a day of boot camp; and no one would ever get another trainer, because we are like a family. The point is, there's a certain amount of loyalty that's built right into rallying the troops with a compelling story (in this case feeling alive, being healthy, and being fit for life).

Where Do I Start My Tribe-Building?

Do you see the power of the tribe? It is important to note that a tribe leader – like you will be in your local community (and beyond) – makes real, meaningful, and rich connections. A tribe leader does not hide behind social media, even though news of the tribe and its activities will likely spread this way. Leading a tribe is about getting out and about, and as we go along, I am going to give you examples of decorating-related events that you can do that will actually help you create and lead your own amazing decorating tribe.

With the help of social networks, it's easy to think about making a name for yourself all over the globe, getting sidetracked with connections that use up a lot of your time but that don't really pan out into sales and profits. To make money (and a great profit) as a design professional, you have to have jobs; so to build your tribe, start out thinking LOCALLY, especially if you are building a local business. Focus on securing local design jobs even if you want to be a regionally or nationally known designer. You may as well design in the homes where you live first, since you have easy access there and travel is not an issue. It's great if your fame spreads from your local area to other communities because your design jobs are so stunning (share photos – without names – with the tribe), but focus first on building your business where the most convenient sales are.

Building a local decorating tribe will set you apart from any competitor, and in a substantial way. A lot of people say they are going to do a lot of things, but I don't see very many business people really applying the concept of the tribe in a successful way in a business model that actually works, so this information will give you a real competitive edge. I think I was a really good example of leading a decorating tribe when I ran my own local decorating business a few years back (now I do business development and training exclusively). I built a wonderful tribe, and I did it without the social media tools we are so fortunate to have developed over the last few years. You are in an even better position today! You have a greater opportunity to build a solid tribe by leveraging these phenomenal social tools to help you and your tribe members connect, share news, impart ideas, herald your events, talk about design and color trends, and contribute your problem-solving abilities.

Real-Life Events in Conjunction with Social Media Interaction

A tribe can thrive through social media networks, but it is even better if there is the real-life human component in conjunction with it, too. Let's say you could create some kind of regular event (on site, and also online) where every week people are coming and exchanging thoughts, ideas, excitement, and advice. Imagine a weekly or monthly decorating event that you host, where you talk and share and infuse everyone with passion, and where you get people talking, exchanging information, sharing their decorating dilemmas, and finding solutions, too. Onsite events allow people to see and feel real examples of what you sell and create. When you are able to publicly give great advice, meet a challenge, or solve a dilemma with your expertise, everyone witnesses it and everyone benefits. Then, everyone has reason to share with THEIR tribes and their social networks!

Out-of-the-Box Thinking:

Tribe members want to be heard, listened to, and respected for their ideas, too. If you can connect meaningfully and well, your tribe members can really put your business on the map through their own social media networks and through their own local mini-communities!

What if you could do something like that? What if every month people were gathering to you (and to each other because of you), over and over again? That's the mentality that I want you to get. You become *the tribe's decorator.* In the same way somebody will call on their doctor on a regular basis, or their nutrition expert, or their hair colorist, I want them to come to you as *their design professional* on a regular basis, not just when they need window treatments or flooring, but when they want to talk about design concepts and ideas just for the passion and thrill of it! For you and your members, being a part of the tribe becomes a fun experience with regular interchange that tribe members look forward to.

You create a type of local social media outlet and inlet for people (both on site and online).

You build your local decorating tribe through local activities. I'll share with you in just a bit some great activities you can do to rally your tribe and get your tribe engaged.

Is Leading a Tribe about Being a Big Leader with Subordinate Followers?

It's important to note again that the tribe leader should communicate with the tribe members on a regular basis. In addition, the tribe members have to be able to communicate with the leader of the tribe on a regular basis as well.

The last thing you will want to do as a decorating professional when you're building a local tribe through local activities is to come off as the *BIG I* approaching your tribe members as the *Little You*. You must leave your ego at the door and instead take up the mantra of being a passionate leader and mentor and see yourself as having equal importance and equal value to each tribe member, someone who wants to educate the tribe members and continually bring forth and share new ideas, new industry developments, and herald change.

With this approach, your tribe members will always have a need for you and desire to stay connected.

Sometimes we all make the mistake of behaving like the "know-it-all designer or decorator." But you should really allow the regular input of your tribe members because the tribe is much bigger than you. It is the leader's responsibility to find out specifically what the tribe members (people) want. One thing we want for certain is connection!

> ### Out-of-the-Box Thinking:
>
> The future belongs to passionate leaders, innovators, and those who think creatively. No machine can copy that!

I will say it again. We want connection to a leader, and we want connection to other tribe members so we can inquire and share and interact, and we certainly want connection to new and exciting ideas. We actually want a combination of all that. We want to use our voice. We want to have input. We want to be heard. We want to be listened to. Most importantly, we want to be respected and valued and respectfully responded to.

So in other words, as a leader, you create a framework for communication and activity in many directions. It's not just you and your tribe members having this good interchange where you're listening to them and they're listening to you, or where you're respecting them and they're respecting you and there is input both ways. Even though that's great, it is more than that. They have to believe in the story – the mission – because you want them to be tweeting and posting online about that interchange to the other tribe members AND even more far-reaching, to THEIR extended networks, giving you opportunity to increase your tribe by *meaningfully* connecting with more people. That's where the real tribe-building power and momentum starts to come in. It's like referrals on steroids!

A tribe can start out small and really grow, but it never has to be over-the-top huge for your business to benefit financially, especially when talking about the local tribe. Loyal tribe members become loyal customers. If you use this model with even a few local tribe members at the start, and you get them engaging with you and with one another and being involved in activities together, then you have the makings of a great business model. It's a totally different approach to business than "business as usual" and "regular" selling. It is dynamic, powerful, and very motivating to homeowners who are interested in working with a design professional to design and decorate their homes.

The Power of Social Media and Social Word-of-Mouth Marketing

We all wish we had more time for a lot of things, like more time to communicate through online social networks. So many decorators and designers have gotten a little "freaked out" about social media and the time it involves. Some may say, "How am I supposed to be tweeting and posting all day if I'm running a business and delivering window treatments?" Here's the great part. Building a tribe and using the power of social media is not so much about you personally getting out there day after day and being on social media networks all the time (although you will do some of that on a regular basis – some daily, some weekly, and some monthly). It is more about engaging in a very effective, word-of-mouth social marketing strategy that offers exponential influence and reach.

Once you begin to build a tribe and create social media networks, you have begun to build a following. At some point, you won't have to do all the work yourself! Here's where your tribe can really help you out. This is powerful not because you're the one tweeting and posting all the time (yes, of course you will do this sometimes).

Instead, you engage with your tribe in a meaningful way through your passion, through your amazing ideas, through good content, through your good business practices, through delivery of great products and services, and through events and activities that people want to attend, share, and talk about.

So, when your tribe members are at work and they're tweeting about that trunk show they're going to go to or the color class they just attended, or when they are posting about the stunning window treatment they just had installed (and posting photos), or the free redesign seminar they were invited to by their decorator (who did their flooring), it gives many more people opportunity to learn about you and about how wonderful you are.

Activities and Techniques to Build a Loyal Tribe

I've got a lot of activities and techniques to make you an amazing tribe leader who is full of the kind of fun and excitement that your followers will be extremely interested in. We are going to look at how to engage your tribe through community events. We will discuss doing trunk shows. We will look at a local real estate program that you can put into place. We'll discuss designer showhouses and we'll even touch a little bit on home shows. I'll also share with you some great information about a couple of coaching programs that I think are where the future lies. As a decorating or design professional, you have so many incredible opportunities for building a solid business.

Innovation and the Right-Brain Thinkers

For your business to move forward, innovation must be the name of the game. You must keep things fresh and alive so people always have something to talk about. In the past, you may have looked at some of the important research on right-brain/left-brain studies. There is a lot of impressive information about that topic. It seems that right-brain thinkers may have a serious competitive edge going into the future. Of course we all use both sides of our brains, but some people focus on that kind of thinking, and research indicates that there is and will continue to be a need for leaders who are right-brain thinkers.

It is to our advantage to focus on becoming more innovative, and on thinking more outside of the box. You see, computers and machines and even online services can replace some of our activity, but nothing can replace the energy of creating new ideas or the energy of leadership and interactivity. The innovative efforts – as well as the social aspect – of human interaction cannot be replaced by other means.

> ### Out-of-the-Box Thinking:
>
> Don't wait for someone else to give you permission. Be a leader! Embrace your great ideas and just put them into action. Your tribe is waiting!

125

So if you are already an innovative, right-brained thinker who loves dreaming up new ideas and coming up with stimulating ways of connecting with people, you are many steps ahead of most business owners and most designers and decorators! If you are already leading and engaging others in what you do, you are headed towards raving success. That's where all the fun is anyway!

Specific Tribe-Building Activities

Just do it!

I am now going to discuss specific activities that you can do to build your tribe and establish yourself as the local decorating expert. With each word on this page, know that I am encouraging you to take action and not wait for someone else to tell you that you have "permission" to build an amazing business for yourself.

Out-of-the-Box Thinking:

Trunk shows facilitate exceptional interactivity. Attendees connect with you and each other, helping you to make more sales!

We've probably all been in situations in times past where we wanted to be leaders. Perhaps we wanted to be a speaker at a show or maybe we wanted get up in front of a group in our local or national community and share. Maybe we wanted to share on decorating or perhaps on another topic.

Many of us were prevented from speaking in public and sharing ourselves and our ideas with others by other "leaders" who acted as "gate keepers," telling us when we were going to do something and when we weren't. Now, I do believe that experience very necessary and extremely important, and we have to have skills in order to do those things, but I find that many decorating professionals have a lot of rich experience and tremendous skills – tremendous gifts. Why in the world should some gate keeper tell that individual that they can't use those gifts or share them with others in a public setting?

So I say to you, that with everything we're going to cover on trunk shows, designer showhouses, real estate programs, color consulting, certified interior environment coaching, and the like – *just do it*! Again, what I am telling you loud and clear is *just do it*! Don't wait for somebody to give you the go-ahead, the permission. Give that to yourself and just get out there and live and breathe your passion, and lovingly share it with others. Grow some holiday balls, take hold of your confidence, and just begin creating your own programs. Again, you just need to do it!

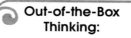

Out-of-the-Box Thinking:

Partner with a non-competing biz for your first trunk show. Your high-end customers love to cook and entertain. Why not partner with a kitchen center?

Trunk Shows

Trunk shows began in the fashion industry. Back in the day, top designers hosted events they called *trunk shows* to showcase their new lines for each season. Before the new lines came out, there was a "buzz" in the air. *Oh, the designer is coming. We're going to get to see the new fall line. You're invited to this exclusive trunk show where the cat is going to be let out of the bag (or out of the trunk, so to speak), and you're going to get to see the goods before anyone else does.* There was such a posh-ness and a mystique about trunk shows. For most people both then and now, it just feels good to be invited to an exclusive specialty social event.

The designers actually carried their clothing lines to the shows in large trunks, and many of the designers held their trunk shows for several days. People could come and pre-order the fashions for the next season. Sometimes multiple designers would get together in the same place for a large multi-designer trunk show.

In Europe, trunk shows really took off and became extremely popular. They became so popular that it got to the point where designers were showing their lines just from pictures in books. They weren't even bringing the clothing and the fabrics anymore, just the trunks and the pictures, and they sold right from the photos. After a while, people began to get tired of this, and trunk shows started going off into all kinds of different directions. However, they originated as designer events to show forth the new season and the things that were soon to become the current fashion.

Why Is It Important to Do Trunk Shows?

I love new media and the Internet, but you know what? We can't just sit around on Facebook, Twitter, and social outlets all day. We need to get our and about in our towns and communities, and I know we can tweet, text, and post from our cars but we probably shouldn't be doing that. We should probably be driving!

Honestly, what people really want is interaction. They really don't want social media to totally take the place of face-to-face activity, where they can be around other people, where they can see colors in true light, and feel textures, and put their hands on fabrics, and be excited, and get together with other decorating enthusiasts. That is what's important!

When you deal with a customer in their home one-on-one, or when you send an advertisement, or even a hand-written letter or card, you're just talking to THAT client – you and them. There is no interactivity in another direction – horizontally. Trunk shows allow people to directly interact with you AND with each other, and that's where your potential for big sales comes in, because the audience members (or tribe members) who go to these events actually help you sell your items. Once you break the ice and get going, and once you get the audience warmed up to each other, they actually start helping each other to like you, helping each other to like the things that you're showing. They start giving each other the "aha," "great idea," "oh yeah, that's really nice." This solidifies you as the expert and as a valuable asset to them, and establishes your products and services as interesting, attractive, desirable, and important. At a certain point they are actively helping you to sell.

Out-of-the-Box Thinking:

Trunk shows are, by their very nature, sales-driven events. People love to buy things at a trunk show. Seminars, on the other hand, are mainly lead-generating events.

Trunk shows are also about creating community and creating exciting events that set you apart from other decorating and design professionals in the area. The last thing you want to be viewed as is just another store front or another semi-serious person working out of their house, and you definitely do not need to be struggling over and over again for a sale. "I hope I get a $2,000 sale this week. I hope I get a $3,000 sale this month." You just can't live that way.

You need to (and should want to) have a regular stream of decent-sized sales coming in on a regular basis, and the way to do that is by continuously keeping your name out there. The way to do it with ease is to be the decorating expert and local design celebrity who people want to connect with. You do that by being innovative, being cutting-edge, being fun, and having events that people WANT to get attend.

The Process of Hosting a Trunk Show

If you want to host a trunk show, the first thing to do is decide for certain to do it and then begin planning! There are several ways to do a trunk show. You can have one totally on your own, or you can partner with somebody for the event.

If you host a trunk show on your own, you can hold it at a public venue such as a local conference center (where rooms are not usually very expensive to rent) or at a local hotel or event center. A private trunk show could be held at a customer's home or a past customer's home.

If you partner with someone else for the event, choose a non-competing business with a target customer and clientele similar to yours, such as a kitchen center or even a bath shop.

Kitchen design centers are ideal partners for trunk shows because some research has shown that people who buy high-end decorating and design services like window treatments and flooring also like to entertain and do gourmet cooking. This is a good correlation to work from, and you can use that information when you approach a specialty kitchen design center about doing a trunk show together. Many such business-people will be open to the idea, because for them it is entertainment for their customers. It's an ideal event to host for their clientele and potential clients since it has to do with the home and decorating and it appeals to their client base. Suggest that you could do all of the planning, provide the props, and do the actual speaking, and they could provide the food and refreshments. They would send invitations to their list and you would likewise send invitations to your list.

> ## ◉ Out-of-the-Box Thinking:
>
> Start planning for your trunk show by selecting a theme first. Once you have your theme, deciding on what to sell – and more importantly how to present it – will be a breeze! Tie the latest products or fabrics to your theme, and feature some traditional items as well. Oh, and please, don't sell clearance items at your trunk show!

Get a Buzz Going

You can publicize the trunk show as a "what's happening in town" event. A lot of local radio and TV stations have "what's happening

129

calendars," and even though your trunk show is an event held by a business, you can play it up as an informational and educational event. Just let the radio or the TV station know that that there is going to be a fun and informative trunk show at a certain establishment at a certain time on a certain date, and they will likely put it in their "what's happening" section, and that's FREE publicity. That's one way to get to the word out.

Once you pick your venue, start to invite people and get a buzz going. Obviously you are going to get the word out by using your social media outlets, but you will also tell everyone you can, and let your customers know as you visit them in their homes for design jobs. Ask them to spread the word, too, and mail invitations to past customers as well.

Out-of-the-Box Thinking:

Email me for a very cool FREE gift that will help you create special packages and "show specials" that you can sell at your trunk shows. Reach me at Margo@Decorating-School.com

You should plan ahead so that you have enough time to promote the event and plenty of time to have a number of attractive, custom, home fashion samples made up to show to your audience (especially if you are a window treatment professional).

One thing I want to say before I go on with more trunk show details is that on the day of the event, just be yourself and have fun with it. Don't worry too much about whether or not everyone will like you. Be sincere and be yourself, and your event will be a huge hit!

How Are Trunk Shows Different from Seminars?

Trunk shows are different from decorating seminars in that trunk shows are selling events (like when the designers of the past sold their fashion lines) and decorating seminars are lead-generating events (where instead of selling, you inform the audience about decorating topics and ideas).

You can mix them around and use a trunk show for gaining leads and you can also sell at a seminar, but traditionally a trunk show IS a selling event. People who come to a trunk show most always expect to be able to purchase something. A trunk show is a sales-driven event, so you're actually going to be selling something at the show. You don't usually charge people to attend a trunk show; if you must, you can simply charge a nominal fee.

Some designers and decorators run service-only businesses, offering such services as staging and redesign without selling products. They may only rent their merchandise out, as many stagers do with furnishings (some redesigners and stagers actually do sell products).

If you do not sell merchandise in your business, you can still host a trunk show, although it will be more of a decorating event or demonstration. During your event, you can have some of the props that you use in your work stored in the trunk. You can take them out as you demonstrate ways to decorate an area such as a mantel or table. You would do the decorating right in front of the audience, giving them inspiration and ideas for their own homes while showing off your talent and sharing about your services.

If you do sell merchandise in your business, of course you would sell it at your trunk show while demonstrating wonderful ways to use the products in the home. If you are going to make your trunk show a traditional selling event, then you will have to decide which items you will sell at your show. Don't try to sell everything you carry. You will also have to pick a theme for your trunk show. Selecting a theme will actually make it easier for you to decide what items you will feature for sale at your show. Your theme could be "Holiday Decorating," or it could be something like "Summer Breeze." Select products to sell that will support your theme.

> ## Out-of-the-Box Thinking:
>
> Be a giver! During the decorating presentation at your trunk show, don't push hard sales. Rather, plant seeds and give great ideas and tips for clever and interesting ways to decorate as well as ideas on how to use the items you are selling. Give some general decorating advice so people who don't buy can still go away with something valuable for FREE! After all, they did invest their time to come. This will increase the likelihood of later referrals and increase sales during the shopping experience portion of your trunk show.

Your Trunk Show Will Have a Decorating Presentation and a Shopping Experience

> ### Out-of-the-Box Thinking:
>
> Increase the value of your shows with tickets! Make your trunk show an exclusive ticketed event. Although they are free for guests, they have to pick them up at a particular location, or you can mail the tickets when someone requests them. People have a hard time throwing away REAL TICKETS. They would rather give them away to a friend. This method can also help you build your mailing and email lists if you tie the ticket requests to gaining names and email addresses.

Your trunk show will have a decorating portion and a "shopping experience" portion. During the decorating presentation (which can last 20 to 40 minutes), people will take a seat, and you will share decorating ideas and talk about design solutions. You will also showcase some of the special items you have for sale at the show. The shopping experience takes place after the decorating presentation. After your talk you will say to the guests, "Thanks so much for sharing in this presentation. I hope you will take away with you some helpful and fun ideas for your home. I'd like to invite you to stay a while longer to enjoy a fabulous shopping experience. Feel free to mingle about and look at the many exceptional home decorating items we have for you. You'll see that we have put together some wonderful show specials, too. Again, thanks for coming to the presentation." Then, you mingle about, too. Let people be free to shop and ask you questions as they do. There should be no pressure put on people to buy. Keep the atmosphere fun and festive.

Selling at Your Trunk Show

I recommend that you implement a trunk show *system* into your business as a form of marketing where you host a different trunk show at least every few months, perhaps quarterly. If you did a trunk show every three months, you would never cry for business again! If you're doing regular trunk shows and putting effort into them, and showcasing wonderful samples and merchandise, they will drive your sales.

If you're a window treatment designer or run a workroom, you would not sell window treatments at your show because they are custom products. What you could do very easily to drive appointments and future sales is to make up a selection of different window treatment samples mounted on 36-inch-wide boards. You can take each board out of the trunk one by one and touch it and dress it as you talk about the treatment and its styling.

You might explain for example how a Kingston differs from an Empire valance. You might show (with the running across of your fingers) how a swag pleats perfectly from left to right.

I hope you are getting the picture. As you are speaking, you will be dropping seeds along the way about other custom products you sell. You will also be sharing your knowledge of fabrics and trims, and giving guidance on which ones are in season now and which are coming into season.

> ### Out-of-the-Box Thinking:
>
> Regular trunk show events are an ideal way to keep in touch with past clients (and their friends). It is a no-pressure and fun way to stay connected, while also adding value to your relationship!

And then of course, even if your business focus is on custom products, you would have some items there to sell, items like sofa and bed throws, pairs of throw pillows in neutral colors that will go with most interiors, mantel scarves, and other home accessory products made with fabrics.

A _Free_ Gift for You!

The throw is a really HOT item and a very good seller at a trunk show. More on that in a bit, but first I want to stop right here for a moment and offer you a little free gift that I think will help you with your trunk shows. I personally LOVE to get free stuff (and so do my sisters – we always give free stuff to each other)! So, I want to give you something free that you will really benefit from. If you email me at margo@ decoratingschool.com, I will send you a PDF audio that I created. It is part of my Trunk Show Success System. I sell an entire system to help you implement a trunk show program into your business, and this PDF is a small part of that system. It will give you some really good ideas of a variety of specials that you can put together for your trunk shows, including sample pricing. It is really just a cool little thing, so please email me and request it and I will email it to you.

133

Selling Decorative Throws at Your Trunk Show

Out-of-the-Box Thinking:

When you partner with a real estate company, be loyal! Focus your efforts on creating and implementing a solid program with a single company. Build trust and you will see the referral tree begin to take root.

Now back to the decorative throw. If you are decorating on a regular basis and seeing clients all the time, you are going to have lots of leftover fabric. Let's face it, we've all got piles of fabrics in our workrooms and studios. You can make up (or have made) a selection of gorgeous throws to sell at your trunk shows. Use a yard of fabric for the front, a yard for the back, and a yard and a half of trim (bullion works best) for the bottom edge. Voilà – you've got yourself a sofa throw, bed throw, or chair throw.

Make up 10 or 20 of them. This is normally an item that can sell for around $300, but you can sell them as a "show special" for around $125, or sell them for $95 if you have fabric that is just going to go to waste. Also make up several throws to showcase some of the new and trendy fabrics (always a good idea at a trunk show). These throws would likely sell for a little bit higher price, because you would have to order new fabric.

Keep the prices at your show a bit lower than you would if you were selling them directly to your custom clients, because people at your show will be impulse shopping, so you don't want to go with a full mark-up.

Even though your costs will be higher, go ahead and feature some brand new and trendy fabrics on some of the throws and pillows (remember I said that designers should do trunk shows to show the new season's fashions). New patterns are usually available from your books for at least two or three years, and you will likely sell the items at your show, giving the customers more reason to call you later to match the pattern.

You should certainly feature a few nice jacquards in the more traditional fabrics on some of your items for sale, but definitely throw in some punchy fabrics that are just really cool and that people can't resist.

If you still have some of the items left over from your trunk show, you can sell them at the next home show.

If you are a redesigner, stager, or color consultant, and you don't sell window treatments or custom products, you can do a show with the theme I previously mentioned, "Summer Breeze" and showcase crisp summer home décor, or "Lighting for a Midsummer Night," and just feature lamps.

Consider doing a trunk show on bedding or baby bedding – or both – and call it "From Cradle to King." In my own design business, I sold custom baby bedding for many years in addition to our grownup bedding, so I did shows on bedding, and I sold lots and lots of bedding. I also did baby bedding shows, and they were very successful.

Here is one word of caution about something you should NEVER sell at your trunk shows. Never sell clearance items – NEVER! Never sell junk. The whole point of hosting exciting, exclusive, talked-about trunk shows is that they have to be upscale and even trendy. That does not mean that the items you sell should be overpriced, because it's still an impulse-shopping situation. Focus on selling beautiful, interesting (some traditional, some trendy), quality products at very good prices.

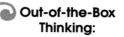

Out-of-the-Box Thinking:

When you create friendships and solve peoples' small decorating dilemmas, you open the door to larger, highly profitable projects that require trust.

Offer some show specials, and have a separate special for future custom sales that you make by appointment (which would have a deadline or expiration date, to move people to take action and make an appointment).

Implementing a Trunk Show System

I personally believe it is so important to implement a trunk show system into your business and play on a variety of themes to get people excited, talking, and looking forward to each and every show. Make them fun events that create a stir!

My *Trunk Show Success System* is chock-full of extraordinary information and ideas for your shows. There are about 8 videos, 21 audios (8 are duplicates of the videos), 28 additional PDFs and document files that make up your *Decorator's Tool Kit*, and 11 more such files that make up your *Hostess Kit*. Some of these files are made so that you can personalize them for YOUR business. I mean, it is just power-packed. I have included every detail of everything you could imagine, including all kinds of wonderful themes and fabulous marketing ideas as well as tips on speaking and body language, and a session on my money-making units model, and I've included some great ice-breakers, too. It is meant to help you create a buzz-generating trunk show system to increase your sales, your profits, and your local celebrity. If you only want to have one trunk show, that's fine. It will be fun and a good experience for you; however, if you want to generate consistent revenue and a stream of leads and word-of-mouth marketing, you have got to implement a trunk show *system* in your business where you are doing a trunk show every few months. Because then, people start looking forward to your shows, which become something people want to talk about to their friends and on their online social networks.

Get Your Tickets!

Seriously consider putting on a ticketed trunk show event. Mail tickets to your past customers, and use your online networks to let people know they can pick up tickets at a certain location. You should have a few designated places where tickets can be picked up. I think it's just so cool that people have to come to The Kitchen Design Center or another upscale establishment to pick up their tickets.

Out-of-the-Box Thinking:

A regular column with your picture, contact info, and a question that you skillfully answer helps establish you as the local expert and celebrity. See an example at www.MargoDeGange.com/ask1.

What happens then is that your trunk show co-host – the guy from The Kitchen Design Center, for example – is going to like you even more and feel like you are really working for him when people come to his studio to pick up tickets for the trunk show.

Part of the reason that we do trunk shows is to build the tribe and to build our reputation as a noted designer or noted decorator in our community. Ticketed events will help establish you in this way.

Another little trick I will share with you is to find the nicest restaurant in town, and try to frequent it a few times and kind of get to know the people there. Ask to talk to the chef after your meal. Tell him (or her) how great the food was. Then, send him two tickets to your trunk show.

136

Get real tickets, or print some tickets on nice paper (we have some for you to print in the *Trunk Show Success System*), and send them to him in an attractive, hand-addressed envelope thanking him for a great dinner and letting him know, "I want to personally invite you and a guest to my very exclusive trunk show." Let him know it is a VIP event with limited participants, and write, "If you are not available to come to the event, please feel free to give the tickets to somebody special." Well, that guy knows everybody in town! He'll probably tell at least a couple of people about it, including his wife, and she'll probably tell at least three or four people. She will also likely be the one who uses the tickets, and that's how it works!

Keep in mind that you cannot build celebrity status with just one trunk show. You have to get to a point where people are saying, "I cannot wait for her next trunk show, and I don't want to miss it, because she can only hold 50 (or 30 or 80) people".

In the beginning you are going have maybe 12 to 15 people at your trunk shows, but that is just in the beginning, and you may very well have a lot more than that if you market the event well. Even if just 12 to 15 people attend, that's okay! 12 people can be just as powerful as 40, and the leads, referrals, and word-of-mouth from 12 can really impact your business. Plus, after you have done several trunk shows, you'll be able to get 20, 30, 40, even 80 people to a show (and more), depending on the marketing and the venue. No matter how many people come, try to make the event cozy.

> ## Out-of-the-Box Thinking:
>
> A weekly Q&A column in the real estate section of the local paper sets you apart from your competitors and sets the real estate company that you are working with apart from their competitors.

Trunk Shows Help Us Stay Connected with Past Customers

Besides encouraging new business, trunk shows are also a great way to stay in touch with past customers in a meaningful way, keeping the relationship strong. If someone was just a one-time customer, being invited to your trunk show gives them a reason to come back around. Then, perhaps three or four years later, they may need decorating ser-

137

vices and they will think to call you because you've stayed in touch.

There is nothing worse for customer relations than to make a sale and then forget about the customer. Would you like to be taken out on a date, and after having a really nice time, be dropped off at the curb in front of your house? Of course not! Hopefully, you are walked to the door. But how would you feel if you never heard from that person again? You might feel kind of used, and that's what happens with our customers. We connect with them and allow them to buy from us, and we have a great time, but then once the sale is made, we never talk to them again. Inviting them to a trunk show is a way for us to connect with them again without putting pressure on them to buy.

Out-of-the-Box Thinking:

Don't be afraid to be a giver. Target your giving to the right audience and it will benefit you greatly.

Trunk shows drive sales, but they also drive leads for future, bigger sales. When money – even small amounts – is exchanged in a positive way, we connect emotionally with a person and increase the likelihood of future transactions. Once someone has purchased something from us, it is much easier for them to purchase again.

But that's not the best part.

The great thing about trunk shows is not only that people purchase items on the spot, solidifying our relationship with them and increasing the odds of serving them again, but because they had a good experience, they become sources of quality leads and referrals (birds of a feather flock together) for future sales.

Trunk shows are really so much fun. People will come. Some people will buy and some will simply come for the excitement and entertainment value of the show. Either way they are helping spread the word of your exceptional design abilities and your decorating products and services.

Real Estate Programs

There are a couple of powerful real estate programs that you can put into place in your business. I will share one in particular with you that I used in my own business. It is a program I called "Ask the Decorator."

"Ask the Decorator" Seminars

Ask the Decorator starts out as a series of a few decorating seminars that you do for the clients and potential clients of a local real estate company, and then the program leads into an newspaper column in the real estate section of your local newspaper. The column includes your photo and a short Q&A article where you answer a question that begins, "Dear Decorator". The best part is, this program can cost you very little money (just a bit of time) and possibly no money at all! You begin by first getting to know a local real estate professional, building trust, and then joining forces to implement this easy program.

Here is the way that I created my program. I partnered with a local real estate company. I focused on only one company (if you pick one, you get greater loyalty, and most companies are not going to work with you if you are working with other companies). I got together with the owner of the real estate company (or, you could get together with an agent). I just approached her and said, "I've got some ideas for my business that I think will really appeal to your business." We had some coffee and we chit-chatted.

You can do the same. Just approach someone in the real estate industry who might be interested in building their business in a meaningful way and at the same time contributing to the community as a whole. Just pick someone and call them, then plan to meet for a cup of coffee. Be very relaxed about it – just be yourself. If they like the idea, they like it; it they don't, they don't; but you approach them with the idea of doing some free seminars for them at their place of business, perhaps in the evenings. This allows you to get in front of people who are likely in or near your target group in a venue that you do not have to pay for.

> ### 🔊 Out-of-the-Box Thinking:
>
> Join in on an existing designer showhouse or just create your own. Gain real celebrity status by starting up your own showhouse, and help a local charity while promoting other design-related professionals in your community.

Plus, you are doing something for the real estate company. You are going to give a fun and informative decorating presentation to their prospects and clients, making their business more exciting to their contacts. They will send invitations to their list (and you will do the

139

same with your list). They provide the refreshments – which you should keep simple – and they provide the venue. Doing the seminars allows the real estate professional to give something special to their clients, and sets you up as the local expert. It also serves to increase your list of contacts.

There are so many possible topics for your seminar. You can tie it into buying or selling a home and choose a topic such as *10 Terrific Staging Ideas to Sell Your Home Fast While Improving Your Decorating Skills, or 8 Golden Redesign Tips to Make a Home Your Own.*

The seminars come before the article series because the articles cost money, and someone has to pay for them. You want to first build trust and prove that you are someone they definitely want on their team. You work to gain a relationship with the real estate company showing them: "I'm good, I'm very good, and I can help you become more valuable in the eyes of YOUR clients." They will see how well you present, and how much the audience connects with you. During your presentation, make the agent or the real estate company look good. Thank them and compliment them for making this seminar possible.

Out-of-the-Box Thinking:

Be the lead designer or the project manager in your very own show-house. You make the rules and you get the credit! Your project can be a simple but elegant showhouse or an elaborate event. You decide.

You may have 10 people show up at a seminar, or you may get 30. It does not matter. Do your best even with 10 people and build the relationships with both your real estate team and the attendees, who will likely enjoy themselves so much they will come to future events. Share your decorating tips for about 20 to 30 minutes. You do not need PowerPoint, although you certainly can use it, but holding up fabrics and accessories and talking about them provides great visuals to keep people engaged. Pass a piece of fabric around once you have talked about it, adding to the interactivity.

After the presentation, have a meet-and-greet where you have tea, cookies, and conversation. Walk around the room and mingle. Let people share their decorating thoughts, ideas, and questions with you. In advance of the event, let the real estate team know that you will be available after the seminar to help their clients with decorating questions. That way when they email or mail the invitations, they will mention it to their list. Encourage attendees to bring pictures of their trouble areas or decorating dilemmas. They can even bring a laptop with a picture or two.

The entire decorating seminar should be very relaxed, matter-of-fact, and fun. You start by introducing yourself and the real estate partner, and then do your presentation. Afterwards invite everyone to share in refreshments in a laid-back, relaxed fashion. You will be so surprised at how effective these events are at getting you leads and even appointments on the spot.

Out-of-the-Box Thinking:

If you are more comfortable working on an existing showhouse instead of creating your own, then be sure to be considered one of the showhouse designers with your OWN area. Don't settle for being someone else's HELPER. They will get the credit while you do most of the work.

In case you are unclear, let me point out that the seminars should be geared toward the homeowner, not geared toward real estate professionals. These seminars are designed to engage both your potential clients and the real estate company's potential clients. This is a fabulous program because it sets up you and the real estate professionals as givers, and allows you to connect with homeowners in a friendly, no-pressure setting.

When I did this in my business, it was a huge success. Everyone loved the free seminars on decorating. We did an entire series. People came and they loved the events so much, and we had amazing connections during the meet-and-greet time. I got appointments and made sales from these events.

"Ask the Decorator" Newspaper Column

By now you may be asking how the seminars tie into the *Ask the Decorator* column that I mentioned earlier. Well, once you do one or two or three of these seminars, and the real estate agents or the broker or the decision maker sees what a success they are, and some level of trust has been established, you can then approach them by saying something like, "I'll tell you what, to further the appeal here, let's just do a whole program. I noticed that you advertise every Sunday in the home magazine of the local newspaper. [NOTE: You should do the free decorating seminars for a real estate company that advertises in the

141

real estate section of the paper on a regular basis – most local newspapers will have a Sunday Real Estate Magazine section that is just for homes.] If you would like, I can do something that would really add some wonderful appeal there and at the same time set you apart from all of the other companies. I can do an **Ask the Decorator Q&A** in a corner of your space each Sunday. That way people will have a reason to go to your ad each week, and I won't charge you for writing it since I may get some leads from it, and I know it will be good for you, too, because it is a fun and consistent thing that people will look forward to reading. I'll talk about color and texture and decorating, so it will give your readers more of a reason to go to your space rather than to the competitors' space."

Out-of-the-Box Thinking:

Really play up the areas that other designers often dismiss as unimportant. If you can make these small, seemingly insignificant spaces shine, you'll make yourself a bigger star!

The real estate companies really like this idea because it is valuable to them. They may have a regular space in the paper that they rent each week, and they may give you a portion of that space for the article, or they may want to split the cost with you. You can work out the details in a way you feel is beneficial to you. If you would like to see an example of the *Ask the Decorator* column that I did, go to www.MargoDeGange.com/ask1. The entire space you see there used to be reserved for the real estate company's ad (the company I partnered with for the project).

They gave me a large area for my column and my photo. As the column became popular, people would send in questions for me to answer. In the beginning I had to create my own questions for a while. Sometimes, creating your own questions can work to your advantage because you can touch on very important topics and then answer them. Sometimes I would take a number of questions and create my own from several because I knew the readers would benefit more this way.

You Don't Even Have to Be a Writer!

If you need questions with exceptional, well-written answers, just contact me. I have a wonderful product which is an assortment of terrific questions that people really asked, as well as some that I combined to create even better questions and answers. It's called *Ask the Decorator* (which makes sense)! You can buy them in packs of 12 for a monthly column or in a pack of 52 for a weekly column. Then all the work is completely done for you. Each question and answer combination has been strategically edited down to 178 words or less with good writing style, which makes it ideal for this type of a column since it uses little space and allows room for your photo, name, and contact information. Having your contact information right there in the article is so important because it makes it very easy for readers to contact you quickly.

Great Impact and Celebrity Buzz

This type of real estate program has great impact and brings a targeted audience for the types of products and services a design professional sells. What a way to make yourself stand out and not only partner with a great team, but also secure an advertising venue that really brings forth what you're trying to sell. All eyeballs go directly to you! Best of all, you are either not paying for it or paying very little compared to a regular ad this size that is not even in a section of the paper that is so targeted.

> **Out-of-the-Box Thinking:**
>
> Get the conversation going through your social media networks. Let people know that something exciting is happening. Others will start inquiring. That's how the tribe grows!

When I did this column, it created a buzz. People would stop me in the community and ask if I was the *Dear Decorator* (because they saw my photo). I remember going to the post office to mail a package, and the lady who worked there said with excitement, "You write that article!" It's really fun because you start getting that celebrity status.

So remember, you start the program off with seminars (or even trunk shows) for the real estate company, and lead into the *Ask the Decorator* column in the weekly home magazine section of the Sunday paper. It's a great program. It's exciting, it's fun, and you meet a lot of really wonderful people. You also end up saving money in more ways than just getting inexpensive advertising and more customers. You save money because you meet people who are givers and who go out of their way for you when you need it. For example, your agent may lower their fee for you when it comes time to sell your house. It's really cool to get the perks!

143

Give Away High-Perceived-Value Gift Certificates

> ### ⦿ Out-of-the-Box Thinking:
>
> At a home and garden show, don't struggle for days to design a product-heavy booth, or waste hours setting it up. The whole idea anyway is to gain people's attention. Why not just drive your wrapped business car right into the home show area and let that be your display? Give away candy and fun trinkets, and make lots of new friends.

Once the real estate agents really get to know you, they will tell others about you, and many of those "others" are buying homes in the area. The agent can invite them to one of your seminars, where perhaps you could give away a few gift certificates for your services, valued at $100 or $200. These are not $100 or $200 OFF, they are straight-out gifts for your products and services, no strings attached! This has a very high perceived value.

A $200 certificate will cost you around $80 to $90 – at the most, and that is if the bearer of the certificate uses it for products and not services, and doesn't purchase anything else, which is not very likely. If you realized that an advertised lead in the design industry can cost hundreds of dollars, you would see that giving away a gift certificate – even a $200 certificate – to a targeted client is a real bargain for you.

Free Decorating or Staging Consultations

There is another simple program that you can offer to do for the same real estate company you are already working with. You can offer to do staging consultations or decorating consultations (consultations only) with every one of the people who buy or list a home with them (or who buy or list within a certain price bracket – one that is targeted to your services). The real estate company pays you a fee for each 1-hour consultation (a fee that is lower than you normally charge), and they give the 1-hour decorating consultation to their client as a gift or as part of a special listing package.

Many people who sell a home buy one in the same area. If they list with and then buy with the same agent, you may end up doing the staging for the home that is selling as well as the decorating consultation for the

144

new home. Again, the agent pays you to do the consultations.

The result for you could be a lot of appointments, with a lot of people who are prime candidates for window treatments, flooring, custom bedding, cabinets, and other products and services with substantial price tags.

Designer Showhouses

Basically, a designer showhouse is a community event that generates a lot of talk, publicity, and expert status. In a nutshell it goes something like this: You design a showhouse, tickets are sold, people go to the showhouse, they wear rubber-soled shoes to protect new flooring, they look at all the of the pretty rooms, and they talk about it to all of their friends!

Designer showhouses are projects that several design professionals work on together. These are almost always a fundraiser event for a local charity. Each design-related professional is assigned a room or an area to decorate or design, and they are usually asked to name that area (by the way, come up with a wonderful name for your area). The showhouse gets lots of local promotion and local publicity, and each designer or professional involved benefits from that. There is also a certain celebrity vibe attached to being a designer who has worked on a showhouse. Many design professional do them for that reason alone.

> **Out-of-the-Box Thinking:**
>
> There is a strong market for coaching services related to the home and how it affects us in terms of our happiness, our productivity, our creative pursuits, and our sense of personal empowerment. The *Certified Interior Environment Coaching* program is reaching homeowners right where they're at in terms of their desire for personal growth and fulfillment.

Pitch Yourself for a Designer Showhouse or Create Your Own Event

Now, there are two great ways to get involved in a designer showhouse. You can either approach the committee of an upcoming designer showhouse to be chosen as one of the designers or decorators in the project, or you can just create your own designer showhouse!

145

There are many wonderful designer showhouses that you can be a part of. Some are sponsored by the same organizations each year. If you want to be a part of an existing project, you first have to pitch yourself and your design ideas to the showhouse committee, and hope that you are chosen.

Another way to get involved in a designer showhouse is to grow some holiday balls and create your own event!

Why do we always have to wait for somebody else to tell us that we can be a star? Why do we have to wait for somebody else to say we can be a leader, or a speaker? Just go do it. Of course, you have to have skills first, but if you do, then just do it.

You can be the lead designer or the project manager on your own showhouse. You can take on much of the designing yourself, or simply design a small area and share the designing and the recognition with a team of decorating and design professionals that you personally select.

Ideas for Hosting Your Own Showhouse

For your own designer showhouse, you could approach a homeowner (someone you know or a recent or past customer), or inquire through one of the local sorority houses or museums, or even contact the heritage society to ask about a historic home. See if any of the homeowners would like to have their place beautified and cosmetically face-lifted by local design experts.

Then you would put the word out that you are looking for other design-related professionals to join the team for this project. You could even put your own small committee together to help choose who will work on the project. Those who want to be involved would have to approach the committee with their vision and ideas.

This kind of activity takes a bit of effort, but the rewards can be great. The buzz that spreads through the community lasts a very long time, and with your own project that you lead, that buzz will focus on you. Most people don't ever take the time to plan and do these kinds of projects even though they are really not all that hard to do. You just have to break the project down into mini-steps that you plan for and act upon. If you are willing to take on this kind of project, you can quickly become a type of local celebrity. The good news about doing your own

146

showhouse is that you make the rules. The project does not have to be an event where visitors are allowed to view the interior for months. You can actually do something special just over a weekend, similar to a parade of homes, but you focus on just one home and do it well.

Decide on a project and a date. Choose a charity. Select a home. Form a committee. Select a team of design professionals. Assign specific rooms and areas to the design professionals on the team. Let each designer name their area. Create deadlines for the rooms and projects. Sell tickets in advance. Promote the event on your own, through your team members, through local media, through online social media, and through your selected charity. Host the event on the designated day. Donate the proceeds to the charity. Get hailed as the lead designer of your own designer showhouse!

How to Approach the Committee to Be Part of a Designer Showhouse

> ### Out-of-the-Box Thinking:
>
> A home environment should support living your best life. A Certified Interior Environment Coach (CIEC) helps people live more authentically by bringing them through a step-by-step process of seeing what they want and helping them to plan for it. A CIEC helps clients look at the way the home is set up and the way they function within the home and outside of the home. Then a plan that supports personal growth, life enrichment, and personal empowerment is co-created.

You may not be interested in doing your own designer showhouse. Perhaps you want to join the team of an existing one instead. Here are some tips to help you get selected and have a positive experience.

The last thing that you should do if you are pitching yourself for a spot as a showhouse designer is to join the team as another designer's helper. That is not a good career move, as it positions you as subservient to a peer instead of equal to them. In addition, you will end up doing a lot of work and getting little of the recognition.

Every showhouse committee will have a specific process you must follow to become a designer for the team. Do an Internet search in your area for the local showhouses. Many organizations do them every year. Contact that organization or the charity that they help and find out who

147

you should contact for information. Once you contact the right person, you can ask about the selection process.

You will first approach their committee. You will pitch for a specific room or area of the showhouse. If the committee chooses you as one of the showhouse designers, you will be given about four to eight weeks to work on your room or area of the project. You will also be responsible for all of the costs associated with designing that space.

Here is an important tip if you are just starting out doing showhouses. Don't necessarily try to bid for the rooms that everybody else is trying to bid for. I think just doing a really small room or a special area can be even better because you can dress it to the nines and for a relatively low budget.

Have Fun with Small Areas and Rooms That Other Designers Dismiss

> **Out-of-the-Box Thinking:**
>
> Take Action:
> 1. Select an activity or event.
> 2. Take one simple action toward it.
> 3. Create a timeline for the activity.

Play up a tiny little room where a big room would break your pocketbook, if you're just starting out. Don't dismiss the great opportunities waiting for you from designing a foyer, an entryway, a mud room, or a pass-through area, for example.

Let's say you are a designer who does a lot of work with photography and wall art. Pitch for a hall area and really play it up with exceptionally framed art on a rich background wall color. Further showcase the area with a narrow table displaying amazing floral arrangements or topiaries.

In a foyer, express your home fashion design skills by layering a table with floor-length table covers piped at the bottom edges and topped with a beaded runner and an elaborate floral arrangement. Or perhaps display a grand case piece with key tassels, situated on top of an amazing area rug.

Consider pitching for a bathroom that is not necessarily the master bath. Other designers might snub at the idea of requesting to design a small guest bathroom, but not you! Why? Because you are creative, and you can do a head-to-floor gorgeous, thick, lush, fully gathered (on a tension pole) shower curtain in a stunning fabric. Most people never think to order a custom shower curtain that is very full and luscious and that goes all the way to the floor. Trim the bottom of it in a stand-out trim. Or display two such shower curtains pulled back on either side with a huge chenille tassel, with another coordinating floor-length shower curtain draping down in the middle.

You could absolutely play up your window treatment ability in a bathroom. Since the windows are small, selecting a top-of-the-line fabric might not stretch your budget too much. Customize towels with luxurious decorative trimmings such as braid or fringe.

Showhouse Housekeeping

You will most likely be asked to submit a list of resources for your area, so keep a running list as you are working on your project. In addition, you may be allowed to sell off your samples at the close of the showhouse, so price out what you want for your samples. You'll be surprised at the interest you receive for them. Publicize in a subtle manner that your samples are for sale.

Your space is your advertising, it's an opportunity. Make it stunning. You will be picking up the tab for your designed area at a showcase home, but you can likely call on your vendors and your fabric reps for help. That's why I always say not to have too many fabric lines. Have a few good fabric lines because you want loyalty and a good relationship from your sales reps. If you request it, your vendors may send you fabrics and other items to help you with your showhouse (or trunk shows).

How to Leverage the Traffic

When the showhouse is open to the public, you will have to man your own area, and believe me, you will want to have help. There is likely going to be a lot of traffic. You should also put together attractive packages or folders, but don't just do the typical folder. (You may have to do folders because of the cost of other giveaways such as gift bags, but you can still make them stand out from the crowd.)

If you have a lot of leftover fabric in your studio or workroom, and if

149

you have lots of time in the weeks before the event, just sit at the sewing machine – or better yet, hire somebody to help you – and make up some attractive little fabric bags. Put some candy and a business card in each and tie the bags with a variety of leftover trims from your workroom (or use ribbon instead). Do something to be different. If you want to do folders, that's fine, but perhaps you could place a nice sticker on the front of each folder with your business info, and place a special offer inside along with a page about your approach to working with your customers, and of course include a business card.

Whether you use a bag or a folder, make sure you have plenty so that everyone who comes through gets one. Use a closet or cabinet to store them out of the way, and pull them out as you need them.

Promoting Your Showhouse Efforts

The sponsors and promoters of the showhouse are going to be promoting it the whole time that it is in the planning, design, and visiting stages. All along the way, from the very start, you should be engaging your tribe about what is happening with the showhouse. Encourage your tribe to tweet and post about it right along with you. Again, you are building and leading your tribe, keeping them informed of all of the interesting and exciting updates concerning the showhouse and your area. Did one of your fabrics come in? Post it. Did you complete the window treatment? Let the tribe know, and include pictures when you post. Make it fun and exciting so that they start asking you more about it. Lead them, and keep the conversation going – that's what a tribe leader does. Use statements like, "Guess what? I did another window treatment for the show house. Can't wait, only six weeks away!" or, "What do you think about this fabric – is it what you would expect to see in a showhouse?" This way, you are a great facilitator and also a catalyst for conversations. You're getting the tribe to contribute back and forth on Facebook and Twitter, and people start saying "What are they talking about? What show? Why are these people telling the decorator what they think looks good? Why is she even asking them? Decorators don't ask us!"

And there you go. Get the social buzz going. Get your tribe moving, talking about you, cheering you on. It's kind of like a marathon – they want to see you win. They love you; they're your tribe members! Just stay connected to people through your social media sites, and send out a weekly or monthly email update, and even send a mailing to your mailing list. Why not create a document to give away? Call it *10 Great Tips for Visiting a Designer Showhouse*. Allow people who sign up for your newsletter to get that for free. Put it on your Facebook page – lead them from Facebook to your website to sign up for your mailing list and get the free document.

During the showhouse event, there will be a brochure that's handed out by the sponsors and event planners. It will have the names of all of the designers and professionals who contributed to the project. It will have your name in it, too, with due recognition. I recommend even buying an ad in the brochure if your budget can handle it, because some people hang onto that brochure for a long time.

If the showhouse sponsors allow it, I would put out an attractive bowl in my area, and ask for names and email addresses to give away a beautiful prize by email. This helps you build your list. Let people know that they will be getting your free monthly newsletter and a chance to win the item you are giving away. I would also do this for your trunk shows and home shows. We have not talked much about home shows, so let me very quickly touch on them with a tip or two.

A Bit about Home Shows

Each year, most cities and towns put on a home show for homeowners. This helps give them ideas for designing their interiors and yards. Sometimes they are called *The Home and Garden Show.*

You can rent booth space at these shows, and you can decorate your booth or area in any way you like. Be creative with your display. The goal is to get attention. Instead of bringing in all of the typical home accessories, fabrics, trims, and window treatments, drive your business car (if it has a wrap on it) right into your booth. Let your car be your display, and have a table with some cool stuff and yummy candies to give away, and don't forget to collect names and email addresses and give away prizes by email. I like to give away a sofa throw because it's about a $300 value and it doesn't cost much to make if you use fabric left over from another job. You could also give away a couple of nice coffee table books, or 3 yards of beautiful fabric. I always give away lots of prizes, and I let people know we will contact the winners by email. This way I am sure to get plenty of people to register for the drawing and at the same time sign up for my newsletter.

A Domain Name for Any Event

When you do any event to market your business and engage the tribe, you should give the event a name so that promotion is easier. As I mentioned earlier, if you're going to do a showhouse, you are likely going to be required to name your room or area.

For each of your events that you name, why not get the corresponding domain name? This allows you to set up a website specifically for that event. Use a blogging format so that you can keep everyone in your tribe up-to-date on the latest event happenings, with the most recent posts at the top of the page.

All in all, keep your tribe posted and involved in all that you are doing. This gives them plenty of reason to stay connected to you and plenty of opportunity to share great decorating tips with others, leading more people back to you.

Coaching Programs

Coaching is another way to build your tribe. Some decorators don't want to sell window treatments because they don't understand them. Some designers are uninspired by flooring or furniture, and for others, a product-based business is losing its appeal. These are the decorators and designers I would point toward coaching.

There are two types of coaching that homeowners are very interested in, and for which there is an increasing demand. One is color coaching or color consulting, and the other is interior environment coaching.

There is a strong market for both of these services, and they go right along with the way more and more homeowners are thinking today and where people are going – to a more esoteric place – a place of connection to family and to their own sense of personal and professional development and empowerment.

Color Consulting

If you are interested in providing color consulting, I highly recommend becoming a Certified Dewey Color Consultant. Dewey is a brilliant man who is world-renowned, and he has put together a fabulous program that is popular in the U.S. and in many other countries.

I happen to be a certified instructor of that program through our decorating school (www.DecoratingSchool.com), and we offer the Dewey Color Consultant Certification both online and on site. We can even do one-on-one sessions by web conference. There's no reason not to be trained as a color consultant, which is also an opportunity for coaching. Coaching is a way to build your tribe, and it also opens the door for you to speak to business groups. Because coaches (even color coaches) are always coaching and mentoring, they tend to have great content to share with business groups. They also seem to "get" where people are coming from emotionally. Many coaches are able to get up in front of business groups and talk to them about topics like color and mood, or how our interior environments affect our productivity. Incidentally, these business audiences are filled with homeowners who are too busy working to do their own decorating, so color coaching or interior environment coaching acts also as a lead source for other decorating and design services.

Certified Interior Environment Coaching

Many homeowners who dabble in design are really not looking for decorating and design services as much as they are looking for life direction, assistance in getting "unstuck," or help in finding a way to live creatively, effectively, productively, and empowered.

A fairly new and groundbreaking coaching program that is incredibly exciting and powerful, and that is meeting an increasing need and demand, is Certified Interior Environment Coaching (www.CertifiedInteriorEnvironmentCoach.com).

This is a phenomenal and inspiring service that decorators, designers, and also life coaches can offer to individuals and homeowners to help them create lives of peak productivity through the way their homes are designed, set up, and used to support them.

A Certified Interior Environment Coach brings individuals through a process of assessing what they want and how the setup of the home can help to support and actualize those wants and goals. This coaching service can be facilitated by decorators who are trained in the program or by life coaches who are also trained in the program. The actual decorating or designing of the home is a separate process, so the coach does not have to be a design professional. Those who are can offer the client additional services (design services) once the coaching process is complete.

153

A Certified Interior Environment Coach helps people to live more authentically and in a more fulfilling way. The premise behind the coaching is that people want more than decorated houses. They want to be able to jump off from their home and jump into their world in a productive and inspired way.

Many of us have let our lives and our homes get away from us, yet our home is the starting place for living lives of peak productivity and happiness. People have forgotten their dreams. They've forgotten that they love art and they love music and fragrance, and they have forgotten how to be creative in the home and in life.

The fragrances and colors we surround ourselves with, the music we allow in, the way we organize our spaces, the opportunity we have for fostering our personal creativity – these all affect our level of personal satisfaction and our sense of life fulfillment and enrichment. In addition, the types of products we use, the way certain materials affect how we feel (such as with allergies), how furnishings are placed, the way we feel in a space, whether or not we are using our creative talents, whether or not we are in tune with and reaching our goals, and even the energy that a home emits are all things that a Certified Interior Environment Coach helps individuals to look at, through a simple step-by-step coaching process. Then they co-create an action plan for life enrichment.

If you are interested in the program, contact me directly (margo@ DeGangiGroup.com) or check out the website (www.CertifiedInteriorEnvironmentCoach.com). This program is simply amazing. It has struck a chord with so many people and I just know in my heart that this is going to be huge, because people are stuck in their lives, they're stopped up, and they're living in stagnant homes. It's not just about the way a home looks. It's about the way the home supports their dreams and aspirations. Certified Interior Environment Coaching helps free people up to a better and more empowered way of living every day.

Summary: Putting It into Action with 3 Action Steps

First and foremost, in your design career, you must stop decorating as if it were a hobby and start decorating for profits. The way you begin to do this is to take action.

154

1. Start by selecting one thing you want to do in your career that really resonates with you, and focus your attention on that one thing for three months.

Whatever it is, it keeps coming back to you. There might be three or four things that you are interested in doing, but there will be that one thing that keeps coming back. THAT'S IT! (There shouldn't be any confusion, but if there is and you have too many ideas on your mind at once, just pick one thing to focus on. Just pick! You can't wear eight dresses to the prom, and you can't work on five activities at once, either. You must choose one and go with it, and don't second-guess yourself at that point).

2. Take one action right away on whatever that one thing is. The action can be very small, but the point is to get the momentum going and build motivation. Let's just pretend that your one thing is to do a trunk show. Then this week, go and talk to one person who can help you with that goal. Whatever that thing is, go talk to one person about it. Start with someone you know if possible. You may even want to go talk to the owner of a local kitchen design center. It does not matter whether they want to work together or not. The point is to just get a dialog going.

3. Create a timeline for yourself related to that one thing that you want to do. Whether you decide to partner with someone on the project, or do it all yourself, set up a timeline that includes a start date and a completion date to bring that event into existence. Then come up with about six or eight mini-activities you can do to bring you to your goal, and put them on the timeline with a specific due date for that mini-activity.

Here is an oversimplified example: Get out a piece of paper and write My Trunk Show at the top. Make a numbered list from 1 to 6. Now list 6 activities you are going to do to bring that trunk show into existence in real life. Finally, put a date on each of the 6 steps. You have now created a timeline for your activity or event.

My Trunk Show

1. Choose someone to co-host the trunk show – by April 10
2. Choose venue for trunk show – by April 12

3. Set the date, time, and theme for the trunk show – by April 14
4. Prepare samples and props for the trunk show – by April 24
5. Start the promotions for the trunk show – by April 26
6. Send out invitations to the trunk show – by May 1

ABOUT THE AUTHOR

 Business Empowerment Coach **Margo De-Gange**, M.Ed., has helped thousands of entrepreneurs worldwide startup and super-charge their businesses. With 20+ years teaching design, 30 years probing business and marketing, and 15 years online, Margo will empower YOU to easily succeed beyond your WILDEST expectations.

Increase profits FAST with Margo's help. She's authored groundbreaking marketing tools for decorators and designers, like trunk show systems, fun tribe-building plans, ready-made seminar kits, pre-made and auto-sent newsletters, pre-written decorating and color articles, websites, and blogs systems. Her training programs include online certification courses in Interior Environment Coaching, Color, Interior Decorating, and business. Visit www.MargoDeGange.com

Credentials: Certified Human Behavior Coach, university-degreed Communication and Adult Motivation Expert, master's degree Instructional Designer, Dewey Color Instructor, Certified Window Treatment Consultant, WF Certified Professional, Certified Professional Decorator, WCAA National Vice-President, WCU National Training Director, Exciting Windows! Network Business Coach, WCAA Education Chair, industry panelist, and marketing strategist. Margo is Executive Director of the *Decorators' Alliance of North America* (DANA – www.DecoratorsAlliance.com) and Director of the *DeGangi School of Interior Decoration* (www.DecoratingSchool.com).

7
CREATING YOUR DESIGN CELEBRITY:
A Designer's Guide to Being Published through Articles and Awards

by Terri Taylor
www.designbizblueprint.com

In this chapter you'll learn:

* How to get great photography that you can repurpose over and over
* How to create winning relationships with magazine and newspaper writers so that you become a resource
* 5 simple steps you need to know to have the "edge" for winning design award competitions
* How our family histories can keep us from creating our own celebrity and becoming a design star

Creating Celebrity around Your Work Is Incredibly Valuable

When photographs of our beautiful rooms are published in local magazines, newsletters, and newspapers, we become "design celebrities" in our communities. The public sees those photographs with the designer's name associated; they assume that this designer must be the very best. This kind of publishing "celebrity" creates enormous credibility for the designer.

> ### 🐟 Important!
>
> Getting published creates your celebrity, which adds to credibility, which solidifies your expert status, which leads to more work.

When a designer gains credibility, she has been elevated to expert status. When she speaks, her clients listen. A designer or decorator who has created celebrity around her work is well known in her community and is considered to be the person to call when design work is needed.

Interior design is a highly visual art and business. interior designers and decorators have the unique opportunity to show the public what they do, by publishing photography of their work. It's true that "a picture is worth a thousand words," and we can utilize that fact to let the public and our potential clients know who we are and what we do.

What Design Celebrity Can Do for You

When your work has been published, people recognize your name. Vendors and suppliers pay more attention to you and your needs. Samples and price quotes arrive a little faster.

The receptionist at the doctor's office recognizes your name and is excited to have met you. She may never be a client, but she is going to tell all her friends that she met you. This creates the "buzz" around your name, so that when someone recommends you, the potential client says,

158

"I've heard of her – isn't she in the magazines all the time?"

Can Design Celebrities Charge Higher Fees?

Interior designers and decorators who are considered to be the experts can and do charge more for their services. The public expects to pay more for the "best" designer.

When you have achieved this expert status, it is up to you to raise the bar. You must provide the client with outstanding service and excellent design advice, and then you charge what you are worth and get it.

Design Celebrities Have Good Self-Esteem

Imagine yourself standing in line at the grocery store checkout, next to the row of magazines. You reach over and pick up the local home and garden magazine and flip it open. There it is, your beautiful room, a full page in color, right there. Wow! How cool is that?

This kind of public recognition of your talent and style changes the way that you think about yourself. Doubts and worries about not being good enough begin to disappear. You have been shown to be the best.

As for designers who are published often, are they interior design geniuses? No – they are not better designers than we are. What they are much better at is marketing and publicity.

There are designers who are true experts at creating celebrity. Barbara Barry is an example of the absolute best. She has created a brand and an empire through good public relations. Her work has been widely published, she has captured every prestigious design award available and she has moved on to designing and endorsing products for national brands like Kravet Fabrics and Baker Furniture.

> **Did You Know?**
>
> Public recognition of your work changes the way you think about yourself: doubts and worries tend to disappear.

Another great example of design celebrity at the top of her game is Candice Olson. Candice is the brave woman who created and stars in the only HGTV show that actually shows what an interior designer

159

does. She has turned her expert status and credibility gained from the HGTV show into her own brand. When I was at Winter Market in Las Vegas this year, I saw her endorsement poster in at least six or seven different showrooms. Way to go, Candice!

I find these women truly inspiring. While all designers don't aspire to climb to the very top like these women, we can use their stellar example to begin to create our own version of celebrity in our communities.

Getting Your Work Published Is More Valuable than Advertising

The public is aware that anyone with enough money can buy a full-page ad. While that expensive advertising does bring recognition, being featured in an editorial piece is far more powerful. Editorial coverage brings enormous credibility to the designer who is being published. The public believes that if the magazine has chosen this designer's work, then that designer must, therefore, be the best.

Important!

Editorial coverage, unlike advertising, brings an enormous amount of recognition and credibitlity.

One of the great benefits of being published in magazines and newspapers in an editorial article is that it's *free*. The designer is not paying an advertising bill, and often the coverage can be multiple pages in the magazine.

Why Don't More Designers Create Their Own Celebrity?

Many designers and decorators don't understand that celebrity is something that they personally have to desire and decide to create. Designers are not "discovered" by magazine editors and then they end up on the cover of *House and Garden*. There is no "celebrity fairy" who taps a designer on the shoulder and says, "You are the next design star!"

Many women (I know that there are a few guys out there, too; please hang in there; there is something for you in this as well) often have beliefs and behaviors in their family histories that have taught them as children, that proper behavior requires them to be quiet, helpful, and modest, and not draw attention to themselves. This may have been a useful behavior as a child, but as a businessperson, it is a disaster.

160

In order to have a successful business, designers and decorators must adapt a new belief and step up to make themselves known as the best designer in their communities. They must stand out from the crowd of other designers and decorators and be noticed by potential clients for their credibility and expertise. This is how a designer develops a following of loyal clients and juicy, interesting, profitable jobs.

When a designer has decided to step up and *create celebrity* around her career, she has made the personal decision to stop playing small, and has stepped into becoming who she can truly be.

Benefits to a Designer of Obtaining Celebrity Status

Creating your own design celebrity is all about standing out in the crowd and getting yourself noticed so that the clients you want to work with consider you to be the expert that they want to work with. Sometimes when designers have unresolved issues about their relationship with money, they are held back and have difficulties stepping out and creating that celebrity for themselves.

You must actually decide to make yourself into a celebrity and methodically, through a step-by-step process, create what you desire. You need to plan how you're going to get your name known, how you're going to let people know that you are very special and really good at interior design.

> **Action Item!**
>
> The first step of creating your own design celebrity is to DECIDE that you want to be a design celebrity.

Who Can Be an Interior Design Celebrity?

I started my career as an interior designer in the design studio of a high-end furniture store. I gave away my time and ideas for free in exchange for commissions on furniture sales. This is where I discovered that there was no one to tell me how to have a successful interior design career. Everyone I asked acted like it was a big secret, as if sharing anything with me they would make them lose business.

You might have guessed by now that I don't agree with this philosophy. I believe that we must share information and best practices in order to have a strong and respected industry.

161

> ### Did You Know?
> When you become "a star," prospects ask for you by name!

I began the slow process of reading every design business book I could find, going to CEUs and conferences, and making many mistakes but always learning from them.

It took me many years of trial and error to reach my goal: my own design studio doing $1,000,000 a year. The turning point in that process was discovering what happened when my design work was published. Suddenly I became a "star." People, potential clients, started asking for me by name. I felt competent and secure in my knowledge and level of expertise. Many good things came out of "accidentally" winning a design award and being published.

It doesn't need to take years and years to get your interior design career started and successful. Anyone can follow these easy steps for creating celebrity in your interior design career.

Don't Allow Beliefs about Money to Stand in the Way of Your Success

Money is simply a form of energy that acts as a measure for how many people we are touching with our gift of beauty and comfort. The big jobs that can "change the world, " the ones that affect a lot of people and the way they live and experience the world, have a lot of money attached to them. The people (clients) who hold the keys to these jobs expect to pay handsomely for great design work. The designers who do these jobs know their worth and are well paid for their exceptional work.

Designers who want to step up into the jobs that influence people and create change must learn to value their work and create a good relationship with money in their lives.

Money thrives on attention. The more attention you pay to money, the more it shows up in your life. When we ignore money, it has a ways of getting our attention, in ways that are not nice. Just leave those bills on the floor under the desk and don't pay them, don't balance the checkbook, and see what happens. Money will get your attention, and it's in a fairly negative way.

162

Money loves to be welcomed and accounted for. I keep a running list on my desk, and I write down the amount of money that comes in every day. Sometimes it's a big chunk from a large job. Sometimes it's just a few hundred dollars. I celebrate every one of them equally because money likes to be paid attention to, and I want to keep that flow going. I want my relationship with money to be good and I want it to be my friend. I want it to be supportive and to be there when I need it.

Don't Allow Family History to Get in Your Way

When I was a child, I asked my Dad how much money he made. He said, "Oh, we don't talk about money. That's not polite." I took this to heart and I didn't talk about money for 35 years!

Sometimes the things that were right when you were 12 years old aren't right as a businessperson in 2010. As a designer and as a business owner, not talking about money is a really bad move: You don't have any idea where you are with your clients if you are feeling fearful or uncomfortable about talking about money.

Great Tip!

Money loves to be welcomed and accounted for, no matter how big or small.

If this is true for you, go back take a look at the belief and replace it with one that makes more sense for where you are in your life today.

Feeling Worthy of Success and Celebrity

A designer I was coaching was struggling with feeling uncomfortable about creating celebrity in her career. This person had all the "right stuff" to be a great designer but just could never get her business going.

She shared this story with me. When she was 16, she began her first job and was so excited about earning her own money. When she received her first paycheck, she couldn't wait to go home and show her dad. She raced into the house and proudly said, "Dad, look, look, here's my paycheck! Isn't it cool?" He examined her check and said, "They paid you THAT MUCH?"

Now this is a good man who loved his daughter. He wasn't intention-

163

ally trying to set her back, but when your dad says you're not worth it, you believe him. This has had a huge effect on the way she approaches everything. No wonder she was uncomfortable creating celebrity – she felt that she wasn't worthy.

Action Item!

Create a new story and belief that supports who you really are!

Now her Dad was an old-world guy, who didn't realize that women can have good jobs outside the home, and be well paid. This is not about fault-finding, and it doesn't mean that you should get rid of your father.

If you relate to this story, you need to go back and find out what story you are telling yourself that isn't true. Creating a new story and belief that supports who you really are and where you want to be will allow you to step into the prosperity and good design jobs that you really want.

Why Don't More Designers and Decorators Photograph Their Work?

The most prevalent belief that I come up against, the one that I hear all the time when I'm out speaking live to designers and decorators, is: "I'm not good enough." "My next design job will turn out better – I will photograph that one." This dance goes on and on, and the photos never get taken.

You need to know that if you wait until you are good enough, you're going to be in the ground! It will never happen.

We as artists are always striving to be better than we are now. That is a good thing. However, being too self-critical can stop you from growing. Designers must realize that the work that you are doing now is a good solid job and it needs to be shared with your community. Just because you will do it a bit differently next time doesn't mean that this current project is bad.

You get better by doing more jobs, and you get to do more jobs if people know what you do. Holding onto this "not good enough" belief keeps you separated from the opportunities that you would have if you stepped out.

164

You get better at your craft by taking on jobs that are a little bit broader or a little bit bigger than what you're used to. You stretch, you research, you learn, and you do a beautiful job.

You know more than you did six months ago. You know more than you did a year ago. You know more than your client. You know what you are doing.

This "not good enough" belief is a big, common problem. I see it over and over again – designers who are very good at their craft, holding themselves back from the success and attention that they deserve.

Don't beat yourself up if you're doing this, but do try to recognize when it is happening. Realize that you personally have to make a decision to step out of this diminishing belief to make your career and business grow.

> **Action Item!**
> If you're doing the same thing, you will get the same results. In order to change your results, you have to be willing to be uncomfortable.

If you keep doing the same thing you're doing, you will keep getting the same thing that you are getting now. Nothing in your business and life is going to change. You have to choose to get out of the comfortable zone and into something that has a little bit of edge to it in order for you to grow and change.

Working with Editors and Writers to Get Work Published

A designer only needs two or three good publishing contacts to be very successful with editorial opportunities. Begin "creating your celebrity" with publishing locally, because you want to build your business and this is where your clients are located.

It is important to learn how to speak to magazine editors and newspaper writers, and understand what the challenges of their jobs are. When you understand what they need and are actively looking for, you can package your work to fit their criteria. Take the time to research the publications that you want to be seen in. Discover what kind of articles they publish, and what they like to show. Are they "homeowner do-it-yourself" articles? Are they small inner-city homes, or big high-end showplaces? Choose the publication that showcases the kind of work

165

that you do. Then submit a well thought-out package to the editor/ writer that is a fit for their publication.

The strategy here is to be remembered by the writer as a resource for good photography and design stories. Of course, you have to photograph your work in order to have something to submit for publishing.

Wouldn't it be great if that writer called and said, "Jane, do you have any colorful bathroom photos? I have a bathroom article coming up." This can happen if you take the time to establish a personal relationship your writer.

> ### 📖 Great Tip!
>
> The strategy with any publisher is to be remembered as a resource for good photography and design stories.

Once you have some good relationships and successes with writer/editors, you can look to some national publications as well. Again, for quick success, look for publications that match up with the sort of design work that you are doing.

Sunset magazine published my National ASID Award Winner in 2000. I entered the national awards with this project because (a) it won nothing in my local awards competition and (b) it just looked like something that would be in a Sunset magazine. The room I had photographed was a bit contemporary, with sleek cherry cabinets and some bold color.

I took the exact package that I had submitted in the local awards and put it in the National binder, completed my entry form, and sent it off. It seems that I was right: I received a call six weeks later saying that I had won.

This was the beginning of a terrific relationship where the editor would call me and say, "Do you have any great patios we can shoot?" Or "We are doing an article on shutters. Do you have anything?" When they got to know me and the quality of my work, I could just send a snapshot for reference. If they were going to use it, they would hire their own professional photographer to shoot it properly for the magazine.

As you can see, publishing success is all about the relationship that you develop with the people who produce the publications.

I have also received invitations to be published from someone researching and finding my website. I keep a large portfolio on the site, and it attracts writers and editors looking for material to cover. My work was featured in the Wall Street Journal in an article about home libraries. The writer found me through the website and interviewed me, and I was in!

This story illustrates how important it is to photograph a lot of your work and show it off on your website. You never know who will find it.

All of your publishing credits belong on the website as well; this is part of establishing your increased credibility and celebrity status. When potential clients go to your website and they see that you have been published in *Sunset* magazine, *Interior Design* magazine, *ASID Icon*, and *Wall Street Journal*, they naturally make the assumption that you must be very good at what you do.

Getting Good Photography without Spending a Fortune

If you can afford the best photographer in town to shoot your spaces, do it! These people are marvelous – what they do is magic, and they are true artists. If you can't afford a "celebrity" photographer, though, that doesn't mean that you can't get great photography.

Do NOT try to do the photography yourself – you will not get noticed, you will not get published, you will not win any awards. Don't do it. Today it takes an enormous amount of expensive equipment and software to create photography good enough to end up in a magazine.

Beware!

Great photography, much like great design, is best left to the professional. Do not attempt to photograph the work yourself.

There is, however, a part that you do need to learn and do yourself that is huge part of getting great photography. It is all about research. Go back to those magazines that you want to be in and start studying those photographs. Spread them all out in front of you and start looking for what they have in common.

Now what you'll find is that they very rarely shoot full-room shots. When we finish a space, we want to take a picture that shows everything we did. We want to see the fabulous drapes, we want to see the chaise over there because it's got this really great pillow we did, and we want to see that little detail on the lamp, and on and on and on. That is NOT a recipe for good photography. The shoot would be so busy that a reader couldn't see what was going on.

Look at an *Architectural Digest* feature; you will rarely see big, wide shots. You will notice that the shots are fairly small and narrow, and they're composed like a piece of art. I am sure that you have an understanding of composition from your art classes. A photograph is composed the same way, looking for movement, rhythm, and balance. This is the same way you compose a furniture plan on paper or a painting on canvas. Your job is to find the really nice compositions in your room so that you can capture them.

Start looking at magazines, and you're going to see these smaller shots. An example would be a French Bombay chest with a lamp on it, a mirror behind, and some flowers. There is a cat on the floor in the corner, and that is the whole shot. That is all you're seeing of the room, but it's very evocative of what the room is about. It is not telling all, but it is giving the idea and the flavor of the room.

Action Item!

Look at design magazines to understand the type of shots you want to take.

You will also notice they use little detail shots, little close-up shots of textures or patterns. Sometimes it's just a shape of a lamp as it relates to the furniture piece behind it. You will see a few wider shots of a room, sometimes with a little more depth, but note that you will not see the whole space.

Research is hugely important to understanding what the shot is that you want in your space. It doesn't matter whether you're using the best photographer in town or somebody you found who's just graduating from the local university and needs to build their portfolio: You are going to have to communicate to them what you want.

You can choose a professional who's been in business for 20 years, or you can choose a recent graduate wanting the experience and credit. Make sure that they are good artists, have good equipment and software, communicate well with you, and understand what it is that you're after.

I would recommend viewing some work that the photographer has done, preferably architectural work. Somebody who has never done architectural photography, and specializes in portraiture, might not be the best choice.

How to Get the Best Photo Possible

I recommend that after you have done your research, you walk around with your own digital camera and start looking through the lens of the camera at what you want. You will find that your space looks far different through the lens of the camera than it does to the naked eye. Far different! So walk around the room looking through the camera for interesting compositions, find one, take a picture. And when you find another composition, take a record shot. Now when you come home you can put those up on your computer screen so you can really see what's going on.

You can choose out that group of record shots what your best shots are going to be. These are the shots that you're going to ask the photographer to create. When you are very specific about what you want, then the photographer can tell you what it will cost and how long it's going to take. This of course is good for the budget.

The other part that you have a lot of control over is the styling of the shot. Imagine that you are on a fashion shoot. There would be a stylist to do hair and makeup, and put clips in the back of your jacket so you look narrower, and all that stuff that they do to make you look exceptionally good.

> **Action Item!**
>
> Start looking at the room through the lens of a camera to identify the best shot.

You, the designer, are in charge of doing the exact same thing in a room shot. You have permission to rearrange furniture, to make the shot composition better. Go back to Architectural Digest and notice the same chair in the foreground in four different pictures. Now, we know that same chair does not live in four different rooms. They have moved it into their shots so that they have an interesting object in the foreground to balance what the rest of the room is in the back.

You can do this furniture moving, but you need to plan it out ahead. Use your record shots to see whether you need more accessories, and

169

then go shopping for what you need. Usually the homeowner ends up buying them from you. If not, return them to where you bought them.

> **Beware!**
> Be very mindful of getting all the details right!

Your goal is to make this shot 10% better than it would've been without your input.

Talk to the photographer ahead of time about lighting, what is available in the room, which way the windows face, what time of day does he or she thinks it would be at its best. For instance, if you were shooting a room that has big east-facing windows, you wouldn't want to shoot it in the morning, since the sun would blow out your windows (unless that is what you want).

When you do all the research, figure out what you want, have all your accessories ready to style your shot, and be very mindful of getting all the details right (pillow stripes all going the same way, no wrinkles in the rug, sofa cushions all lined up, etc.), then you can have beautiful, polished, and professional photography.

Getting a WOW Photo

The WOW photo is the one image that you find in your space that is absolutely fabulous. It is important to take enough photos to illustrate your work, but once in awhile you end up with one photo that is absolutely stunning. This is the one that could be a magazine cover (always a vertical), or the one that will win a design award.

Always be on the lookout for the WOW photo: Its market value is huge.

How to Get Magazine Editors to Look at Your Work

There is very common perception out there that it is difficult to approach the magazine editors and writers. That perception is simply not true; editors and writers welcome quality information. It can make their job easier.

Here is an interesting story. While I was in the process of writing "Creating Your Celebrity: The Designer's Guide to Getting Published," I ran

170

into the local editor of one of our home and garden magazines at the mall. I asked her whether she gets many submissions from designers wanting to be published.

She said, "No, we never do, and I don't know why. I go to designer meetings and tell them to send me everything that they are doing, but nobody sends me anything. I am constantly searching for the next project for the magazine. I said I was out on a shoot today doing a garden. I went inside and to look at the kitchen because I've got a kitchen article coming up in a couple of months. I think I will use it because it is new construction."

Here is this magazine editor peeking in back doors and scrounging in corners trying to find photographs to put in magazines because the designers don't show her what they are doing.

Predicting What the Magazine Will Be Covering in the Future

Yes, it is called an editorial calendar. They create one at the beginning of each year and map out what that edition will be about. Just call the magazine and request a copy of their editorial calendar, and they will give to you.

It will tell you, for instance, that in four months they're going to do an issue on bathrooms. Call the editor now and tell her that you've got a couple of bathrooms that they might be interested in.

> ## 🔘 Action Item!
> Request the editorial calendar from every magazine you're interested in – today!

You simply call a magazine editor and ask whether they have a minute to talk to you, tell them about your project, and ask whether you can send it to them for consideration.

It is important that you have your package put together before you make this call. You must send your package out immediately so that she remembers who you are. Running around trying to put your photographs together and write something three days later simply will not work.

If you don't hear from her tomorrow, call her back. Just tell her that you want to know what she thought of it and whether she could ever use something like this. Don't be disappointed if you don't get an immediate "yes." Your timing may not be right; you don't know what they are working on right now, and it can take awhile.

> **⊚ Important!**
>
> Remember, the idea is to establish a relationship, and the opportunities come as a result.

Often they will call back in a few weeks and ask whether you have any photos of kids' rooms or whatever they are working on. Remember, the idea is to establish a relationship, and the opportunities come as a result.

Magazines are running on tight budgets these days, so they don't have as much money to spend for photography. They are always looking for good material that has been professionally shot. If you have it, you have just become a resource.

It's our job, when we approach these publishers with our photographs of our work, to give them an idea for the story that has a human-interest element in it. When we present our work to these publishers in this fashion, we're helping them do their job more easily.

You don't have to write the story, but you need to outline it a bit. Most of us are not writers, so we don't need to write four pages. You do need to outline the story; otherwise they've got to guess what are they going to do with these pictures.

Other Thoughts about Submitting Articles to Publications

First of all, you need to know that it is not about you.

Suppose I submit this great photo of a family room that I finished last week to a magazine and I say, "Look at this family room; I did a great job on it. I got this rug from Tibet, and I found these cool fabrics that support it and it connects it all together." Are they interested in printing this story? No!

Had I researched a bit, I would have found that they don't write stories about what the designer did. That's not at all what they write about.

When I go to that magazine ahead of time and I take a close look at

172

what they cover, I discover that they write something about the people who live in the space, and how the design supports the way that they live. And it's not about the tile on the floor or the color on the wall. It's about these people that came from Minnesota to Arizona and they wanted this wonderful sunny space and they have grown children who are going to stay in all these guest rooms and the designer did all the things that they wanted. In other words, there is a story that has human interest, and the pictures support it.

So your name is in there a lot, and you get plenty of credit, but the story is not about you.

The Importance of Participating in Design Awards Competitions

The reason I feel it's so important to participate in design awards competition is because it has enormous social proof attached to it. Remember, social proof is when the public believes that if others have chosen you as the best, then you must be the best.

Awards are almost always published somewhere. So winning an award is guaranteed publishing. You don't have to do anything; it is all pre-arranged, and your work ends up in a magazine. When people see that you have won something (and it doesn't really matter whether it's a first place or a merit award), your credibility has increased measurably. This gives an enormous boost to your career, and amazing things happen.

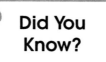

Did You Know?

Social proof is when the public believes that if others have chosen you as the best, then you must be the best.

Is It Hard to Win a Design Award?

It is not nearly as hard as you might think. The biggest problem that I encounter is designers telling me that they enter a competition once, don't win anything the first time, and get discouraged and never try again. They say, "The same designers always win every time. I'm not going to do it anymore!" It is important to understand that the same designers always win because they always enter. You have to play if you want to win.

173

I started entering ASID Chapter Design Awards in 1989. My studio has won a chapter design award every year since 1989. That is a lot of good free publicity.

> ## 🔘 Great Tip!
>
> Winning an award is not as hard as one may think. The key is to submit consistently.

Now the reason that my studio can do that isn't because I am the most amazing designer in the world. I'm pretty good, but the reason that I win consistently is because I have figured out a method that works.

That is why I wrote *Creating Your Celebrity: The Designer's Guide to Publishing, Awards, Show Houses, and Home Tours*. It explains in detail my repeatable system for celebrity publicity around your work, using these opportunities. You can find this book and CD package at www.DesignBizBlueprint.com under "tools." It is not hard to be successful at awards; you just need to know some of the "inside secrets" to make it work for you.

Every year we enter four or five projects. Sometimes we win only one, and that's okay – we get published. Some years we win three or four awards; a couple times we have won five out of five. But you never know how it will come out because the judges are from somewhere else in the country, and you have no way of knowing what they are looking for.

So remember, when you see the same people winning those awards year after year, it's not because they're really better designers than you are. They win because they are participating consistently.
Here is one of those places that the "not good enough" gremlin comes up again. It is so important to your success to get rid of that belief and just leap in there and do it!

How to Be Successful at Awards Competitions and Get Published

One of the first things that you would be paying attention to is choosing the right competition to put your project into. For instance, if you are going to enter the Sub-Zero kitchen competition – which is a fabulous one because it has prize money and it is published in a great hardcover book – don't send them a project with Kitchen Aid appliances in it!

You're not going to win, and it would be a waste of time. If you are entering a local chapter competition, choose the right category. If you have three great pictures of a large house, you probably should not to enter in the big house category. The reason is that others will have seven or eight photos to tell their large-project story. The key here is to be able to communicate to the judging people how terrific this project is and that you met and exceeded all the criteria in the judging form. It is very hard to do that with three photographs, and a lot easier to illustrate with eight photos.

Remember that the goal is to be published as a winner. It doesn't really matter what you win – the public doesn't remember, generally.

You would be better off to take those three photos and put one in the kitchens category, one in bathrooms, and one in product design, for instance. You might win two out of three! It doesn't matter which category: Win for the publishing, and get seen in the magazine.

The next most important thing to remember is to follow directions precisely.

I hate to say that some judging person would be so petty as to disqualify your entry because it was missing a piece, but it is true – they will. Because there are a lot of entries to look at, anyone not following directions will be immediately eliminated.

> **⦿ Important!**
>
> The key is to be able to communicate to the judges how great your project is and that you met and exceeded all the criteria in the judging form.

So follow the directions carefully. Pay attention and read all the "mice type." Make a checklist of all the things you have to do, and put the completion dates on them so that you can get it all done on time.

The third thing is to include one WOW photograph. The more photos you have, the better, and "before" photos are great, too. The reason that the WOW photo is so important is that the first judging cut is based on that photo. The judges are going to flip open that book and say "Yes, that's pretty good," and it goes on the *good* pile. Or, "Ahh, that's bad," and goes on the reject pile, and nobody is ever going to look at it again. So opening your presentation with the WOW photograph is absolutely critical.

175

Judging Criteria at Design Competitions

In most cases the judging criteria will be on the entry form. It will often state how many points will be awarded in what areas. For instance, 10 points for space plan, 10 points for lighting, 5 points for presentation; pretty simple. The harder things to make sure that you address and show the judges are *rhythm* and *balance*. You must address all these things with your photography and 600 words in a design statement. If there are 10 things that the judges need to see and grade on, you must make sure you clearly address each of those 10 things. It's either in the photograph, in the drawings, or in the design statement. Your job is to make sure that all those pieces are clearly and obviously defined.

> ### 🐭 Action Item!
> Be sure to read and follow all the criteria precisely.

In most cases, you will be assigned a notebook to put your project in. Do not decorate it! This will detract from your project and could disqualify you.

The packaging and matting of your project is very important. Everything must be very, very crisp. The last bit of preparation that we do is take brand-new plastic sleeves that are really clear and crisp, and slide everything in. When a judge opens a book that it is so different than the other ones, they can feel the care that went into it. This feeling translates into the quality of the project that they are looking at.

When a judge looks at a package that is sloppily put together, the edges of the mats are a little bent or something is not mounted quite straight, or the plastic sleeves are a bit scuffed, the feeling of quality is diminished. It says that this designer doesn't care much, and that's probably reflected in the project as well.

Giving Your Project a Little Something Extra

Think of this as just going for 10% better. If you can squeeze just 10% more out of your photography, 10% cleaner, crisper drawings, 10% better packaging, you will be a winner.

This tactic of a presentation that is beautifully put together is very important. The back of pages are as important as front of pages, and the captions must all be written nicely. You will have someone proof your design statement so that it's grammatically correct, with no misspellings. All those pieces add up to really put your project presentation over the top!

176

Finding Design Award Competitions

Unfortunately there is no central listing spot for design competitions; however, they are not hard to find.

First, most design organizations organize them locally and on a national basis. These are well organized, are published, and are one of the benefits of being a member of a design organization.

Many magazines sponsor competitions; they're usually found online. Recently a designer who I mentor with entered an online *Architectural Digest* contest and made it all the way to the finals.

> ## ◉ Great Tip!
>
> Look for these places that sponsor design competitions: magazines, industry organizations, and product vendors. While you have to do your own research, they are not hard to find.

Another spot to look are the trades that we utilize. For instance, the glass and mirror organization has one; also check out the woodworkers'/cabinetmakers' groups. Each kind of specialty trade each has its own contest. I recently discovered one from the National Association of Home Builders' own marketing group. This would be a good place to be if you want to be noticed by homebuilders.

Then there are the large product manufacturers. They almost all have competitions with their product as part of their marketing programs. I saw one from Shaw Carpet on my email just last month. These industries are looking to show good examples and build enthusiasm for their product. Sometimes these wining photos show up in the company's national advertising, which is another great benefit for you.

Besides the publicity from the awards publication, you can create some more "buzz" and write and submit a press release about your award.

Allocating Marketing Time for Submitting Articles and Competition Entries

In my studio, about 80% of my marketing time is about getting published and getting our name out there. We go after feature articles, we do awards competitions, and we do show houses and home tours – all those things that create fantastic publicity for us.

177

That is where I create my celebrity status, and it's how clients know who I am. This is the most important thing a designer can do to promote her career.

Action Item!

Decide to be a design celebrity and make it a priority in your marketing calendar.

More of this information can be found in great detail in my home study course, *Creating Your Celebrity: The Designer's Guide to Publishing, Awards, Show Houses, and Home Tours.* It is two CD's and a bound book where I candidly share what I have learned from my years of developing successful designer publicity. This course is packed with more information on how to get great photography on a budget, how to get your design work published, and how to win awards at competitions. There are also two big sections on how to not spend a lot and get really excellent publicity out of show houses and home tours.

3 Things to Do NOW to Start Developing Your Celebrity Status

1. Take a moment of quiet time and reflect about what belief (s) or person(s) in your life could be holding you back from stepping up into your true brilliance. What is keeping you from achieving the design career that you have dreamed of? Is this something that you can let go of now?

2. Get started now. Pick one of your projects to photograph. I know you have at least one that is fabulous!

3. Take action. Research, call, and interview three photographers. Hire one to photograph your work.

It's not spending money – it's investing in your career.

ABOUT THE AUTHOR

Terri Taylor, ASID, IIDA, IDS, IFDA, teaches and mentors designers and decorators about business and marketing strategies to grow their businesses and get paid what they deserve.

Terri supports entrepreneurial design professionals in blending their passion, money, and relationships, and in making a difference in their lives. She provides a unique mix of proven design business systems and inspirational tools to create meaningful success.

Terri is a practicing interior designer and contractor with 32 years in the interior design and construction business. Her design studio, Taylor Design Group, is a diversified design practice that works in the areas of high-end residential design and remodeling, model homes, hospitality, and medical and professional offices.

If you are an inspired interior design entrepreneur, visit www.Design BizBlueprint.com for business-building resources.

179

8
DIRECT MARKETING:
Use Proven and Simple Techniques to Build a Strong, Affluent Clientele

by Steven C. Bursten

In this chapter you'll learn:

* Why you need to know and care about Lifetime Value of a customer
* The difference between Direct Marketing and conventional marketing
* Find out exactly how much to spend – and what results to expect
* Proven appointment generators
* What's holding you back from success and how to overcome it

Two Ways to Create Customers – Time and Money!

There are only two fundamental ways to create customers in your business. One is through time and the other is with money. And if a person isn't willing to risk and invest time and money, in a correct balance, then they're really not serious about the business.

> **Important!**
>
> A serious business owner strikes just the right balance between spending time and investing money in order to get a new customer.

Sometimes it's hard to know how much time and effort is really worth it. So I'd like to share with everyone what the lifetime value of a customer is according to literally hundreds of people that we've queried in class.

Here's what I've asked when doing this survey: First of all I want everyone to write down on a piece of paper what you think a customer is going to buy from you, knowing that if after they buy something, maybe they buy $2,000 or $3,000 the first time, maybe they never buy anything again, maybe they buy $50,000 three years later, whatever it is.

On the average of all the customers you sell, what would be the lifetime value, say, over the next 10 years of every customer. Now if you've got your piece of paper written down, let's ask how many of you put down about $10,000 as the value of the customer. Many of you probably have a higher figure.

Lifetime Value of a Customer – Most Say $20,000!

We find that few professionals look at the lifetime customer value as less than $10,000. Most say more than $10,000. Now I'm going to take it one step further. On the average, would each of your customers refer you to one other person over a lifetime?

Attendees at Window Coverings University believe they would. That means the true lifetime value of a customer is more like $20,000! What does that tell us? Most people in our industry hate to take a risk. They don't want to spend money for advertising or time for marketing.

What Would You Pay to Acquire a Customer?

If I ask a business owner, "Would you be willing to give somebody $100 to become a customer?" many would say, "Oh, no way, never would I do it." If I said $200 or $300, there wouldn't be 1% of the people in our industry willing to invest $300 to get a customer. But when you look at the lifetime value, it changes your perspective. Start thinking about the time you put into it, the money you put into it, to acquire a customer. This is critical, it's essential, if you want to grow. You have to love customers before they are customers if you want to build a good business. This is the main difference in small business owners and large ones. Large business owners actually love customers more and are willing to invest marketing effort to acquire them.

If an advertising opportunity or some sort of promotional opportunity brings with it a certain price tag, I'm encouraging you to not shy away from a specific price tag but rather think of it as on average and over the next several years – what you're getting is one or two customers, and the result that opportunity will yield to you.

"$100 Lead Cost is Golden. $200 Is Still Very Good... Today with Newspaper Advertising, You Can Spend $1,000 and Not Get a Single Lead!"

In media advertising, if you can get anywhere near $100 lead cost, that's golden. If it's $200 lead cost, it is still very good. But most business owners say, "Do you mean if I put a $400 ad in and only get two leads...and possibly only close one of them, that is acceptable?" The fact is, yes, it is acceptable.

> ### Did You Know?
> The main difference between small business owners and large ones is that large business owners are willing to invest marketing effort to acquire new customers.

In years past you could invest $500 in a newspaper ad and expect four to five leads. Unfortunately, the truth today with newspaper advertising is sometimes you can spend $1,000 and not get a single lead. That's why direct marketing is so important to the window coverings business with limited ad budget. So let's consider what direct marketing means.

Direct Marketing

> ### ◉ Did You Know?
>
> The definition of direct marketing is simply going direct to customers using flyers, mail, phone, and face-to-face activities.

Direct marketing is when you do things direct in non-media. That's not using TV, not newspaper, and not radio and broadcast. Instead, you go direct to the customer in selected neighborhoods. You use flyers, you may use postal mail, you may use telephone call techniques to be in direct touch with people.

Direct marketing includes all the things that interior designers and window covering specialists hate to do: *Go meet a potential customer face-to-face.* Oh, isn't that terrible? That's direct marketing.

The definition of direct marketing: flyers, mail, phone, and face-to-face.

In face-to-face I would include a thing we call "Trunk Shows" at our company, Exciting Windows! They were developed by our Vice President of Consumer Marketing and Member Support, Kathy Cragg. A trunk show is a special event. It can be in a customer's home for a half-dozen friends and neighbors, or it can be for 100 people at a country club, senior community, or something like that.

Decorating Seminars – No Buying, Just Fun

It's an event where you really have fun. We call it "like having a Tupperware party but you leave your checkbook at home, you can't buy anything." Decorators show products, talk about color trends, and usually have a little ice-breaking quiz.

Sally Morse is terrific at that. Anyone who's ever listened to Sally Morse, who works with Hunter Douglas, will know what a decorating seminar is. Sally Morse started with me originally at Interiors by Decorating Den, years ago. She bought a franchise and became the best

184

in the system on PR to build a fabulous business. She's a great person to listen to. If you can ever see one of her decorating workshops, you will learn a lot.

Leave Your Checkbook at Home

Here is a bit of clarification on decorating seminars...

When you announce and tell your customers – say, send out a mail piece or email, or you call them on the phone – make it clear that this is a fun get-together – no buying! Tell your customer to invite her friends. You don't want just to get the people you know, you want them to bring a friend along. You want a customer present to rave about your work and how much fun it is to work with you.

> ## ⦿ Great Tip!
>
> At decorating seminars you can show products, talk about color trends, have a little ice-breaking quiz, and have fun, but leave the checkbook at home.

Most decorators will have one good customer a month – if you're selling one or two customers a week – once a month you'll have someone who's really special and the creative treatment is really beautiful. Tell that customer, "Your window treatment design is so exceptional; I know you want to show it off to your friends. Why don't we have a little event – you can have four or five friends over, maybe a couple of neighbors, and we can all have fun. It will be a little decorating workshop with color trends and new products. Wouldn't that be a fun thing to do?"

It's a fabulous way to create awareness and build your business with the right kind of customer.

Don't Try to Sell – for Custom Products, Build Awareness

It's an awareness-building event. Awareness is critical. If you are in the custom business, you cannot sell anything to attendees. If you have knick-knacks and small-value products, then you are not in the custom business. Yes, many direct-sales companies – Home Interiors, Pampered Chef, and Longaberger Baskets, for instance – sell products by party plan. But those are not CUSTOM product companies. You have

185

to decide the business you are in. I am thrilled to get in front of six or eight homeowners like the one who is my customer. If I don't get an appointment today, I will in the future if I make a good impression.

Important!

Use decorating seminars to build awareness!

This way I've made new friends with high-potential customers; I can now get their email address, I can start sending them email every month. I can send postal mail every couple of months. I can call back by phone to keep reminding them so that maybe six months or a year from now, *when they're ready to buy window coverings*, they will think of me.

"Awareness" – It's Simple, but Hard to Grasp

The fundamental of awareness that the business owners have to understand is very difficult to grasp. Awareness means that the right, high-potential target customers know three things about you:

1. Name. The name of your company – and your personal name. They've got to know your name or else they will never call.

2. Products and Services. Potential customers must know what you sell and the services that make you special compared to competitors. Do you mainly sell draperies? A lot of businesses only sell draperies, but not blinds or shutters. A lot of blinds businesses don't sell draperies. Some businesses only sell from their store and do not have at-home service. Customers need to know how you sell your products. Do you come to the home? Do you charge a fee? Do you offer decorating ideas at no cost? Until homeowners know what it is you sell, there's no reason for them to call you even if they know your name.

3. Consideration. Finally potential customers have to consider you before they will call. You have to be on their short list of 2 to 3 companies they want to call before they buy. Customers have to be almost "brainwashed." They have to hear from you many times – advertisers say anywhere from 9 to 20 times that they have to hear of you – before they're willing to *consider* you when it comes time for them to buy something.

Mailings: Do They Really Work?

The answer is yes, if they're done correctly. And let's clarify between flyers and mailers. For example, mail sent to your past customers is fabulous. Mail to open up a neighborhood is not good. Years ago when I started a new person in a franchise business, my goal with the franchise would be to achieve sales of $100,000 the first year in business from a standing start. (This compares to a typical six years to reach $100,000 in sales with "Word of Mouth," which our industry preaches as the main way.)

Our system is to take 1,000 homes and distribute flyers every single month. Flyers cost about 10 cents apiece or less, to print – 7 or 8 cents, often – and maybe another 10 cents if you pay somebody to distribute them. That's a maximum 20 cents and if you do it yourself, very inexpensive.

> **Beware!**
>
> Mail sent to your past customers is great. Mail sent to brand new neighborhoods is not effective.

First Class Mail Costs Too Much

On the other hand, if you want to send out 1,000 mail pieces, you're talking 50 cents to 60 cents with your printing and postage and everything like that. That means you're looking at $500 or $600 to send 1,000. You may not get even one appointment. You cannot not afford to develop a new area with First Class mail.

Now when it comes to your past customers – and most businesses have a past customer list of at least 50 people and generally 100 or more. You may have 400 or 500 and even more. If you prioritize and budget your mail, you can afford to do it every other month, or even every month.

If you have over 200 customers, then you prioritize them. Your best customers will get mail every month; others every three months. But that's the way, if you're using mail – and we call that Preferred Customer Marketing – then prioritizing your customers is the way to go. How to do it is in itself is a separate trick, and we'll cover that a bit later.

Using First Class mail should not be a method of opening a new neighborhood; it should be a method of staying in touch with past customers.

Opening a New Neighborhood

I just want to make it real clear that the first dollars and the first time that you spend is always to go back to your past customer base. It is critical to start there.

Once you've done that, then you want to open up a new area – you want to be able to select that area, and it's very important that you select it correctly. Remember, I'm again talking window coverings, shop-at-home. That's what my expertise is and that's all I'm talking about in marketing.

Only 1 in 6 Can Afford High-Quality Custom Window Coverings

If you're going to market upscale products, know that only one out of six people can financially afford beautiful window coverings. There's a lot of people that can afford metal blinds and even wood and faux blinds. If you sell commodity products, there are more people who can afford them.

Action Item!
On average, your best results will be in neighborhoods whose home values average $400K to $1MM. Research, find, and target those homes.

But I like to get into drapery sales and some shutters and things that are beautiful and elegant, and that only one out of six people can afford. So to open up that neighborhood, the first thing you do is to find homes that are in that value.

On a national average basis, that'd be $400,000 to $1 million homes. A lot of people might say, "Why should I stop there? I want to go where the $2 million homes are." Well, the $2 million homeowners are probably not going to use a window covering specialist as often as the people in $1 million homes. You don't want to go either too high or too low.

Select the Right Neighborhood –
Not Too High or Too Low

So the first thing to do is to be sure you've selected the neighborhood; but there's another trick, there's a real pitfall here, a trap that can get you. And that is if the neighborhood is more than two years old – in the first two years, most people get privacy light control and some beauty in a couple of rooms.

But then they may not be doing anything until their neighborhood is around eight or 10 years old. And in between, you could spend a lot of time putting out flyers and trying to open that neighborhood, you're going to go nowhere. Even though it looks like a neighborhood across the street that should be buying from you.

Run a Survey – Save Money and Save Months

So the first thing I say to a person if you're going to open up a neighborhood, you need to run a survey first – that's where you survey 10% of the people, and that's a special little thing I can't get into here, but it's one of the forms that we provide at Exciting Windows! We provide a system to survey the neighborhood so you're sure that by spending 6 hours now, you don't waste six months trying to sell in the wrong place.

> ### ◉ Beware!
>
> People invest in some window treatments in the first 2 years of a new home ownership. They won't return to doing more window treatments until at least their 8th year in the new home.

The first thing you can do is find out the median household income by ZIP Code, or even better, by using U.S. census tracts. You can go with the census tracts, break areas down into usually as few as 500 to maybe 1,000 households. ZIP Codes are typically anywhere from 3,000 to 5,000, and up as high as 20,000 households.

Target Customer Income

You want to be able to find out what is the income and go to the upper-income-home areas. If you find a median household income on a national average basis that is somewhere between $60,000 and $80,000 per year that's probably going to be a good area.

189

Let's say, for example that there's 10,000 people in a certain ZIP Code. That would be about 4,000 households. There's about 2.5 to 2.7 people per household. So if you go into a ZIP Code that's got 4,000 households and it's got a median household income of around say $70,000, that means half the people are above that, so you take the top 2,000 homes in that area, and you make that the area that you really want to work in, and that group is probably going to have a median income of $100,000 to $150,000 which is an ideal level for your kind of business.

This information is available online. You can Google it, and get census information, or at www.custEmers.com/potential you'll see a little thing called "market potential." And you can put in a ZIP Code and it will give you exactly the sales potential and the median household income.

ZIP Code Sales Potential

You can take any ZIP Code and just put it into Google and say household income for that ZIP Code. The advantage of going to the custEmers.com is that we not only organize it as to the income but we actually extrapolate the sales potential if you just do a modest amount of development, or if you try to develop it really well, it will tell you exactly what the sales potential is for that ZIP Code.

Then we want to start sending out flyers. Now most people say, well, flyers don't work. I put out 300 flyers once and I didn't get any response. That's because the person doing it doesn't understand the fundamental marketing principle of awareness.

> ## ⬤ Important!
>
> Understand the fundamental marketing principle of awareness: people must know who you are, they must build up confidence in you, and they must consider you when they're ready to buy.

That's what we talked about a little bit earlier, and we have to remember that people must know who you are, they must build up confidence in you, and they must consider you when they're ready to buy. In a typical neighborhood where there is buying activity, about 8% to 10% of the homes are going to purchase something for their window during the year.

So if you have 1,000 homes, and it's really an active target neighborhood, that means 80 to 100 homes will buy something for their windows sometime this year. Most people think that when you put out

1,000 flyers, you should be flooded with leads, or if you put out 200 flyers, you're going to have a couple of appointments, or you're going to get 1 appointment for every 100 flyers; but that's crazy – it's not going to happen.

You may put out 1,000 flyers and get nothing, especially in the beginning. Now the challenge is that you don't know whether that's because they're learning who you are and they're really buying something from somebody else, or whether the neighborhood is not a target neighborhood. That's the challenge.

What to Expect from Your Flyers

Assuming it's really a target neighborhood, you should expect from 1 to 3 appointments for every 1,000 flyers you get out. There are two ways to get the flyers out. One way you can do them is by punching a hole in each, putting a rubber band through it, hanging it on the doorknob, and kind of walking them around one at a time. It takes about 16 hours to get out about 1,000 flyers; so in about 4 hours every Saturday, you'll get out about 250 at a time.

Using a different method, which I teach in our class in Window Coverings University, you can get out 250 an hour – about 4 times as fast. How? You roll them up and you use your car for delivering them. Some of the best time to do that is early morning on Sundays before people pick up their Sunday paper.

> ## ◉ Great Tip!
>
> Assuming it's really a target neighborhood, expect 1 to 3 appointments for every 1,000 flyers you get out.

Either way, the main thing is that you want to get your flyers out. Your flyers should always have your picture on it, and have your phone number very visible, right at the top, in really large type, maybe 48-point type.

Call Homeowners after 2 Flyer Distributions

After about two distributions, you want to start calling people in those neighborhoods, and you can buy crisscross directories where you can get the names and phone numbers of the people living in those target neighborhoods so you can call them by name. And you just tell them,

191

"Hi, my name is Susie. You've probably seen my flyer, my picture there, and I wanted to put a name to the face and just tell you that I'm in the area, the neighborhood all the time. If I can ever be of any service, I'd love to stop by and help out." That's the way you build a target neighborhood.

Again, you should be able to distribute 1,000 flyers in 16 hours, which is about every Saturday for about 4 hours, that is if you do it by foot. If we do it from the car, that's about 250 flyers per hour.

From every 1,000 flyers, we should expect to get one to three appointments. Because from each appointment on average you can get $2,500, right there you've just completely paid for the cost of the flyers and the time that you've spent to distribute it.

You Must Want Success

> **Did You Know?**
> The foundation for your success starts with a burning desire to improve your business.

There are two things that are really important here. First of all you need to know the long-term value of getting a customer, and that it's worth investing 16 hours or $300 or whatever it takes to get that one customer.

But secondly – and I find that only a tiny group of leaders really possess in our industry –is the desire to improve their business. And what we're talking about figuring out what it takes to build a successful business and make money. For example, our firm's signature class, Professional Window Coverings Sales, costs $2,000, but you have to put that into perspective. I appreciate that $2,000 is a lot of money, especially today; but it is a drop in the bucket if you can add $50,000 to $100,000 in sales in the next year as a result of that, which I would expect any graduate of that class to do.

Are Flyers Appropriate for Upscale Homes of $1 Million or More?

Yes, but if you have only a few of them, you may want to use postal mail. Do use flyers if you have a subdivision with lots of them close together. Some designers may feel that putting out flyers is demeaning and will create a negative image, but that's 180 degrees incorrect.

192

The Elephant in the Room

Designer Vitalia Vygovska explains this thinking as follows: That is sort of one of the elephants in the room in terms of flyers, so let's explore that. Where I live, the northern suburbs of Philadelphia, a lot of lower-priced services distribute flyers. Businesses like lawn cutting, low-end landscaping, maybe some house-cleaning services – those are the types of businesses that I personally get flyers from. Why is it still a good idea to use flyers in a more upscale business like ours?

To answer that, consider a few points: First, what does the flyer look like? And if it's a flyer that's loaded with coupons and discounts for cleaning or get your drapes cheap and things like that, you don't want to do that. And second, what is it that you're offering?

Customers Welcome Quality Promotions

It shouldn't be free lining and free this and free that. What you want is something that every month has a feature. And maybe that feature might be beautiful draperies, maybe the next time it's shutters, maybe the next time it's swags, and you have picture of the product that you're featuring.

> ## ● Great Tip!
>
> If you make it a quality flyer with a decorating tip and a special offer, your prospects will want to save it and refer to it when the right time comes.

Then you will have a special value. You might say something like "We know that the swags are so beautiful that we're offering a special: Any top treatment is 50% less when you buy the draperies." So you can offer a very dignified value with your products but the main thing is to give them a decorating tip maybe a paragraph long, like a quick tip about using colors. Show a feature about how beautiful window coverings can be and maybe about using throw pillows, or things like that.

But if you keep it as a quality piece that people will want to save, they're going to put that on the refrigerator, they're going to put it in their kitchen drawer, and they're going to save that until the time when they're ready to get their window coverings and then they'll give you a phone call. So the first thing is to make it a quality flyer.

Should "Real Designers" Knock on Doors?

The main reason most designers do not do flyers is they feel that it is demeaning to their image to go door to door looking for business. And they fear rejection, so they downplay the value of using flyers.

By the way, part of developing a neighborhood is when you see a home that has a window without draperies – when all their neighbors have beautiful draperies and you can see the tie-backs and the top treatments, and here's a home with bare windows – you want to knock on that door and give them the flyer personally and just tell them you're in the area and be glad to help them if you ever can. Also, a home with a real estate sign is another good place to stop and meet the homeowner. This canvassing philosophy goes back to your decision about your target customer.

How does the customer think? Many people tend to project to customers the way they think customers *ought* to think, which has nothing to do with the reality of the way they really think. What do I mean by that? We'll explore who should be our target customer.

Who Earns Enough to Qualify as a Target Customer?

> ### Beware!
>
> Many decorators tend to project the way they think customers ought to think, which has nothing to do with the reality of the way customers really think.

We're going after people who are generally making a $100,000 a year to maybe $150,000 or $200,000 a year. You know that the average Joe doesn't make a $100,000 a year. It takes somebody who does something special. It takes a lawyer, a doctor, maybe a schoolteacher whose spouse works, it maybe takes a he's an accountant and she's a lawyer, two-income professionals working together. It's people who are in sales, people in management, people in computers, people in technical skills that are highly paid. Well guess what – when those kind of people got out of college, they had to go out and create a future for themselves.

And the doctor or the dentist who had to spend $300,000 on equipment had to send out direct mail. They had to send things out and say teeth cleaning or free evaluation, or $5 off or something like that. My wife, Valerie, answered a coupon from a dentist for $5 off and wound up spending probably $10,000 over the next several years. So you've got to realize that these are the people who had to do something extra to pull themselves up by their bootstraps and to make a future for themselves.

Target Customers WANT You to Knock on Their Door

And when somebody comes and asks them for business and they or their spouse is doing the same thing, they respect that. They appreciate people who go out and work hard to build a business. And you're actually creating a highly positive image, not a negative image. And that's where a lot of people go wrong on this.

So the whole thing is understanding your target customer. If you're going to be really successful, you want to get into a community and be a part of that community and know the way that the community thinks.

You want to do things with that community and for them – if they've got a country club, if they've got a little clubhouse; you want to lead any charity groups. When you're a part of that community and you give to them, I assure you you're going to get rewarded in the long term.

Great Tip!

The key to success is really knowing and understanding how your target customer thinks.

And once you decide that a customer is worth investing time or money in and you decide that you want to have a good, successful business, you're going to spend your time out there in the neighborhood and seeing them. And you're going to spend a lot less time on the back side of the business with paperwork and going to work rooms and things like that. You're going to spend the time out front, making friends in the neighborhood.

Direct Mail – Send to People You Know, and Who Know You

And as we said earlier, direct mail is not a good way to open up a neighborhood. But it is a great way to stay in touch with your past cus-

195

tomers. In fact, it's the first marketing effort you should make, assuming you have at least 50 past customers. Now, if you're brand new and you have no past customers, what's the next best thing? How should we use mail when I said we don't want to use it in 1,000 homes because it's too costly?

How to use it is that you send your mail to people who know you and who want to see you succeed. Start with your Christmas card list or other such greeting card list. Or start with all of your friends that you've got on Facebook. Get the names and addresses and send direct mail to people who know you and want to see you succeed. Your church directory will have a list, any organization you're part of, any networking group – that's the place to use mail. It is not to open up a new neighborhood to send out mass mailings.

Mass Mailings – Yes, They Work

Now I will explain an exception to the advice against using direct mail to open up a new area. When we say direct mail, there are two types. I was talking about First Class individual mail to individual people. But there are mass mailings like Super Coups, Valpak, and a variety of other companies that do that. And they usually sell 10,000 at a time – in other words, their minimum purchase is 10,000 and they're usually around 3 cents apiece. So that means that if you pay $300, you're going to get 10,000 of them distributed. Well, you might get an appointment out of that; it could happen. And a lot of people think, Well, that's beneath me, and it's only coupons, and it's junk, and things like that. But the fact is that those things do work.

Action Item!

Don't disregard the power of co-op mailings, where your mail piece is packaged together with several other companies'.

And if you take 20,000 of them and send them out consistently every month and you make that an investment, it will pay off if you have the right kind of little coupon in there that is both dignified and a value – it has to be something that people want to act on. But don't throw that away if you're willing to invest money. It can be good way to invest.

Frequency for Direct Mail

In terms of frequency, how often should we expect to do any kind of direct mail, whether it's targeted to individuals or done as a mass mailing?

Let's talk only about individual mailings – I'm going to take the Valpak-type mailings off the table. The first thing we do is get a database. There are a lot of online databases right now, but you want to get a database that you can put the names and addresses of people into, and you want to have at least a couple hundred names if you possibly can.

Getting Your List – Joe Girard Tells How

Joe Girard, listed by *Guinness Book of Records* as the world's greatest salesperson, said everybody knows 250 people that they would invite to a wedding or a funeral. And so that's a good place to begin with for your list. You can get your list from your church directory and other places like that. Actually, you must build a database. Then you're going to go through that list and prioritize. Let's say you have as many as 500 names. Whenever you get over 200 names, I would prioritize them.

If you had only 200 names, it only costs about $120, 60 cents apiece, and you can send mail every other month. If you work out the math, that only costs about $60 a month to send mail to 200 people every other month. But you want to prioritize if you can get more than 200 names, and

Great Tip!

Prioritizing your list helps you stay on budget!

that's where you decide who are the customers or the people that you have the greatest affinity for. That way, if you want, you can keep it within a budget.

How to Prioritize Your List

If you start with, say, 500 names and you go down it, you can know – especially if it's a past-customer list – you'll remember them from three years ago. "Oh, yes, I remember, they were nice young couple just out of school, had a great future ahead of them. I really liked them; I want to stay in touch with them." You check them off as keepers. Even if maybe they only bought $300 back then. Or maybe the person bought $20,000 worth of services – "Oh, boy they're great. They're going to be

197

not only finishing up this home, they're going to be buying a vacation home about 50 miles away on the coast…" or the lake someplace like that. So you want to take people who you like because they bought a lot, or because you had good chemistry, whatever it is, and you want to check them off.

That might be 30% to 50% of your customers; for some it will be 60% or 70%. These are "Preferred Customers." You want to have a separate preferred customer marketing program, as we call it at Exciting Windows! Now you can send mail to those people more frequently than your others and still stay on budget. I would start off sending them every month for about three months; then I would back off to every other month for that group.

After Selecting "Preferred Customers"

> ## ◗Action Item!
>
> Preferred customers should get your mailings every month for the first three months, then every other month.

Then I would look at my other people and I would send to them less often: Some people would get four times each year, some people maybe only once a year. So that's a way you want to manage your direct mail program and keep it within a budget. Of course, you'll need to decide on your advertising budget before you plan all of this.

The preferred group get mail every month after the first three months, and then you go to every other month with those preferred customers. These are your preferred customer mailings.

What Makes a Mail Piece Work?

Creating an effective mail piece is more art than science. But always go back to your marketing principle and remember that they must know your name, they must know the products you sell, and they must consider you as an alternative. In a mail piece, you want to take it a step further. You want to have some urgent, timely call to action, a reason that this is a good time to buy.

Actually, sometimes it can be strictly informational. One of our best mail pieces had a beautiful drapery, almost like a theatrical tie-back,

198

with a huge tassel, and it's really opulent and overdone. But the piece says that we still make house calls. That's simple enough: It tells that we come to the home, and then on the back side it gives more detail about the products that we sell and the fact that we come to your home at no cost and we offer these services and things like that. We didn't offer a specific value or a promotion.

Want Appointments Now? Offer a Special Value for Limited Time

If you have an established business and you have enough appointments, you may be able to build a business with strict awareness mailings like that; but if you need a customer right now, you may want to offer a special value.

> ## Action Item!
>
> Offer a special offer called "a drapery trade-in sale."

One of the best that we've had at Exciting Windows! is something we called a drapery trade-in sale: "Call us this week – we'll give you a trade-in on your old draperies and remove them for you and take them to a local charity." You don't have to put all that on the thing; that's part of your discussion on the phone. But customers like the idea. You can tell them, "Just measure how wide your windows are and take $10 a foot, and we'll give you that much off on your purchase" – that's an easy way to do it. So there are lots of ways.

Watch your competitors. But, only "borrow" the ideas you see them use over and over. Many business owners get creative, but most of our ideas don't work. So watch for the ones that do work – and use them, not the others. I will tell you that the idea of percentage-off is not as effective; in fact doesn't work nearly as well. People like fixed dollars – sometimes a $50 gift certificate or $100 gift certificate. (We have found there isn't much difference between offering $50 or $100.) And by the way, when I say a gift certificate, I mean a gift certificate for them to use now – it's a coupon if you say it's a discount against a purchase.

Don't Be Afraid to Offer a Real Value

Some people are afraid of being abused, and so they say, "Well, I don't want to give a $50 gift certificate and then have them just buy $50 worth of products. I am willing to give $50 off on a $150 purchase."

199

But, that is the point of a GIFT certificate. I've never seen anybody who could buy less than $200 worth of custom window products. So we like to call ours a "No Strings" gift certificate, and let the person choose the purchase amount – that's a pretty good way to go.

As for other things that have worked effectively: added value is a big thing today. Getting the beautiful window coverings is nice, but now you can have the beautiful valance to go with it for only half price or maybe even – you might even make it a fixed cost of $100 extra as an option to have for your window coverings.

Value Added Is Better than Discounts

> ### 🌀 Great Tip!
>
> Offer to put up top treatments free of charge for the first 30 days. If customer likes it, sell it to her at half the price.

It's always better to make it look like we're giving something extra to the customer versus taking off money or a percentage. I saw it starting to happen about two years ago. It's still very firm that people like to get the extra, and I like to do it as a business owner. The more I sell to them, the more beautiful the window is going to be, and the happier and more excited she's going to be, and the more referrals I'm going to get when people walk in and see it.

So I would always rather add the value – in fact, I've got a little idea I use to sell top treatments. If they don't want the top treatment – they think they can't afford it – I say, "Oh, don't worry – I need some displays in this area. Let me put it up here for you to see how it will look. We'll leave it here for 30 days. If you decide you don't want it, we'll take it back." And so I always like adding on a little bit more to the room. I would rather sell the top dressing for half price and get my cost – then it is silently selling for me to her friends. It costs me nothing out of pocket, and I will get referrals for years.

What Should the Mailer Format Be?

There are fabulous creative agencies that have come up with unbelievable things in envelopes or colored envelopes, beautiful mailings, maybe with three-dimensional things. Those fabulous offerings have a place – on a limited distribution or for a company that's got a lot of money for marketing. Frankly, they're very tricky: They may pay off…they might do something. But probably 8 out of 10 times they're going to flop and you're going to spend thousands of dollars and not get much out of it.

The safest thing is just go for simple standard postcards. We were using 6 x 9-inch postcards. We like the oversized postcard, but when you compare the price, it costs 50% more than just using a small postcard because the postage is higher, and the printing cost is higher. So remember that 60% or 70% of the value of your message is simply the fact that it got out and people got it in their hands and they know the name of your company and the products you sell, and they'll consider you.

If you consider that the formula for professional advertising people is something like this: graphics is 20%, text is 20%, and the fact that it got there is 60%. So I would recommend keeping it low-cost: Use a standard small postcard, and get more of them out, and have high quantity. That way you're likely to get better results.

Great Tip!

Calling past customers is the best and easiest way to build your business.

The Phone Is Your Friend

Phone calls are one of my favorites, and it's something I know most of you really kind of dread. Every time I teach a class on this, people say, I don't want to call somebody – I'm going to interrupt their dinner and I'm going to make them mad, and things like that. But again, it's like many things: We have our ideas of the way the world works in our thinking, but we haven't had a chance to look at it from the way the other people who are out there really think about it.

Past Customers Want to Hear From You

Let's start with the easiest phone call of all: your past customers. We spent tens of thousands of dollars on research, and one of the most salient points that we – a good friend, who has worked with major companies, and I – still use today is the fact that it may take two or three appointments with the decorator to really select the final thing they wanted. Then they bought it, and then it's four or five weeks and they talk to the decorator once in a while, and then the job is installed, and the decorator may come back and they certainly should be there. But at that point, it's all over with, and this wonderful friend that they've built up over a period of weeks that has been so friendly during the process of selling – all of a sudden, they never hear from that person again.

Do You Like Being Jilted?

Now for the women out there: How would you feel if you were going on a date with somebody and they were really great, a wonderful person? Told you how great you are and then all of a sudden you never heard from the again. What kind of feeling does that leave you with? What they told us on the survey was that the customer felt she was jilted. And so the first thing to know is that customers are not offended by you calling back; they are offended by the fact you don't call them back.

> ### 🔊 Did You Know?
>
> If you're a good business person, you not only welcome complaints – you encourage and thrive on them.

And what's a major barrier in addition to the fact you think you're going to offend and intrude on their lives and interrupt them during dinner, which is all a bunch of hogwash? Many people simply won't make calls. Many people think this way: "I don't want to call back a bunch of people… There might be some problems… They're going to complain about something…

And tell me how much it is, and I'll have to go out there and fix it again or spend money on it. I think I'll just let sleeping dogs lie; I'm not going to find out about that."

Welcome Complaints! Turn Them into Sales

The fact is once in a while you'll receive a complaint, but if you're a good business person, you not only welcome complaints – you encourage and thrive on complaints. A complaint is your chance to show what you're made of. It's your chance to get another sell, your chance to make that customer remember forever and tell all of their friends how wonderful you were when there was something wrong with that job, and they'll never forget you for it.

If there's something wrong with a job, chances are that you're the only one out of the loop. Everybody else, friends and colleagues and neighbors and everybody who comes into the house, has heard of the problem, and you're the only one who doesn't know about it. You're the only one that doesn't know – if you did know, you'd be working to fix it.

> ## ◉ Great Tip!
>
> When calling past customers, be sure to emphasize their great choices and good taste.

If you receive a complaint, the first phone call to make is always to your past customer. What to say to them? Just be a friend; just call back and say it was nice to work together last year for – if you remember what the product was, that's better. If you don't, just say I just wanted to kind of call and let you know that I was thinking of you and I want to be sure everything is working right.

We like to check back periodically to be sure that you know the drawstrings are working that everything – the tie-backs, the draperies are pulling, and everything is really looking good and working correctly. They'll almost always say that it does. Then you might ask whether they've had any friends in, and if so, did they like the work that you did. And don't talk about yourself as the designer and how great you are. Talk about her and her wonderful good taste to make the final selection. And ask them about it and they'll tell you about how wonderful their friends thought about them and everything.

When You Visit a Customer, Get Photos and Set a Trunk Show

If it's a really nice job, be sure to take pictures for your portfolio. Then suggest to the client, "Wouldn't it be fun to have a few friends over sometime? I'd love to put on a little design workshop for you and a little decorating Trunk Show." You can open it up to other things, but mainly if you just call and let them know that you are thinking of them, you will wind up making people remember you, and they will be much more likely to tell their friends.

Customers Are Not "Yours"

We tend to think that if we sell to somebody once, that's "my" customer; I own them for life; they'll never buy from anybody else; they'll remember my name forever because they thought I was so wonderful. We feel that this is how the world should work.

203

Well, that's hogwash. In three to six months, they'll have forgotten the name of your company and your name. They'll remember you as that sweet little lady who dressed so nice and everything; but what was her name anyway? And then all of a sudden they want something for another window and they see an ad in the paper, and by golly they take that ad, or somebody else puts a flyer on their doorstep and loyalty is right out the window. We do not own customers; they have minds of their owns. They're going to forget you, so that phone call reminds them who you are. And your direct mail piece and your email do that, too.

Email Follow-up Is Essential Today

You want to have your email going out every month reminding customers, contacts, and friends who you are. When you do that, your name is on their mind, and will think of you when they're in a cocktail party or they're over at an event and they're talking to some friends and somebody mentions needing something for their window. Your name will be right on the tip of their tongue.

Because they've been hearing from you all the time and they remember. And they'll say, "Gee, I just heard from her a few weeks ago; she called me and told me it was okay to refer her. I thought that maybe she was too busy; I didn't want to refer and make her too busy." A lot of customers think they shouldn't refer because you're so busy with all your other people, and you've got to let them know to refer you.

> **Great Tip!**
> Use email as one of the most effective and least expensive ways to stay in touch with your customers.

Well, this is the way, and you'll find that if you call or if you reach 30 to 40 people, you'll probably have one person who will say, "You know, I was meaning to call you; I was thinking about it."

If a past customer wants a product, they might call you and they might not. But because you called them, you're going to get that sale again. So that is extremely important to follow up with past customers.

Marketing Is Creating Awareness with Multiple Contacts

Jo Ann Brezette said it first, I think, and Kathy Cregg has repeated as a mantra for all of our Exciting Windows! training sessions, that the goal is multiple points of contact over a short period of time. The more ways that they can see you on Facebook, on an email, with a postal message, a phone call, a flyer – no matter where they turn around, they're always seeing and hearing from you. Then they talk to a friend who's had you out to their home. That's how marketing is done. It is not just by sending out one flyer that's got a giant discount or taking a full-page ad in the newspaper – that isn't it. It's multiple points of contact over a period of time.

Making Friends, Building Relationships

The whole idea is to build the relationship, build the friendship. In fact, the whole basis of the seven-step selling process is called *make a friend*. That's the whole thing that's behind it.

> ### 🌀 Great Tip!
>
> Leaving a message on someone's answering machine is just as effective as speaking to them on the phone live.

After you have distributed flyers two times, you want to start calling, and you've got 1,000 people there to call. You can call about 20 people an hour, so spend 3 to 5 hours on the phone every week and just start calling people and leaving a message on their machine – that's almost as effective as talking to them live. I don't have time today to go into why, but simply leave a friendly message. You definitely want to start making phone calls to your target neighborhood after you put out the flyers: They've seen your picture, they know who you are, and so they'll have a very friendly reception.

Facing Your Fears

In our industry even more than in most, the folks who would like to have success are often business owners who are afraid, and have multiple fears. Some owners are afraid of too much success that it'll take them away from their family. They won't be able to treat their family with the time and care they want to. Some people are afraid of rejection. They don't want to knock on a door or put out flyers or ask a customer for permission to put a yard sign out, showcasing your company's name.

We have business people who come into interior design and decorating because they love color and design. Also, they're kind of perfectionists.

And perfectionists are very much afraid of being rejected. They just feel totally uncomfortable, which means that their fears dominate them and prevent building their business. In a nutshell, "Successful people do what unsuccessful people don't like to do, and will not do." That is the difference in those who conquer their fears and succeed.

In Summary: 3 Action Points for Success

1. Make a list of people you know. Start with Past Customers.
If you want to build a successful business, your first task is to decide where your business will come from. Who are your customers, and how will you open up new areas? Start with a list of past customers, then your holiday list, then your church or club. Make a list of people who know you and like you and want to see you succeed.

> ● **Important!**
>
> Successful people do what unsuccessful people don't like to do, and will not do. That is the difference in those who conquer their fears and succeed.

2. Select your high-potential target neighborhood.
Open up new areas by creating awareness with flyers, phone calls, knocking on doors, holding trunk shows and events. Make an effort to stir things up and get to know people who want business.

3. Get on the phone.
Follow up with phone calls, especially to past customers. Call homeowners in the neighborhoods where you distribute flyers. The idea is to remember that you must create awareness if you want to create appointments. And if you want to have sales, you must have appointments.

ABOUT THE AUTHOR

Steven C. Bursten is Chairman/CEO of Exciting Windows!, a national network of experienced window-fashions professionals who feature stunning ideas and expertise in all products. Now celebrating a half-century in window coverings, Mr. Bursten is a recognized author of more than 100 articles in leading industry magazines and a how-to book on business startup, *Bootstrap Entrepreneur.*

He is co-founder of Window Coverings University; co-founder of the International Window Coverings Exchange; and founder of the world's largest interior decorating franchise, Interiors by Decorating Den.

9
PARTNERSHIPS:
How to Use the Power of
Joint Ventures
to Grow Your Business

by Margi Kyle

www.doctormargi.com

In this chapter you'll learn:

* 3 ways to look for the right partner for you
* 5 types of Partnerships, including
sole proprietorships
* The advantages and disadvantages
of partnerships
* Whether mission statements are attracting
the wrong clients
* How partnering outside your industry can grow
your business in new and exciting ways

I have had 10 partners in over 40 years that I've been in business and have no regrets – well, not too many! It has been a journey that has taken me to places and professions I never would have gotten to on my own. I am grateful for all I have learned and am pleased to share it with you.

Design was not my first passion. My first career was in Early Education with a minor in Child Psychology. I worked with children for about four years, only to learn that I didn't want to spend my life with just children. Cooking was something I did every day and loved it. So why not create a catering business? A great thought and very easy to get it going! After a very busy year, that business ended with a cocktail party of 500, a very intoxicated bartender, and my husband begging me never to do that again. I didn't have a partner in the formal sense, but a friend who was working with me in a joint venture. Nothing gained and nothing lost if it didn't work out. So now what to do that would create that passionate feeling you get when you are living your dream? Why not Fashion!

With my love for clothes and looking my best, fashion seemed like a natural thing to do. I went back to school and learned how to make patterns and sew, and life was good. I had even learned how to make underwear – who has time for that? No one will ever see your talent! It still was not pulling at me, saying Let's do this forever. So what is my passion? Interior Design, but of course. Why didn't I think of that sooner? At that point my now-former husband thought I was crazy and was not going to pay a cent to send me back to school. He felt that I just needed to grow up!

Important!

In life there are no roadblocks!

In life there are no roadblocks, so off I went, and kept sewing and cooking, allowing me to go through design school. I worked, went to school, and cared for my family: two children and a 13-year-old foster daughter. It is not easy starting all over again, but well worth the time, money, and devotion.

After I finished design school, I wanted to be solo. I wanted to be on my own. I knew I would make a terrible employee, so I just started my own business by myself. We were living in Vancouver, British Columbia, and I was working for builders and teaching. We transferred to Toronto, Ontario, and back to school I went to learn about Canadian furniture. The original plan was to move back to the States, but once again, that wasn't a decision I could make.

I took the last-year courses at Sheridan College, to learn more about living and working in Canada. I missed school, and the next year I found myself teaching the full three-year program. While taking a class on a field trip to the International Center in Toronto, I found that almost nobody was open, and if they were open, they were not receptive to talking to students. They are our future, and I was shocked at the attitudes in almost all of the showrooms.

We finally found a showroom that was open, and this nice little man was there who literally gave us a tour of 10 other showrooms. He was a furniture broker, and we started working together the next week. In the real world, there are three different prices: wholesale, designer, and retail. Michael – or better known at the time as Mr. Stern – knew only wholesale pricing. Pricing I had never seen before, and he was sharing them with me. He was a furniture broker, and a good one at that.

I realized that he knew his stuff. He could bring furniture to me that I didn't even know existed. We worked as a joint venture for about a year and did a lot of business before we got serious about forming a permanent business.

So, let me explain briefly about a joint venture versus sole proprietorship, two common forms of business organization.

> **Important!**
>
> Know the difference between joint venture and solo proprietorship: two common forms of organizations.

Joint Venture: This is a temporary contractual association of two or more persons or firms that agree to share in the responsibilities, losses, and profit of a particular project or business venture. Plus it is temporary and a great way to see how you all will work together. When the project is over, so is the joint venture. Because it is not a legal entity, it cannot be sued, but the individual members of the joint venture can be sued. Each firm independently, and the joint venture as a whole, are liable to the client.

211

- For me it was a great way to gain experience in new fields.
- It provides a strong design team for a tricky client.
- Increased staff and business.
- We were able to keep our individual identity.

Sole Proprietorship: This is the simplest and least expensive form of business – all profits are yours. Today when you are working with contractors as joint venture partners, contractors need commercial general insurance, which is liability insurance. If you hire a contractor as a subcontractor, they need to have their own workers' compensation policy in case they hurt themselves on the job. You need to see a copy and save a copy of their insurance. Get it from their insurance agent; or you could cover them on your policy, but that is not recommended. This is extremely important in every field. Designers need professional liability insurance to pay for any errors or emissions. If you are in a joint venture partnership, make sure they have at least professional insurance.

Well, I fell into the partnership. I had tremendous goals – that's another thing that I will say: Everybody needs to sit down and make sure that your goal hasn't changed. When I first started, mine was very, very pathetic. You know they always say to write achievable goals. I looked at those and thought, "Any wimp can do this. I'm going to write my most unachievable goals to see what I can do." Some of them were pretty bizarre.

> **⊙ Action Item!**
>
> Write down specific goals that will stretch you and perhaps even make you uncomfortable.

I've been very fortunate. I was invited to listen to Dr. Mark Victor Hansen, the *Chicken Soup for the Soul* guy. At one of his events, a two-day seminar on "How to Create Prosperity," I was the only woman in there. At the break, he said he was selling his tapes for $99. I couldn't afford that but couldn't afford not to buy them.

He turned my life around. I met him again two years later, and showed him all of my goals as we sat by a pool for 2 hours. He said, "I have chills learning that someone took my information and really did something with it." He taught me to write specific goals as to what I want to be, when I would get there, and how I would get there. I also wrote as to what I would be wearing and how it would feel. Thanks, Dr. Hanson.

212

You've got to write it down, you have to read it, connecting with what your goals are today. Have they changed? Has your life changed? You need to know how much business you need at your age and stage of life. Look at writing your goals like creating a floor plan for your clients. They buy twice as much if they can see what can fit in the space. The same goes with your life. So many people look at others they admire and wonder how they did it all. They didn't waste time wondering how to do it; they just did it! After spending two days with Dr. Mark Victor Hanson, I wrote:

• Aim high and think big (my motto).
• I wanted a partner, which surprised me when I changed my goals because I didn't think I wanted one.
• I wanted a "wife" and hired full-time help at home so that I could do what I needed to do in my world – that was the biggest key. Because you can't keep up with laundry, kids, husband, and work the hours I was working. So I had to literally hire somebody who could take the kids to their activities, who could keep my refrigerator stocked, could do the laundry, could have dinner ready, a nanny.
• I wanted to own my own building within five years.
• I wanted every partner to have a new car.
• TV show: I never thought in my wildest dreams I'd have my own TV show. But I wrote it down there and I achieved it within a year.

>
> **Great Tip!**
>
> If you're really driven in your business, consider hiring help around the house – someone to help you clean, do laundry, shop for groceries, etc.– so that you can concentrate on your creative passion.

   * So don't limit your goals – we only have one kick at the can, and we need to aim high. I don't want to be down there in that box saying I wish I had. I want to be saying Oh, I'm so glad I did.
   * We added two other partners to our partnership as well, so there were four of us. It was my goal to be the biggest residential designer in the Toronto area. And we were a very dynamic group. It just about killed me, but I did it.

Questions to ask yourself:
• How long do I plan to be in business?
• How much money do I need to make?
• How big do I want to grow?
• How many employees do I want working for me?
• What is my time commitment?
• What will my partners be: Do I need designers or other people in the

213

industry who will add to what I already have?
• What are my main business goals?
• How long is it going to take to accomplish them?
• How will a partnership affect my marriage?
• How much involvement should my family have in my company?
• Will it be a win/win situation?
• Where will it be located? What will our name be? What will our Mission Statement say about us?

   * Remember, you are building a business. If you need a friend, that is one thing; but if you are serious about building a business, find someone who can do all the things you can't and don't want to do.
Another key factor before you put pen to paper is to decide how you are going to disagree and how you will end your partnership should anything happen. Who gets what and how it should end? There can be a buyout agreement, split everything equally, sell everything. You don't want to pay a lawyer's fee; arbitration might work better. Do this in writing before the partnership is formed.

🔘 Action Item!

As you consider a partnership, sit down and write down answers to key important questions!

We had great personalities together, and then Michael added or introduced me to two other manufacturers that joined with us, and we really had a good thing going until unfortunately Michael got very sick and eventually died.

We were buying tremendous goods from Ralph, who was the manufacturer that carried upholstery, bedding, and case goods. Michael had been buying from Ralph for years, so our pricing was terrific. Ralph wanted a piece of the action and joined us in our venture. He needed a designer to do his showrooms and an outlet for his samples that manufacturers couldn't sell in their own showrooms. So he used us as the outlet and we became partners.

And then I sent one of my students to Ralph to work with him as his head designer. The student was also named Ralph, but I called him Ralphy. And so Ralphy just got thrown into the partnership with all of us. And it was great to have another designer on our team, even though he was working full-time for Ralph.

Splitting the money was probably the hardest thing that we had to do – who makes money where, and how, and why. But we all added a different twist to that partnership, which was wonderful because we never were idle; we were always on the go. And if one person didn't think of something, the other did.

Talking Money with Partners

It's all about communication – in a partnership and in a marriage – so don't hold it back. This, too, is extremely important. I had to let both my partners and husband know how I like to entertain my clients or friends, what I will never compromise on, and areas where I can cut back. We were running a full-service design center, silver tea service and all. My clients must be treated like gold, as should my friends.

In the beginning, we split everything 50/50 because Michael was getting me a fantastic buying price that I couldn't get myself. I was bringing in clients, and he was, too; however, I do charge for my design time. We threw that into the kitty and then I started teaching out of our studio. So I'm sitting there thinking, I'm here from 7:00 AM until 10:00 PM, and he is at home having dinner with his family. I got a little resentful, and so we had to go back to square one. So we settled on this:

Important!

It's all about communication – in a partnership and in a marriage – so don't hold it back.

The company will get 25% and I get the rest. It really wasn't a problem, but it would have been one if I didn't share how I was feeling. Money is the hardest thing to talk about, no matter what your situation. You've got to talk about it fast when it comes up; if you let that fester, it'll eat you up.

Then when Michael got sick and he was off most of that year, I was driving down to the hospital to see him and giving his wife a check for half our profits, thinking he's not done a thing. He sat down with me and he said "I know how you're feeling. You're sitting here thinking I'm not doing a darn thing and you're killing yourself and you're giving me half." And I said yes, that's kind of how I'm feeling, so he ripped the check up and he said Let's reassess this. We won't survive if we drain the company. I didn't want his wife to worry, so I asked the two of them what they needed to live on. Then we worked it out and drew up another agreement.

What if some of you are just thinking of starting a partnership or maybe are in talks with someone – is a 50/50 split is reasonable? Yes, I think so, if you're both bringing in equal amounts and spending the same amount of time on projects.

215

When I say that you should bring in equal amount, I mean both revenue and new clients. You need to look at both of these. I was bringing in the clients, and Michael was selling them the furniture; so to me, when it started, it was totally 50/50. It kept shifting as time went on, and we had to keep making adjustments. That's the tricky part, because you want to be fair but you also can't feel like you're taken advantage of.

Given that, would it make sense to structure the agreements maybe for only a year, so that every year when that anniversary comes up, you can review all the parameters of your agreement? Yes, I think that's an excellent idea. We did it anyway; we did it every six months just to make sure there were no hard feelings. Yes, with the economy the way it is, Dewey, my partner today, and I do it monthly. We have had to adjust our course price and profit price to fit the changing times. So it's just communicating. If you are comfortable enough with that person to form a partnership, you should be comfortable enough to talk to them about how you are feeling about money and your workload. You know you have a good partner when the partner brings it up first. That is a good working relationship.

Other Tips on What Made Our Partnership Work

> **Important!**
>
> Be sure that partners bring different skills into the partnership, so that you complement each other, not compete with each other.

What made it work is that we were so different. Ralphy and I were both designers, which helped because we talked the same language and we could do the shows together, and we could create the design very quickly. We had over 10 showrooms that we had to design twice a year, which is a big job.

So we worked really well together but we never were doing the same thing: While I would be drawing the layouts, he would be moving the furniture and specifying the fabrics. I can't stress that enough: You don't need a shadow – you need a partner who can do what you don't want to do, or couldn't do.

Because we were all busy all the time doing what we did best and not hanging over the other one seeing what they were doing, we had a very highly productive company. And we'd get together Friday afternoons, buy a lottery ticket, go home and pray that we'd all win, and discuss the goals for the next week. We all really worked six days a week – it was a very interesting dynamic that just happened, because we all had the same vision. We made our dreams become reality. What a fabulous feeling at the end of every day.

Go slowly with partnerships and don't rush into it. There is no need to rush into it if you can form a joint venture, which I've done many times with great success. That is where everybody has their own little business but you work together on a joint project and you decide how you're going to split profit. When that job is done, the partnerships is over. You don't have any legal papers to sign, and you really get to see how you work with other people. After 22 years in business, Ralph and Ralphy started arguing and their friendship and their working relationship went downhill. We had written the ending, and it was amicable. I didn't expect my partner to die, but that was how it ended with him. I still talk with Ralph but have lost track of Ralphy.

> **⊘ Great Tip!**
>
> Don't rush into a partnership. A good way to test the waters is through a joint venture.

As I was ending my marriage of 27 years, my business was also ending. A tough period, but it, too, had a happy ending. I met my husband Lee, and he wanted to take over the business, but I felt it was time to let it go. Lee needed to keep his identity and I needed a fresh start. It had been a long but good journey, and I am grateful for all I learned. I am the sum total of all my experiences, and that feels good.

Do You Have a Mentor?

So how can we find our own "Michael"? I sure never went looking for mine. When you're out in the world, look with your eyes and heart to see what is out there. I believe so strongly in finding a mentor and mentoring someone yourself. That has helped me more than anything else. I met David Beach on TV while living in Vancouver. He was on TV selling a book on color. He was doing everything I wanted to do and I admired him greatly. I tried for 2 years to find him. He had moved to Toronto, and as life would have it, came to me in my studio, one week before I started my own TV show. David was a guest every month and added such flair to my show. I wanted to be David. We talked weekly, and when he found that my company was closing, he sent me a dozen long stem roses, with a note: "I am retiring and want you to take my job. No one can walk in my shoes better than you. Please say yes!" I worked at Para Paints for two years and loved every minute.

> **💡 Important!**
>
> Know the difference between different kinds of partnerships!

While I was at Para, I created four new color cards in two years but didn't know that David did one a year. I feel that things happen for a reason, and Lee and I then moved to Charlotte, North Carolina, to be closer to my aging parents.

Another joint venture while I was still in partnership with Michael, Ralph, and Ralphy involved Anita, Pat, and me. We three were selected 25 years ago to design the first R2000 house in Canada, which was an energy-efficient house. IRIDO picked three designers, all residential designers who had our own companies, and for two years we had a joint venture to build this R2000 house together. We all shared in the responsibility, workload, suppliers, and goals. We never formed a real partnership, but became and have remained really good friends. We had more darn fun, and it was wonderful because if one company's staff didn't have time to do something, the other one did. The night before we opened, we all worked as a team and didn't leave the house until we all had our rooms the way they were designed to be. The way designers should work together.

A Look at the Types of Partnerships

General Partnership: When two or more people join for the purpose of forming a business and these people alone share in the profits and risks of the business, a general partnership is formed. It is easy to start; a written partnership agreement is not required – but don't start one without an agreement. You don't need a lawyer, but I wouldn't do anything without one. Some states require that you register your company.

One benefit of a general partnership is that two heads are better than one. Sometimes banks look at you differently if your business is a formal partnership.

One drawback is that you are totally liable for you partners' actions. The partnership does not protect your personal assets or your partners' assets from litigation costs. If you have several partners in a general partnership, any wrongdoing by one will affect everyone. So choose your partner(s) well.

Limited Partnership: This is formed according to statutory requirements, with a limited partnership agreement filed in the state where it

218

was formed. It is more expensive to start up this way. If partners are in other states, the agreement also has to be filed in those states. Limited partners are liable only to the extent of their investment. A limited partnership may be appropriate for a small but growing business that wants to raise money by selling limited partnership interest in the company.

There is also a Limited Liability Partnership (LLP), which is limited only to the company's business debts and to each person's own negligence, but not exposing each partner to financial risk because of the other person's negligence.

The limited partnership or else the LLP may be what you might start with, for your protection. We had to have a board of directors, which made me feel very protected: our accountant, lawyer, my father, my mentor, and two suppliers, plus Michael, Ralph, Ralphy, and me. We had monthly meetings, and it was a two-year term. After our first two years were over, no one wanted to leave, so our board stayed the same for over 20 years. We also shared profits with our staff, if they brought us business. Part of the perks of a partnership is that you can brag about your partner and what they do and vice versa. We did very little advertising and a ton of business.

Limited Liability Company (LLC): This form started in 1980 and is the hybrid for the general partnership. Owners are not called partners but members; this can also be a sole proprietorship. Its members can be investors with little or no management or actual work involvement. States do vary, and I know I have to pay $200 every year for my LLC. Not a very expensive insurance policy.

The primary benefit of an LLC is that it limits the liability of a corporation. The liability is limited to a member's investment; personal assets are protected. A successful claimant can only take what your company is worth, or for me, whatever is in my bank account. Also, it's easier than a corporation. There's flexibility in how profits and losses are allocated among the members. LLC members are not employees, so you don't pay unemployment taxes. You can easily change your general partnership to an LLC.

There are some disadvantages, though. Licensed professionals such as lawyers and accountants are prohibited from registering their business as an LLC; this might affect designers in licensed states.

Corporation: This is sometimes called a C Corporation. It must be approved by the state's secretary of state office or other appropriate state agencies. After the first organizational meeting and the date of approval, the board of directors are elected and the bylaws are prepared. Discussions or actions concerning the sale of stock take place.

Corporate officers are required to inform stockholders of the financial condition of corporation. Annul financial reports must be prepared by an account and provided to stockholders. Reports must be conducted monthly. If a lawsuit occurs, it is against the design firm. Only corporate assets can be used to pay the business's debts. The corporation is legally and financially responsible.

A corporation exists independently of its originators or any other person connected directly with the firm. The originators may sell their interest in the corporation to other stockholders or outside parties at any time, and the corporation goes on.

S Corporation: This type of corporation can be one person or many people. And it provides liability protection and has a different tax responsibility than most of them. And my accountant said by the time you are of the age to retire (which I said I never wanted to and I still don't), Social Security will be gone, so he thought I should have an S corporation and not be paying into Social Security. So that's why I went with an S corporation. In hindsight, I'm sorry I did it. I don't have enough qualifying quarters to even collect Social Security now because I worked too many years in Canada.

I truly respect joint partnerships and have been part of one several times. Another group of us, Tim, Paula, Tom, and I, worked together for two years and then decided we'd all had enough. It just was not the time or place for another design studio. Nothing ventured, nothing gained.

Realistic Expectations from a Partnership

Expectations can be tricky. Michael was not a designer, so his responsibilities were to do all the ordering and all the shipping, check stock all the time, make sure the books were done and samples were in stock, and a whole list of stuff that I just don't even want to think about doing.

He was on the phone morning, noon, and night, ordering, making sure

220

everything was going the way it was suppose to, organizing the window installation, organizing the painter to get out there. We had full-service organizing that did everything from windows to major renovations. It was crazy. I couldn't do all of that plus work with clients. My job was done when I wrote the proposal, they signed it, and

> ### ⊘Action Item!
>
> Write down your expectations and make sure that all potential partners are on the same page.

they gave me a deposit, then it all went to my partner and my secretaries. We had weekly meetings and progress reports and ran a very tight ship.

I was off running to the next client. So again, that's why I feel strongly that if you need a friendship, that's fine, but your business maybe won't grow the way you want it to grow; that's fine, too. Define where you want to go and grow and what your expectations are. How much of the pie do you want? I unfortunately wanted it all. I'm very happy today to have a piece of the pie or action, but I'm a lot older too. So again, I had partners that would support me in my TV, that could go out and get sponsorship so that basically I was the little princess that just said this is what I want to do, and they made it happen.

Consider what you need, what areas you are missing that is preventing your business from growing, and write down the answer(s). If you definitely decide you want a partner and you're looking for one, make sure you know what you want in that partnership, what you expect to get out of it. Too many times I've seen designers get along in class and when the class is over, they want to be partners. And that's great; it depends on what your goals are. To me it was a friendship where they do everything together, they go see the client together. You're paying somebody to be your shadow and to do what you really could do and are good at. Step out of the box and look at industries that can help your business grow. Builders, workrooms, painters, furniture brokers, architects, etc. Find people who excel at what you don't excel at.

Know the person's goals and dreams. Do they fit yours? Do you both have the same energy and passion for your career? Do you both have the same code of ethics? Here's a sample code of ethics that you might want to adopt.

Designer/Decorator Code of Ethics

1. Honesty is the top priority.

• Who you are, how you work and make your money
• Let your client know how you price products and about product knowledge and warranties
• Give the client a list of references: both clients and manufacturers

2. Treat your clients like royalty.

• Your client is always right
• Mind your manners and also call them Mr. and Ms. (or Mrs.) until told otherwise
• Treat your clients the same no matter whether they spend $100 or $10,000
• Send hand-written thank you notes
• Keep your own problems to yourself. Friendships can develop after the job is done

3. Always be professional.

• Dress for success – even when running to the grocery store. You never know who you will see and where!
• Never lose your temper in public
• Get a baby-sitter for your children for site visits: They weren't invited into the client's home.
• Don't talk about other clients in a bad way or give their names without consent

4. Use your sense of humor at the proper time.

Important!

Keep your own problems to yourself. Friendships can develop after the job is done.

• When a client is upset or angry, listen and don't use humor
• Listen and don't be judgmental
• No jokes, please
• Humor is enjoyed only when it is shared with all parties

5. Be prepared – try to be ready a day before your meeting.

• When you are rushed, your client feels it and won't make any decisions

222

• Don't keep changing your appointment times – you will look disorganized
• Always call to confirm your next appointment
• Feel confident with your presentation. If you don't, your client won't either. Make sure they sign the work agreement and all proposals.

6. Pre-plan in order to be one step ahead of your client. This will help prevent problems, and you will look prepared and ready.

• Whether in your office or in their home, organize your samples and presentation so the client won't get confused.
• List your reason for your selections, and then LISTEN and WATCH the client's facial expressions. Don't talk your way out of a sale; less can be best.

7. SERVICE, SERVICE, SERVICE: It is number one today and always!

• Give them several options within their budget – but not so many as to confuse them.
• Let your client decide how and where they are going to spend their money.
• Money kills dreams. Listen to their wish list before you discuss money.

Businesses That Can Make Good Partners for Interior Designers

> **⊚ Great Tip!**
>
> Organize yourself, your samples, and your presentations – anything to minimize client confusion.

We had a joint venture with my drapery workroom. And that was a wonderful partnership for 25 years. They're always looking for designers, and designers are always looking for workrooms.

There are all sorts of ideas that you can work on with a partnership. In Vancouver, I partnered with a couple of builders. Just make sure you've got a contract with them and let them know when you want to get paid – contracts, contracts, and contracts. Be the business person that our industry deserves.

223

If you like someone and think you might be able to work together, take them to lunch or just ask for an hour of their time in their office, saying that you have some ideas that you really would love to discuss with them. And ask them to have a list of what they have to offer, and to have their portfolio and resume ready, and just say that you're thinking of going into or adding to your business. You don't even have to say partnership; just "thinking of adding to my business and wondering how we will fit. Here's what I can do for you; I'd like to know what you can do for me," and see what they say.

> ## ◗ Action Item!
>
> Use this lingo: "Thinking of adding to my business and wondering how we will fit together."

I had another man who joined us too, who specialized in marble. He had his own little marble company, and he ended up doing a ton of work for us. He'd bring me the client, I'd design it, and he would do it. So it was a win/win for both of us, and that's what we wanted.

One of my friends just opened a flooring company, and she commented that this is the worst time in the world to be opening a new company. I did the design for the building, and we went out for lunch to see how I could help her. I offered to get her going with an invitation-only event, with invitations going to all her old and new clients, for a Sunday afternoon. I told her to book her time with her designer, which would be me, and pay her (me) a dollar a minute.

So they would pay me, she'd do the bookings and advertising, and we'd both win. I'd then select the flooring, give the clients back, and we'd split profits by me getting 10% and she'd get the rest. Be creative, and see what clients are looking for.

So there are many forms of partnerships, It doesn't have to be working every day with someone – just when you need help in certain areas. Here's another type of partnership, which I successfully pitched in Toronto. I went to Lansing Lumber, a small hardware store, and met with the owner. I met them at a Junior League cocktail party and had asked whether there would be a good time to talk with them. After we met, I ended up doing presentations at their store once a month. "One Saturday a month from 10:30 until noon, and 1:00 to 2:30, and I'm going to charge you X number of dollars. You advertise for me and I will bring the people in." He laughed and he said "great plan, but you're way too expensive," and I said, "Okay, here's another deal. How many people can you hold?" He answered 150. I said, "If you don't have any more than 50, don't pay me." He was sold out both times.

The Lansing Lumber owner advertised on the radio and on TV about a free seminar, "How to pull it all together." People are dying to find out how to do these things. So all of a sudden, he said, "Hey, I want you every month." Another joint partnership was formed, and we worked very well for several years.

> ## 📀 Great Tip!
>
> Don't shy away from opportunity: It can really be a fabulous experience, even better than you ever thought.

So just look at where you are, what is out there, what the needs of people are, and create a company that can service those needs. Don't shy away from opportunity: It can really be a fabulous experience, even better than you ever thought. You've got to be so honest with them about everything you want from them, and when it doesn't happen, tell them. And don't be afraid to – it's exactly like a marriage.

Nothing Is by Accident

I believe in instincts, and a great story is how I met Dewey, my current partner. I got a phone call on a Tuesday, asking could I fly on Sunday to wherever and meet Dewey and be on a designer council. I didn't know who Dewey was, and I laughed I said I'm honored, but I don't even know the man. I'm getting home from Boston on Saturday night, and I think it's an impossibility to be in Buffalo on Sunday morning at 9:00.

While talking to my husband that night, he asked about my day. I told him about the call and being in Buffalo on Sunday morning. He said, "I've never known you to pass up an opportunity. You love color; go meet him." So I got on the plane at 5:00 AM, thinking What am I doing? I am paying for this; this is insane. But when I met Dewey, I knew. We just clicked, and in an instant we knew we would be working together. He knew what I needed to know and I knew what he needed to know. It's been five years, and we are still going strong.

I wrote a course for designers, Nature's Guide to Precision Perfect Color Combination. Dewey and I formed a company called We Make Color Easy, another joint venture that allows us both to remain working together while keeping our own identity.

Dewey is the brains behind the Dewey Color Coordinator book, Embrace Hue You Are, and several other books. He didn't know how to put it together as a course for the design industry. The man is brilliant but he's not a designer, and so he needed me to go out and train instructors. He needs to just keeps inventing and let me turn his works into powerful information for the industry!

We talk all the time – we are best of friends. When there's a problem, it doesn't matter what he's doing – he will stop and help me solve my problem. It has been an unbelievable partnership, one that I never would have had if I hadn't taken the risk or taken the opportunity to do something different. I am a huge risk-taker because you won't get where you need to be without taking risks.

This partnership wasn't our first rodeo; we both had a pretty good idea of who we were. We wanted to go with his products. Why re-invent the color wheel, since Dewey did it better than I ever could have dreamed? I've always taken my husband to meet whoever I wanted to work with to make sure that they all got along. Five minutes after Lee and Dewey finished talking, Lee stood up and he said, "You two don't need my approval. You both are connected. Go out and form your partnership." Dewey had the papers all drawn up and all I had to do was to sign it. We had already gone through all of this several times, so it just happened.

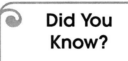

Did You Know?

When you're ready to learn, the teacher will come.

When you're ready to learn, the teacher will come. So if you think you want your business to grow (who doesn't?) and you think perhaps a partnership is the way to go, start looking at people a little differently. We all have needs, and you know there's more power in numbers: Two heads are better than one.

So when I say start looking at people differently, are there some specific traits or characteristics or things to listen for that all of a sudden will make you sit up and realize that this could be a potential for partnership?

Here's what you can do. Go to any of the shows, design centers, and showrooms in your area. Put an ad in the newspaper stating you are just starting a business, and what your needs are. Somebody to install

226

window treatments, somebody to make the custom furniture, a painter, and so on. At the end of the week, I found people to make things and install draperies, a painter, and so much more.

> ## 🔴 Important!
>
> It all starts with your goals. Big or small – you must know where you want to go to get there.

Join WCAA, join IDS, join whatever organization is in your area, and start talking to people who are out there. You might even find that you hook up with an installer and he can bring you a ton of business and so you start a joint venture. You don't have to own the person, but just start working together. Professional groups are well worth their time, Chamber of Commerce, Rotary, networking groups all help. If you are not networking, you are not being seen or heard. Clients don't hire invisible designers.

So really, it all starts with our goals. For me, my goals were huge. I wanted to do it all and be it all, and I knew that in order to achieve all that I wanted, I couldn't do it alone – I had to have partners.

If somebody's goals are to run a small business just go on appointments and just satisfy one client at a time and not get too big, are partnerships maybe not the right path?

Well, I wouldn't recommend it. There's nothing wrong with that, absolutely nothing. Either way is okay as long as every one of us understands what our goals are.

One designer said that they also have sort of big goals and always write them down and use vision boards. But it took them a little while to get to the place where they knew what their goals were. And there's definitely a period in someone's life where it's not quite clear what you're goals are. You think you like your business, you like what you do, you like working with clients. You may sense that there's something bigger and better out there, but you're not quite sure what it is. What do you do in that situation?

I was in that position right after I had achieved all of my goals and met Dr. Hanson, for the second time. I thought, Okay, now what do I do? I always give my clients a fake million dollar bill and put it on their coffee table and say tell me your dreams and I'll help you make them come true. You just won the lottery, money is no object, and that gets people talking. I gave myself that fake dollar bill and said write down

227

the rest of your life. What is your most burning desire? And it was TV, TV, TV – and I thought, I have never done a TV show; I don't have a clue how or where to start. I was already doing radio, I was already writing for three publications, but I wanted to get on TV. And my brother was on TV (for those of you who remember *Barney Miller*, he was Det. Stan Wojciehowicz).

> ## 🐦 Action Item!
> If you're unsure of your goals, give yourself a fake million dollar bill and think as if money were no object. What is your most burning desire?

My dad owned a talent agency; I called him and said I wanted him to get me on TV. I needed an agent. Long story short, he wouldn't help me. His advice: "You are the best person to promote you. Get out there and do it." I was so mad at him, but he was so very right. By the end of the week, I had my own TV show, *Moments with Margi*.

Well, I didn't have a clue what I was going to do – I'd never done this before in my life. Now a lot of listeners are thinking, Man, she's got chutzpa. No, it was a goal that I had to achieve. I've done TV for 30 years now and am looking for a new and better way to be on another show. Live your passion!

How My Partners and I Ran Our Business:

The Jacket

Every client needs a jacket or folder in your office. I use the folders with a pocket on each side. The pockets will retain the Company Policies, Proposals, Change of Order Proposals, all copies of the purchase orders, and the client's deposit card. On the front of this jacket is a white label. On this is written in pencil only-the clients name and telephone numbers, fax numbers, email addresses (both home and business, if both are available and if the client doesn't mind calls to their business). Always ask permission to fax or call the office. Some clients do not want any information to be seen by their employers. (Use pencil so that when the jacket is completed, the same can be erased and the jacket used again.)

I keep these jackets in the desk file drawer under "New Clients." When I get a new client, I am ready to do business, after they sign and agree with my Company Policies. I do not do anything until that happens.

228

Remember, you run your company, not your clients running it for you. Make sure they understand the way your company operates and what you expect from them. Also, what they will receive from you. No one likes surprises, and the hardest thing to talk about is money. Get that topic up front and on the table so you can have fun in your career.

At no time is this jacket to be removed from the office, nor any of its contents. In my jacket, I have a copy of the Company Policies, time sheet, and all personal notes. No pricing is in this jacket; it is all kept in the office file. Some clients love to browse through your jackets while you are doing something else. Don't you want to know what your doctor has in your folder there? Also, if should you leave or misplace this jacket, you will not have lost it all.

Beware!

Remember, you run your company, not your clients running it for you. Make sure they understand the way your company operates and what you expect from them.

If you are a sole proprietor, it is not as crucial, but if you are running a company with a secretary wgi answers the phone, she needs all that information at her fingertips. She, too, will have a time sheet and will record all phone calls so you will be able to track what is going on. Don't forget to make a file on your computer to keep information on each client and also, a file for all their emails. Today, more than ever, we need a paper trail. Make sure you have one.

Customer Proposals

This form should be on your computer so it is easy to access and store in the client's file. Start with their name, address, and all numbers where they can and want to be reached. Also note directions to their space and a good time to contact them.

The Customer Proposal is given to your clients after your initial consultation. It is very different than the Company Policies. The proposal defines what you are going to do for your clients, along with estimating your design time and fees. This can also be your bill for the initial consultation.

• When you receive a proposal with a check for the consultation, an invoice marked *Paid* is then sent to the client.
• This proposal is made up of everything that your company is going

to do for the client, selling price, tax, deposit, and balance owing on the order. This proposal becomes a work order once signed and once a deposit has been received.

• After the proposal is written up and ready for the client's signature and check, photocopy the proposal twice, one for the designer and one for the office until the original proposal is returned and signed. Always photocopy the first check received from a client for your record. This copy is to be placed in the "Proposals Pending" file.

• Keep a copy of all proposals in your file and in the office file. Always include a self-addressed stamped envelope with any proposal or invoice that is sent to a client. You will get your money much faster, and your clients will really appreciate the extra step your have taken on their behalf.

> ## ◎ Important!
>
> The Customer Proposal is given to your clients after your initial consultation. It is very different than the Company Policies.

• Spell out everything that your company will be handling for them, such as delivery, installation, tax, etc.

• If possible, try never to take less than 75% down for a deposit. That usually doesn't cover costs today!

The Client's Deposit Card

This is a card or any system that will allow you to track each deposit and the number and date of each proposal.

• Each new proposal must have a new card. Any office store will have them, and the one I use is like an index card size; it is two-sided to show deposits and paid-in-full.

* When an item is paid to a manufacturer through a purchase order pertaining to the client's proposal, this item will be taken off the deposit on the client's deposit card.

▪ Should a client have paid $1000 down, and an item for $200 is ready to be paid to a manufacturer, we would then deduct it, leaving a balance of $800.

* The cards must be kept with corresponding proposals at all times. The purchase orders are attached on top of the proposal until they are paid to the manufacturer; after that they are marked Paid and show the check number; then the card is attached to the back of the proposal until it is finally attached to the invoice.

• By looking at the client's deposit card, you should be able to determine at any time what is happening on that proposal. For example, if only the deposit shows on the card, then the items ordered on the PO's, have not arrived. As each item is received by your company, then the manufacturer of the product and the PO number is recorded on the card. When the invoice is received, then the amount paid is recorded in the first column. Once everything is marked Paid, that proposal is stapled together and filed in the Client's Paid file.

In Summary: 3 Action Points

1. First, find a mentor. If you don't have a mentor, you're missing the boat because that's where your energy will come from. I don't have one right now, and it's driving me crazy. That is not a surprise at my age, I have had many accomplishments and need to find someone older than I am to mentor me. It will happen and I can't wait. In the mean time, I will be a mentor. I'm mentoring a little high school gal who I'm trying to get into the Art Institute of Pittsburgh, and that's just giving me the energy that I need. When she leaves my office, I'm on such a high because she reminds me of me, and I just can't wait to get her going. Mentoring means to me: They will get you where you need to be, far faster than you can do it on your own.

2. List your priorities. Today that probably should include to take in more money faster. And definitely revisit your goals. Look and see whether they've changed or tweak them. Mind-mapping is fun if you have never done it; Google how to do it. Look at whatever you do well to get your energy back.

I also would say on that same note, go to the library every week and get a new DVD or CD that's motivational and listen to it while you're driving around, which I call dead time. We can't get on the phone while driving anymore, so that's a way to pass the time while doing something motivational.

3. Create your mission statement. If you have a mission statement, go back and readdress that as well. My first mission statement was so long ago that I can't even remember what it was – I was going to cure all the ills through my design work. You can't be all things to all people, all the time. It was so unrealistic, it got me nowhere. After I paid a life coach, we changed it to read: "My mission is to Educate, Motivate, and Dedicate myself for the love of design." My whole life focus changed. I was teaching again, I was mentoring again, and doing what I truly, truly love to do. Today you've got to think out of the box. Set bigger goals so that you can accomplish more. Aim high and dream big – it's still out there. And if you find that you have any other questions for me that I haven't addressed, I am very happy to answer emails or talk with you.

ABOUT THE AUTHOR

Margi Kyle, *IDS, ASID, WCAA, WFCP, DCI, CCC*
For over 40 years, this remarkable, captivating woman has built an astounding portfolio from the ever-important "designer's perspective." Never idle, this New York School of Interior Design and Sheridan College graduate has contributed to this industry as an interior designer, television host, mentor, keynote speaker, educator, and writer. Margi's credentials include Professional level of ASID, IDS, WCAA, WFCP, and DCI – along with being National VP for WCAA (Window Coverings Association of America) and National President of IDS (Interior Design Society). Margi is the founder of the Nonprofit organization Little Smiles of North Carolina, a "mini Make-a-Wish" for any child in the hospital.

Margi has received her Master's in Interior Design and is the Executive Director for We Make Color Easy – The Dewey Color System, and is a spokesperson for Hunter Douglas, We Make Color Easy, and 3Dream. Net. For more information on Margi, visit: www.DoctorMargi.com, DesigningDr@Gmail.com, and www.WeMakeColorEasy.com.

10
SET YOURSELF APART
THROUGH PERSONAL BRANDING

by Terri Maurer

In this chapter you'll learn:

*Why having a brand is crucial
to your success*
*How even individuals and small businesses
can have a marketable brand*
*How a strong brand can level the playing
field with larger firms*
*To understand the key elements
of your personal brand*
*To formulate your Personal Brand
and Brand Statement, and how to use them
to move your business toward success*

Branding: What's It All About?

Branding is obviously not a new marketing concept; it's been around for quite some time. Believe it or not, branding was first adopted by marketers in times much like we're going through right now: the Great Depression, and into the early years of World War II. Things were tough, money was tight, and people were very cautious about how they were spending their money and what they were spending it on.

For businesses to survive, they had to find ways to attract customers and stand out from everybody else in the marketplace. So, branding was born and continues today as the key element of any successful marketing plan.

> **Did You Know?**
>
> Personal branding, unlike branding in general, is a newer concept. It didn't come on the scene until the late 1990's.

Personal branding, however, is much newer. It didn't come on the scene until the late 1990s. Tom Peters, a well-known management guru and author, came up with the concept of branding individuals for marketing purposes in 1997. It has taken off in the past 12 years or so.

Many individuals in service industries, and especially sports figures and people in entertainment and music, have latched onto this concept to help them rise above their competition and make themselves stand out.

Personal Branding vs. General Branding

What is branding? It's a set of perceptions and images that represent an individual or a company. Many people think a brand is simply their elevator speech, or logo, or tagline.

Branding is a much broader concept. It's the essence, or a promise, of what will be delivered by a company, a product, or an individual. In an abstract way, it defines what the business experience will be. Without a

234

solid brand, marketing efforts are generally going to be very weak and ineffective.

Marketing can go off in a hundred different directions as many individuals and entrepreneurs adopt a shotgun approach. They don't develop their brand, and they don't write a marketing plan that focuses their efforts in the most productive way. By taking a branded marketing approach, customers receiving your marketing pieces, visiting your website or blog, or finding you on one of the many social media sites will know ahead of time what to expect when working with you. Your personal brand will help pre-sell you and your firm to customers. They will know you better and understand your business approach.

Everything you do and have in your marketing plan will be based on that brand. Peter Montoya, a marketing guru who does a lot of personal branding, defined personal branding as: *the powerful, clear, positive idea that comes to mind whenever people think about you.* Your brand is what you stand for. It's a representation of your values, your abilities and actions that other people associate with you.

Your brand is like a professional alter ego, designed solely for the purpose of influencing how people see you. In the simplest of terms, it's what people say about you when you're not around. Hopefully they are thinking and saying something positive.

> ◉ **Important!**
>
> Personal branding is a powerful, clear, positive idea that comes to mind whenever people think about you.

Let's take a look at some easily identifiable individuals who have strong personal brands. Oprah Winfrey has a personal brand. Tom Hanks has one. Michael Jordon, Mike Tyson, Martha Stewart, Donald Trump, Dennis Rodman, and Tiger Woods all have very strong, recognizable personal brands, and they market them well.

Let's take a look at Oprah's personal brand. All the experiences we've had with Oprah, whether we watch her top-rated TV talk show or we've seen her in some of her movies, tell us the same things about her. We see quickly that she is open and honest. She tells everything like it is. Everybody knows about her weight issues, everybody knows about her abuse as a child at the hands of her relatives, and everyone knows how she worked her way up to the professional pinnacle she holds today. Oprah encourages people to be all that they can be, almost like Uncle

235

Sam on the Army recruiting posters. There is no doubt she has strived to become the best of the best at what she does. She's definitely in control of her Harpo empire.

She's an extremely hardworking person, and yet she comes off as just being one of us. She's caring and compassionate, and she shares her wealth and influence on some huge projects. Remember the show where she used her powerful influence to have new cars donated and given to deserving women? Or, spending her own funds to create a school for promising students in Africa?

That's the kind of influence Oprah has, and this is the sharing and caring concept of her personal brand. This is what Brand Oprah is about.

Tom Hanks, the actor, is another good example of a personal brand. He's the guy next door, family man, easygoing, with high values and a strong work ethic. If you look at the vast majority of his collection of work, it's all in family-appropriate movies. Even the movies when he moves away from that brand to stretch his wings a bit more, like his role in Road to Perdition, he maintains his nice-guy image. The role he played in that film was of a not-so-nice guy. He was a hit man, plain and simple. While the hit man was not someone you'd hope your children would emulate, he included his family-man side in the part as well. He was a man devoted to his wife and sons and in the end gave everything to save his last son. Even if you hated him and what he stood for, you had to love that family connection. This is the Tom Hanks brand.

Can a Non-Celebrity Have a Personal Brand?

🌑 Important!

Every single one of us can have a brand, based on our unique individual characteristics.

Absolutely – anyone at all can have a personal brand. The celebrity brands we talked about are based on them as individuals and their professions. Every single one of us has a brand, or can have a brand, based on us as unique individuals and who we are. Everybody is unique in some way. We can sit in a room with others in our same business thinking that everyone there is a designer or a decorator or has a drapery showroom and that this somehow makes us the same.

236

Not true. Nothing could be further from the truth. We are all individuals; we have different approaches to the way we work and different styles. We each have a different personality and characteristics that we bring to the table.

Any person can have both positive and negative traits that stand out. If you are fortunate to have presented your best side, you will likely have a positive brand to market. But if your less attractive nature pushes to the front, your brand will tend to be more negative.

Think about some of those celebrities mentioned before. Obviously, Oprah Winfrey and Tom Hanks have very strong, positive brands. On the other hand, think about Mike Tyson, the boxer. Here is a guy that's become known as an ex-convict and rapist who chews the ears off his opponents in the ring. Not exactly someone you'd want your kids to worship, is he?

> ## 🌑Remember
>
> The positive images provide a much higher value as a personal brand.

What about Dennis Rodman, the NBA basketball player? Rodman couldn't seem to get enough attention with Michael Jordon on the basketball court, so he decided to play bad guy to Jordan's good guy image. Both of these guys may love puppies and kittens, and treat their grandmothers like queens, but their brands are saying something entirely different.

Now, take a wild guess which of these well-known people we've spoken about are making the most money and are the most successful – those with positive images, or those with negative images? They're clearly not the ones with the bad-boy images. The positive images provide a much higher value. How many endorsement contracts can you think of that either Tyson or Rodman had? Sure, they had a few, but the other, more positive brand images were much more profitable when it came to endorsement contracts.

What Can a Strong Brand Do for You?

The first thing you need to do is develop your own personal brand. This is not a quick fix for your marketing. It takes working through the branding process, and it takes some time. But rest assured, it will be time and effort well spent in the end.

There are several things that having a personal brand can do for you as you begin using it as a critical part of your marketing efforts. First of all, having a solid brand can help you better compete with the big guys – yes, even if you are a solo entrepreneur working on your own. Many of us have the misperception that we can't compete with bigger firms, and that simply is not true in today's business world.

Did You Know?

Customers trust a person far more than they trust a corporation.

Customers trust a person far more than they trust a faceless corporation. An individual operating their business as a sole proprietor or an S-Corp or LLC has far more to lose than a big corporation. Or, for that matter, even just a larger small business. Those who have more to lose, including their personal reputations, will try harder to please their customers.

As individuals we tend to be much more accountable than corporations. That's all about the people in the relationship. People do business with people. They do not do business with office buildings, brick and mortar stores, or websites. They do business with the people in those situations. We all do business with people we trust, people we like.

The individual's advantage is that customers get to know their company because they are the company. People care more than corporations do. What do you suppose the odds are that you could get through to discuss a complaint with the CEO of AT&T on the telephone? But, you can bet that any customer who called anybody reading this could get you on the phone without any problem at all. It's your company. You are the company – you have more skin in the game, as they say.

What Can a Personal Brand Do for Me?

There are several things a personal brand can do for your business. Marketing focuses on human psychology and emotions. Sales and purchasing are all about emotions. It doesn't matter what the product or service is. If you go to a car dealership and sit in a Maserati or other fancy sports car, you're sitting in that car because you it makes you feel good about yourself. A Mazarati is not about transportation to get back and forth to work, it's about feeling good about how you look in that hot car, how successful people will think you are because you can afford it.

238

It's all about emotion. No one goes out to buy an Armani suit because he needs something to wear to protect himself from the elements. We go try on and buy that Armani suit because it's made from wonderful fabric, it has a great cut, it makes us look like a million bucks, or simply because it has that certain cachet that others will recognize.

Everything is about emotions. So, when customers see your personal brand, it will pull perceptions from their minds based on the positive aspects of your personality and skills. This will result in customers seeing you as being superior to others when you present exactly the qualities they are looking for.

You are different from any other competitor, because your brand is based solely on you and no one else is like you. You are authentic because your brand is based on your personal characteristics and skills. It's not based on five other design firms; it's not based on the person across the street. It's strictly based on your personal you. Every individual is unique in some special way.

> **Important!**
>
> You are different from any other competitor, because your brand is based solely on you and no one else is like you.

Any person or small design firm can brand themselves to improve their marketing efforts. There is nothing magic about branding. It is simply a matter of going through the process to reveal the most valuable things about yourself or your company and capitalizing on them. It will take time, effort, and a healthy dose of soul searching to figure out who the real you is, but it will be worth it in the end.

What Makes a Personal Brand?

A personal brand has three key elements: *who you are, what you do, and the value you bring to the customer.* Another way to put that last element is: Why should customers do business with you and not with one of your competitors?

Who you are: For branding purposes, who you are is not at all about what business you are in. You are not a designer; that just happens to be the profession you chose. This *who* refers to the unique personal you, not your profession. We're referring to the who that is the sum total of all your personal life experiences.

What you do: Again, this is not about your job or professional title, but rather how you do your job in a way that differs from your competition.

What value you bring: This portion of your personal brand highlights why customers will get more from dealing with you than with someone else.

The 4 Components of a Personal Brand

There are four distinct components that go into a personal brand that makes it all about you. First are your personal characteristics and traits. Second are your skills and knowledge. Third are your business attributes: how you work with people in a business situation. And fourth is your personal style.

Did You Know?

Four components of a Personal Brand

1. Your personal characteristics
2. Your skills and knowledge
3. Your business attributes
4. Your personal style

Characteristics can just be your personality. But it can also be what your interests are. What are your hobbies? What's your lifestyle? What things have you accomplished? What possessions do you have? Who, as a group, are your friends? All of those things are characteristics that make up an individual.

Maybe you're one of those bouncy, bubbly personality types. Or, you're interested in fine wine or gourmet cooking. Maybe your lifestyle was growing up as part of the country club set, or you were raised in Kentucky on a horse farm and know all about raising and racing thoroughbreds.

Accomplishments represent any honors, awards, or other special achievements in your lifetime. Remember that they don't have to always have to be related to business. They can be your personal accomplishments because this is a personal brand. Are you an accomplished pianist, or recorded in the *Guinness Book of World Records* for some unique thing?

Consider any special possessions you have that make an impression on your life. Perhaps you own a BMW and belong to a car club that takes road trips and does scavenger hunts. Do you have a collection of fine wines or art? These are all a part of you.

240

As a group, who are your friends? Is there a certain type of people that you tend to hang around with – beer drinkers, wine connoisseurs, or pet lovers? All the things mentioned above are your individual characteristics. They make you who you are.

Next, look at your skills and settle on your most important skill as a part of your brand. You know your educational background, and professional skills that you have acquired. What do you do on a day-to-day basis that might set you apart? Perhaps your skill is based on your ability to work with certain types of customers.

Don't forget to think about skills unrelated to your profession that could be unique when applied to your profession. For instance, if you grew up in a family that owned an art gallery specializing in a certain type of art; you will have that extra something that no one else likely has. Or, your family collected some unique item. As a designer, you may have a wonderful ability of showing off other people's collections. Not everybody has that skill, so this is what makes it personal to you.

Next, address your business attributes: what you're like to work with. Are you detail-oriented, or a big-picture thinker? Are you honest and ethical, are you a team player? Are you a leader? What is it about working with you that makes you more desirable to your client base?

> **Important!**
>
> There are no good or bad answers in any of these areas; it's all just about being different.

There are no good or bad answers in any of these areas; it's all just about being different. Big-picture thinkers are great for some customers, and not so much for others. But, someone needs to take care of the details to get the job done. There are customers who match all of these unique issues out in the marketplace.

In the end, it all comes down to your own personal style. How do you routinely work? Are you that highly creative person, or are you better on the fast track? Are you slower, but detailed and very methodical? How do you work? And how do you relate to people when you're working? You know whether you are an introvert, an extrovert, or an in-your-face kind of person. Do you like to push the envelope whenever you can? These are all things that make you unique among thousands of other people in the same business.

241

How to Apply Branding in Practice

Most of you have probably heard the expression about perception being reality in the business world. There are as many different perceptions as there are human beings on earth. Just like opinions, everyone's got one. Well, you've got your own perception of what those four concepts above mean to you, from your personal viewpoint.

⊘ Action Item!

Once you have finished creating your own list of brand concepts, get input about them from a group of family and friends.

When you sit down and start making a list of these different concepts, it will be based on what you think. No doubt, sometimes we all look at the world and ourselves with blinders on and with a very narrow viewpoint. To be sure that our perceptions have validity, it is best to get outside responses for comparison.

Once you have finished creating your list of brand concepts, it is wise to get input about them from a group of family and friends. These will be people close to you, but a few steps away, looking at you from the outside. There's nobody like family and close friends to tell you what you want to hear – and a lot of things you don't. But they provide an important sounding board in the branding process.

Like it or not, we all have a brand now – today – whether we've worked on it or not. We already make an impression on the workplace. So, it only makes sense to find out what that is and use it to compare to our personal perceptions and that group of family and close friends. With all these viewpoints, it is much easier to see whether our brand is what we think it is, or should be. To find out how you are perceived in the workplace already, seek feedback from not only customers, but architects, contractors, sub-contractors, and others you have worked with professionally.

Getting that extra outside point of view goes a long way to help us see things about ourselves more clearly. Sometimes friends or family come up with things we just don't think of, or have simply forgotten. Their input will be invaluable to the branding process.

When working on your branding process, don't limit yourself to who you are today in terms of who you are, what you do, and what value you bring. Think back to your youth and all the things that were instrumental in making you who you are today. A lot of times we think of things in life that we really enjoyed when we were younger. Somehow they got pushed to the side as we got older and other things like family, education, or work now take the time and space in our lives that they once held.

Our lives and profession are such a natural part of what we do that we don't look at them as being anything particularly special. But you need to know what others think in order to develop a well-rounded brand. You think you are one way, but others think something different based on experiences with you. Hopefully, the perceptions will not be too far apart. The closer the opinions, the easier it is to fine-tune a brand that truly represents you.

Your Personal Brand Statement

Once you've collected all of this information, what do you do with it? How do you sort through it and put it to use? You're now ready to focus in on your brand by developing a personal brand statement.

Great Tip!

Keep your personal brand statement short and succinct so that you can remember it and use it.

When you ask others to help you with your personal brand concepts – characteristics and traits, skills and knowledge, business attributes, and personal style – ask them to limit their responses to two or three key words or items in each category that best describe who you are. This will make the process much simpler for you when you begin writing your personal brand statement. You are looking for the key things that almost everyone thinks about when they think about you.

Okay, back to the brand statement. This falls into the KISS category: Keep It Simple, Stupid. You want to have a short, succinct statement that you can remember and use. Limit your statement to one or two sentences, or 12 to 15 words that convey the essence of you and why people should do business with you. If the statement is too long, it will be difficult to remember, and easy to forget and not use.

You want it to become your mantra: a filter through which all of your marketing efforts are viewed to be sure they are on target and according to your brand. Print it out, tape it on the wall, carry a copy in your wallet or briefcase, use it for a screen saver. No marketing effort or piece will go out without first passing the test of this prism.

Writing the Personal Brand Statement

Go back to the *who you are*, *what you do*, and *what value you bring* elements of your brand. All of this needs to be included in the statement. The *who you are* portion will be made from your list of characteristics and traits. *What you do* will be made up from your education, skills, and knowledge responses. You can also add to this *who your target market will be*. We can't market to the whole world, so we need to define a targeted group or groups. The *what value you bring* portion will be determined from your key business attributes and personal style.

Let's look at an example of how a brand statement is formulated.

We'll assume someone has done their research, gathered all of the necessary input, and tweaked their lists of responses to arrive at the key elements that will define their brand.

Let's assume a person has their tweaked list showing that their key attributes are that they're both a leader and a team player. They find that their key personal characteristics and traits were a great sense of humor and they are highly intelligent. Their key skill is a high level of creativity. In terms of their key business attributes, they are a great leader, but can be a team player as well. As far as their personal style, they like to really push the envelope, always going for that better, cheaper, faster approach and the latest materials and furnishings.

> **Important!**
>
> Your personal brand statement is the basis for all your marketing!

Given that set of criteria and doing a few re-writes to fine-tune the brand statement, the result might be something along the lines of: *A funny but smart team player pushing the envelope to lead the way to highly creative project solutions.*

This statement defines the essence of this individual's personal brand. This will be the basis of all their marketing. Their website and blog will reflect this statement, as will their letterhead, envelopes, and business cards. Advertisements, banner ads, and marketing collateral pieces will reflect this statement.

Their letterhead and business cards should show the light, humorous side of their personality. They should be made from a material that is unusual and slightly edgy. Do they look creative, or standard? Do the font and colors for all printed pieces reflect the statement? Does your work environment reflect the brand? It's all about the brand now, so use the filter before moving forward on any marketing effort.

The brand statement is strictly for your internal use. It is not your tagline or your elevator pitch; it's just a filter through which all marketing is viewed. Again, memorize your brand statement, print it out, tape it on the wall, make it a screen saver, write it on your palm of your hand if you have to.

Everything is now about your brand, and the brand is about you. You need to protect it with your life. You need to monitor and analyze its use. Set up some Google Alerts to watch for brand abuse on the Internet, and act quickly to preserve the brand. There are major corporations whose brands are being skewered mainly because of the Internet and the ease with which customers can now make their issues known to the world.

It's so easy now for a customer who gets upset and files a complaint, expecting it to be fixed quickly. If the problem isn't fixed right away, they may go online, post some negative comments – which quickly spread around the globe – and there's some serious damage to that brand.

> **Did You Know?**
>
> The brand statement is strictly for your internal use. It is not your tagline or your elevator pitch; it's just a filter through which all marketing is viewed.

Remember United Airlines' tagline: "Fly the friendly skies"? United's skies have been anything but friendly to one customer. His guitar was checked with his luggage. While the plane was out on the tarmac, someone on the plane commented that the baggage handlers were tossing around a guitar case – of course it was his case, and it got dropped. He immediately notified the flight attendants that if they broke his guitar, he expected United to fix it or replace it. He also told people out at the check-in desk at the gate. He pretty much got blown off by all of them.

Sure enough, when he arrived at his destination and claimed his guitar, it was damaged. He made numerous complaints to the airline, but to no avail. He finally told the last customer service representative that if they

245

didn't make good he would, as a musician, write three songs about the incident and lack of customer service, and post them on YouTube. They told him to go ahead and do it, so he did.

This guy has had over 9 million hits on his YouTube video. He's gone from being an unknown musician to having a website, recording a CD, and becoming a speaker on customer service. Because of all the publicity for Taylor guitar, the company sent him two free Taylor guitars. United has begged him to take down the video, but he decided to not only leave it there, but to write and post the other two songs he promised.

> ### 💡 Important!
>
> A well-defined personal brand helps you attract the kind of customers who relate to you.

Has the United Airlines brand been damaged? Undoubtedly. Could they have acted sooner and avoided this? Definitely. Is it too late to repair the damage? Probably. You can see now how important it is to protect your brand and what it says about you, especially because yours is a personal brand that represents you.

Now That I've Got It, What Do I Do with It?

One good thing about a personal brand is that it helps you attract the kind of customers who relate to you. You're no longer attracting all different types of customers. You're attracting people who are somewhat pre-sold on you because your brand reveals something about you ahead of time that they connect with. We've all felt a "click" or connection with someone who we felt we could easily relate to or that we shared some commonality with. This is how your brand will work. It will attract like-minded customers to you.

Going back to our sample brand statement: That person had a sense of humor and wasn't afraid to share that with potential customers. A customer who appreciates that will be attracted and will know going into a project that there will be fun involved. But, the customer also knows that this is a funny and intelligent person, and so won't worry that the project won't be handled well. They're a team player so the customer feels comfortable putting them together with their architect to get the project done right. The customer is an edgy, push-the-envelope type who likes to have the latest and greatest, so this is a match made in heaven for them.

246

When people start seeing and appreciating the *you* in your marketing, they will come knocking on your door. But, having a personal brand doesn't matter if you don't market actively. If you don't have a marketing plan, or you have one but you don't implement it, it won't matter whether you have a brand or not.

The marketing plan gives you a focus on where you need to go to sell *you* to customers who will appreciate what you have. How will customers and vendors and other people that we work with know that you are funny and intelligent and brilliant? Because you are going to tell them very clearly in everything you do and everything you say. All of your marketing efforts will tell your story. You'll tell them when you go out and do speaking or when you write an article to build credibility.

I knew a designer some years ago who was kind of quirky, and everyone knew it. She always put some quirky object in every project that her firm did. I went to an open house for one of her projects, and sure enough, tucked over in the lobby seating area was a goofy-looking stuffed rabbit. It had really long legs and big buggy eyes. The clients loved it and left it there, and it attracted a lot of comments from visitors that day. Instead of sending the typical plant to her open houses, she sent these signature quirky little gifts. It could be a piece of art on the wall, or an accessory, or a fabric that they put on a chair, but there was always the quirky reminder of that designer and her firm.

That piece of her brand helped tell customers that this was a creative person with a sense of humor. She might not have been ideal for the customer looking for a traditional space with wing chairs and wood moldings, but she and her firm met the need of another market niche that appreciated their creativity and fun approach to their work.

> **● Important!**
>
> The marketing plan gives you a focus on where you need to go to sell you to customers who will appreciate what you have.

There are always people we love to work with, and others that we work with because we have to. Our fond memories are of the ones we make that special connection with. There are bankers and CPAs, people who are very detail-oriented, and who love to work with that same slow-process, thorough kind of person. They are attracted to people like them. There are all kinds of people who look for all types of different features and traits when it comes to hiring designers. Having a clear brand is just another

247

way to put yourself – the real you – out there for customers to find.

There is no good or bad, right or wrong about this. There is someone for everyone. It's finding the best fit for you and for the customer. They just want to know that you understand them and that you're going to get their job done. But they also want to know that they're working with somebody they're compatible with. Selling your personal brand lets customers have a better idea of who you really are and how you can be of help to them. It's your opportunity to say, "Hey, this is who I am; let's get together and make a beautiful project."

Why Branding Is Important to You

You can't assume that people know what we do just by saying that you're a designer, or a decorator, or this person does window treatments. There is so much involved in what we do that few customers can get their arms around it all. We all know that most clients don't have a clue what goes into putting together a project board. They have no clue how long it takes to select a wall covering or a fabric.

> ### Did You Know?
> By basing your brand and marketing on you – you won't have to work so hard, because you won't have to put on an unnatural professional persona.

And no two of us design or decorate a space in the same way or have the same approach to getting the job done. What you want to do is show these potential customers that you're different. And they want to know far more than the specific services you have to offer them – they want to know about you.

By basing your brand and marketing on you – you won't have to work so hard. Life is too short to have to go out and put on some unnatural professional persona every time you go to meet a client. Wouldn't you rather find the client that would be okay if you showed up in a pair of jeans and a poncho, and just kind a hung back a little bit? Couldn't you be a bit more creative if you were more relaxed and natural? I sure could.

There are customers out there who don't mind that casual approach, and having them find you just makes it better for us to work with people who are like us: people who appreciate the way we work and the unique things we bring to their projects.

It just makes life easier. And it makes the customer's life easier. People who like you are more likely to value you more, and spend more money with you, and that to me is an end goal for anybody who's in business.

People who are very similar to you, or at least people who have an appreciation for what makes you unique, are your ideal customers. You might get a person who is that stodgy banker, that CPA, who really just wants to have some fun in his life even if it is only the designer. Wouldn't it be great for them to just have somebody (me) come over to the house, or their office, we talk about their project, and I can relax and be a little bit more myself. We're not looking for dates here. We're just looking for strong personal business experiences and relationships.

Remember that you're not the only designer in your neighborhood, city, state, region, country, or the world. You're not the only window treatment specialist in those areas either. It's important to find ways to set ourselves apart with that strong personal brand. Or, if you have a bigger company, then your company brand.

> **Great Tip!**
>
> People who are very similar to you, or at least people who have an appreciation for what makes you unique, are your ideal customers.

Say a customer or potential customer calls on the phone and says, "I want this," and you know you're not *this*. Wouldn't it be great to tell them that you're really not the person to help them, but you know somebody else who can? When we start out in business, we think that we can't turn down anybody. The longer we're in business, the more we know about bumps in the road, and the more bad clients and people we work with who drive us crazy.

Looking back, it's easy to see now that they probably weren't really bad clients – we just didn't mesh. We just didn't have what they were looking for. It's ideal if we can sit back and say, "Look, this is what I've got to offer, this is who I am; does that work for you? If so, great; if not, let me help you find someone better for your needs." It's about making the market adapt to you.

We don't want to work with absolutely everybody. We could probably all come up with a list in 10 seconds of five people that we hope we would never have to work with again, and could quickly make a list of two or three reasons why. We could then sit there and say, Well, no wonder I didn't like that job/client – I absolutely hate that type of person or that type of work.

249

It's like defining what we want our business to be. Too often, we're so far into our careers before we even think about doing this. We think of marketing as only placing ads in newspapers or magazines. That's not what marketing is about. Marketing is about using a multi-channel approach, finding the channels that work for you and the ones that don't. As far as I'm concerned, the biggest waste of money is print ads for designers. Unless you've got a ton of money and you can do them over and over again, you can't get that 7 to 15 repetitions about you and your firm out in front of people. That's how many times a customer needs to see your name before they remember it as a top-of-mind resource.

Great Tip!

Marketing is about using a multichannel approach, finding the channels that work for you and the ones that don't.

That one ad is going to be one static piece that doesn't change to meet the needs of different customers. Thankfully, the Internet is making that easier to do advertising. The Internet also makes it easier for us to get out there and market ourselves on small budgets. You can put a website up for a couple thousand dollars or less, and as long as you keep it up to date, and have good relevant content on it, people will keep coming back.

It used to be the Web 1.0 world that we lived in. Everyone thought, Oh, good, I'll put my brochure online. Well, that was still just a static piece, but now it was on my computer. Then, consumers took to the Internet, but wanted to be more interactive relative to the people they do work with. They wanted to get in touch with this person or company. They wanted to talk to them or at least communicate with them before they decided to buy. They wanted to ask questions and get answers. This was the beginning of the Web 2.0 world.

Now, customers don't want to just look at Web pages anymore. Now, we've got people in the Web 3.0 world who not only want to be in touch and interactive, they want to tell you what to do and how to do it. So, finding ways to control your marketing in an Internet-focused world, and having a personal brand, "this is me" approach, is great. You meet people who really appreciate it. I'm on Twitter with a lot of people, but I've got two or three people who will routinely send me messages like "I really like your humor," and I think, "Well, at least it's coming through to those people." Those are the people I am attracted to, and I hope to attract them to me.

Taking On the "Right" Kind of Customers

At times like these, when you start targeting certain customer groups, you sort through the customers, and you make notes. You don't ever want to work with *this* person again, or you call another person up and you tell them you really enjoyed working with them. "You were a great customer. We worked well together. You gave me a lot of excellent input; we bounced ideas around and did some great things. Please recommend me to your friends." You know, their friends are probably a lot like they are. So, what you want to do is start building a group, or a community, or a tribe of those customers that appreciate you for what you are. In our careers we are all going to go through times when we get customers that we don't want. So, why not focus on getting the ones we do want?

You know the scenario: Everything seemed fine when they signed the contract, and then two weeks later, you were sitting there asking what you had gotten yourself into. "How do I get myself out of this? How fast can I get this project done and move on?" Eventually, you do move on, but you still have to pay the bills, so you have to take on some less-than-perfect customers. I'm not telling anybody not to take a customer if you know your mortgage is due, for heaven's sake. That doesn't make any sense at all. But that doesn't mean you can't work as yourself as often as possible.

> **Beware!**
>
> Even when working with less than ideal clients, be sure to be true to your own personal brand.

You can bring your personal brand to it, and that customer may appreciate it, and if they don't, they can go someplace else the next time. So long as you're putting yourself out there, you're being authentic. You're giving them the best that you can give them, based on what they've given you, what their budget is, and you do the best you can under the circumstances. You work with those people and you move on. I know when you first start out, you definitely think you can't possibly turn a customer down. But you become older and you become wiser, and endure the bumps and the bruises that come with being in any profession. You'll come to a point one day, the "Aha!" moment will occur, and the harps and angels will come. You'll realize, "I don't have to work with this person. It's going to be far more trouble than it's worth. It's going to cost me a fortune in aspirin and Rolaids. I'm going to let this one go. They're not my ideal customer."

Action Item!

Give yourself permission to fire a client (or not take her from the start).

So, instead of taking that customer on, that in your gut you know isn't a customer that's aligned with your personal brand, and not the perfect type of customer for you, it's okay to pass, to say, "No, thank you." Instead, it's okay to start thinking about other marketing activities that you can be doing that are more aligned with your personal brand.

Do You Have to Take On a Client Who Goes against Your Brand?

Remember that saying that the good Lord never slams the door unless He opens a window? You know there are other things you can do to find the customers you need. If you're in a desperate situation, and some person comes to the door and has a check, you may have to back off a little bit and do that project. What it does not mean is that you have to get off the road of your personal brand. That's your focus. That's where you want to go. That's what you want people to see about you. Do the job, pay the rent, and then get back on track looking for the right clients.

Turning down unwanted customers is not going to be fun, but it happens. We all know there are people who don't know what the service should cost. You know they are going to be a pain to work with, but they really want you on their project. You understand what your value is, and you charge accordingly. The more stressful the job will be, the more your fee should be. If customers are willing to pay that higher amount, you need to think hard about it to make sure you're going to make enough to offset the stress and headaches. It's one of those situations where you know it happens, but if the client is willing to pay you that much money, you know you can afford the aspirin and the Rolaids it takes to get through the job.

Developing a Brand in Partnership

To develop a brand in a partnership, you need to mesh the personalities and the skills. Instead of having a one single personal brand statement, you would have a combined statement of what you both bring as a firm. The best thing to do when you are looking for a partner or when you're

252

hiring employees is to hire or partner to your weaknesses. Whatever your personal strengths are, don't hire somebody else who does the same things well. Hire somebody who does something that you don't like to do or something that you're not very good at so that you can balance each other out.

To brand your partnership, come up with a meshing of the brand components for your company. It is best to do this before you take that step to hire employees, because then the brand of the company has been set to meet your and your partner's personalities. You then have a strong basis for growing the company and your brand.

If you take that same brand statement we talked about earlier – say one of the partners has a great sense of humor and the other one is the really smart one – you can still have a funny and intelligent design "team" that pushes the envelope.

> **Important!**
>
> The best thing to do when you are looking for a partner or when you're hiring employees is to hire to your weaknesses.

It's just a matter of working through the process, jotting down the concept responses – when you write down your key attributes, just look at the ones that match and the ones that don't, and decide how you can capitalize on this. Maybe both partners have great senses of humor, but only one is a detail person who gets the job done.

What you're doing is building your brand around the fact that you're a team and the team provides these benefits for your customers. When you start getting into who will be your target market, then, obviously, that's probably going to be the same niche unless you became partners for the express purpose of getting into a new market area based on their experience. Your business attributes can be handled the same way, meshed, or they can just complement each other. Ideally, you can capitalize by using the best of both partners to build the brand.

Using Focus Groups in Brand-Building

We talked earlier about getting outside opinions and perspectives to help in developing your personal brand. The easiest way is to use a few focus groups of friends and colleagues. The Internet and email work great for gathering data from your groups. This is how we do much of our communicating these days anyway, so why not for brand-building?

> ## 🔵 Action Item!
>
> If you want good, sufficient feedback, you'll need 8 to 10 responses. So, send out your message to about 15 people.

I have friends through my ASID involvement who I spent years with and who probably got to know me better than some of my family. I was able to just send an email out to about a dozen of them, telling them that I was working on a personal brand. "Will you help me by answering these few questions and returning it to me by next Friday?" I do advise that you make up a list and send it out to more people than you would like to hear from, because some won't answer – they're busy or just forget.

If you want good, sufficient feedback, you'll need 8 to 10 responses. So, send out your message to about 15 people. That way, when a few people aren't able to respond within your timeframe, you will still get a good number of responses. If you just go to 1 or 2 people, you won't get as much input. Remember, you are looking for feedback that includes your key characteristics, skills, and attributes. The smaller number of responses may not be enough to show you a clear pattern.

When you get your feedback, it likely won't be a clear picture and will require some fine tuning. You may receive broadly differing opinions for your key characteristics or business attributes. For instance, when I worked on my brand, I sent out my entire full page list of business attributes to get their minds working, but asking them to send only three that they best feel reflect the way I work in a business setting. On that list, there are terms that some might see as similar, like honest, ethical and trustworthy. So, pick one that you feel sums up those similar attributes and list only that. Try not to skew the feedback.

When you start seeing repetition of the same key words by a number of people, you know that your perception and their perceptions are pretty close. That's when you start saying: "Okay, this looks like one of my key terms; I should use it." Try to tweak the terms to the point that you've got no more than three. Trying to put more into a succinct sentence can be a challenge. Don't feel that you need to use those exact words in the statement; it's the essence of what they mean, after all.

Everything that we do is part of you being a business person, even if it's just going out on Saturday afternoon shopping. What if you run into a customer? What if you run into a customer you've been trying to see and you're in a pair of cut-off jeans, a tank top, and flip-flop sandals? Would that reflect your professional brand?

You almost need to live your brand – if your brand is truly based on an authentic you, and you think like a professional. Even in those times that you're running out to pick up cough syrup for your kids, or milk and bread at the grocery store, you need to make sure when you go out there that you're presenting yourself professionally so that you're not going to be embarrassed with anybody that you run into.

Certainly everything is in the mix – any brand that's based on you is going to have an aesthetic side. If you aesthetically are a cut-offs and tank-top type of person, somehow or another you need to find clients who are okay with that. Clients who can still see you as a professional in spite of the fact that you've got on a pair of cuts-offs, flip-flops, and a tank top. Something to think about.

> **Remember!**
>
> Everything that you do is part of you being a business person, even if it's just going out on Saturday afternoon shopping.

I'm sure there are people out there who can do that. Hopefully some of them have enough money to hire you. Which could be an issue, but that doesn't mean you need to run out to pick up bread and milk in an Armani suit, either. It's just a matter of your wanting people to see you as a professional, to see you as a business person. So you need to, even in the off times, present yourself in that manner.

It is always good to throw these issues up against somebody else, because we're very focused on what we are and what we think we are. The whole idea is to find out what the world is seeing. We may think we're doing one thing and it is being perceived and accepted on the other end as something entirely different.

Remember: You are asking people to help you, to come up with at least their opinions. There is nothing that says "I swear to you I will use every word you send back to me in my personal brand." You're just using them as a filter in your process. You've already answered the questions yourself and decided at some level that "this is what I think I am, what I am selling and presenting to the public, to my potential customers, and to customers I already have."

If you're going to say, "My personal brand is that I'm easy-going and I get along," and 25 of your subcontractors send something back that says, "You're a real pain in the butt, you're unreasonable, you've got a short temper, blah, blah, blah," that's one of those *Whoa!* moments. Something is not aligned with what you want your brand to be and what it seems to be from the outside looking in. If you want your personal brand to be this, you're going to have to make some adjustments to align their opinions with your own.

Beware!

Asking people to share their honest opinions of you is a humbling but necessary process in developing a well-defined personal brand.

As I mentioned, there are good personal brands and there are not so good personal brands. If you go through this process and you find out that your personal brand is not that great after all, you pretty much have two choices. You can either fix it, or if it's really that bad, you might have to move and start over someplace else where people don't know all those negative things about you, which could be expensive.

Going through this process is helpful. Even the people who tell you the things you don't want to hear have helped you. Because – there are people out there who just think they're wonderful and helpful, but then find 25 people who find those same people pushy. That's a whole different perception. So, coming up with those attributes that you have selected and cross-checking them with other people is certainly well worth the time.

How is this process different than the survey that somebody would send out at the end of the job to the customer?

Generally, that survey would ask, "Did you like the work? Did we do what you wanted? Were your expectations met?" In that situation, you are asking more for project satisfaction information. Your branding survey is more about people and how they personally perceive you in several different aspects. But with this survey, you're saying, "Hey, here I am; get the knife. I'm asking you as a customer and as a friend to help me see myself better and see what my brand is."

256

What Should I Ask in My Survey?

For my own survey, I did a brief introduction telling my colleagues what I was doing and asking them for their unvarnished opinions to help me develop my personal brand. Then I just listed the brand concepts: characteristics, business attributes, and personal style. You don't have to ask them about your skills unless you think it will be helpful for you. If you do ask about skills, some of them might feel that this is simply your education and what you learned through the workplace.

Give them examples of what you're looking for. "When you think about me, what characteristics do you think best describe me?" It's as simple as that. They'll say "you're funny" or "you're friendly" or "you're driven." For the business attributes, I developed a list and sent that out with the surveys, and asked if they would please pick three to five that they felt were good descriptions of me in a business situation. You can ask them something like "What would you say my great skills are in this business?" And you may find the answers crossing lines with the business attributes a bit.

When you ask about skill perceptions, the simpler you can do this, the better. It's not rocket science, after all. If it's long and involved and difficult, they won't do it. Especially with customers, if they don't want to fill out the survey, you may need to call them and do it on the phone.

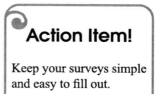

Action Item!

Keep your surveys simple and easy to fill out.

How Can I Get My Focus Group to Answer Honestly?

I set up the woman who does my newsletters and my PR to receive responses to my surveys anonymously for me. She received them all at her email address, compiled them, and passed them on to me. It gave some people a level of comfort that I didn't see their specific responses. This way they feel they can say whatever they need to and not be embarrassed by it or think they're going to hurt my feelings. I also specifically said that I wanted the good, the bad, and the ugly. I said, "I'm not asking somebody to tell me nice things about myself; I don't need that. I really need to know what your perceptions are on all of these things."

257

If your brand is if truly based on you and your uniqueness, it shouldn't change over time unless you drastically change. It is what it is.

When you start working to market your brand – whether you work with a graphic designer or someone else – give them your brand statement and say, "This is my personal brand. This is what this brochure needs to say about me. Regardless of the content we put in the brochure, or regardless of the content that goes on my website, it has to show this brand. And if that means humor needs to show, don't come back to me with it printed in some stodgy old font. And don't do it in dark colors that we always refer to the classic banker colors: maroon, navy, and green. I need something that's light. I need something that shows that I'm a friendly, funny person."

It's the same thing when you're doing your logo. What does your logo look like? I've been to a couple of seminars over the years where they would ask everybody to take out their business card and trade it with the person next to them. Ideally you're next to someone that you don't know from Adam. Then we ask, "Okay, tell me what this business card says about me." Nine times out of ten, it was nothing at all like which that person actually was.

🔊 Remember!

If your brand is if truly based on your uniqueness, it shouldn't change over time unless you drastically change.

Or, you get that card that somebody ordered from a Walter Drake catalog. You know the one – black ink on white lightweight cardstock, in script. They ask, "What does this say about me?" *Cheap. Lack of creativity. No imagination.* It says all sorts of things that this person didn't want to be putting out about themselves.

You may want to ask in a more specific way: "What does this tell you about me in terms of graphics, materials, the font, and the colors?" Very often it's never anywhere near what they hoped it would say about them. Maybe they liked it at the time, thought it looked good, and so they ordered them. They liked the color; the logo was kind of cool. But does it represent you as a person? Does it represent your brand?

In Summary: 3 Action Steps

Let me end with the words of my favorite philosopher, Ziggy. He said "Even the little guy can cast a big shadow, once he's found his place in the sun." That's exactly what your personal brand can do for you – cast a big shadow and help you find your place in the sun. It will make you stand out among the rest.

To get started on personal branding, follow these three action steps:
1. Do your branding survey.
2. Set up focus groups of family and close friends, and customers and business colleagues like architects, contractors and subcontractors that work with you.
3. Finally, work through the process, and develop that personal brand statement and put it to work for you.

ABOUT THE AUTHOR

Terri Maurer
Nearly three decades in the interior design arena coupled with nearly as many years in leadership positions at local and national levels with The American Society of Interior Designers culminated in Maurer's election as national President for 2001. Following completion of a B.A. degree in Interior Design, she added extensive training in speaking and presentation skills, leadership, coaching and mentoring skills, and strategic and futures scenario planning. This combination of skills positioned Maurer to work with interior design firms to recognize business challenges and focus on strategic solutions, and to work with the industry/supply side of the interior design profession, assisting suppliers in situational analysis and strategy development to help capture the interior design market segment.

Speaking and training seminars on business topics, personal branding customer experience, and generational diversity have been developed by Maurer and presented across the U.S. and in Canada at major industry trade shows and for related professional organizations. Included in ASID "Distinguished Speaker Series" 2005–2009, Maurer has written numerous articles for national trade publications as well as being interviewed and quoted in books and magazines on issues related to the interior design profession. She is co-author of *Interior Design in Practice: Case Studies of Successful Business Models,* for Wiley & Sons Publishing. Maurer writes a column on marketing and other business topics for Sources+Design magazine, is author and publisher of *Designing Strategies,* a bi-monthly e-newsletter, and has contributed articles on business and interior design to print publications, websites, and blogs.

11
HOW TO PUT IT ALL TOGETHER AND TAKE IMMEDIATE ACTION FOR FAST RESULTS

by Vita Vygovska
www.vitaliainc.com

In this chapter you'll learn:

** 3 secrets behind setting priorities, so you feel
in control of your time and workload
* The main secret of effective marketing –
and it's not what you think!
* The #1 ingredient for taking massive action*

Congratulations! You'e almost done with the book. And if you've been reading carefully, you've become very knowledgeable about various marketing tactics that make up your overall marketing plan.

What did your marketing plan look like before you started reading the book? For many, it is a mishmash of random activities that aren't clearly defined, that overlap each other, and don't make up a well-rounded plan. Some things get done sometimes when and if there is time for it.

A true marketing plan is comprehensive and balanced. Think of it as your marketing pie. You can see that each marketing activity (and each chapter you've just read) is represented by an individual and equal slice of the pie. What this means is that each activity carries equal importance and therefore must be equally represented in your actions.

But after reading all 10 of the chapters, you may be wondering right now: "How do I create my own marketing pie?" "How do I put it all together? Where do I start? What's important? How do I get it all done?"

That's what this chapter is about. I will answer these and other questions to help you make sense of it all, pull it into a cohesive marketing plan, and spring into action.

Marketing Is the Designer's Number 1 Job

> **Important!**
>
> You are not just in the design business. First and foremost, you are in the business of marketing your design business.

The most important thing I want you to recognize and accept is the very first lesson I learned in all of my marketing classes: You are in the business of marketing. You are in the business of creating and working your own personalized marketing pie.

You may think you are in the business of designing beautiful interiors, staging houses, repurposing owners' furniture, or making beautiful window treatments. Actually, these are the services you provide. They

262

are also your passion. But before you can make your passion available to those in need of it, they have to learn about it, want it, and make a decision to buy it from you. Marketing comes before you can let your passion come through for all to see.

You are in the business of marketing your design services. Without marketing, you will not have clients to give these services to. Educating your prospects about you, making yourself irresistible, and fulfilling your promises IS marketing.

> ## 💧 Remember!
>
> Marketing is a non-negotiable activity!

It is our job as entrepreneurs to continually and methodically educate our clients and prospects about what we do. Nobody else will do it for us. Nobody else has the same stake in it as we do. Nobody cares or knows enough. It is our life, and our "baby." The one word for that process of education is in fact MARKETING.

A college professor of mine, Christine Bell, once said something that I never forgot: "If you're good at marketing, you can sell hammers and nails." What she meant by it is that if we become really good at marketing strategies, if we master the art and science of educating our potential consumers about our services, we can sell anything – even something as boring and seemingly straightforward as hammers and nails. Thankfully our business is so much prettier and more exciting than that!

Marketing is a non-negotiable activity – much like your appointments with your clients, your visits to the design centers, or conference calls with your contractors. These are all the things that you do to move your project forward. In your personal life, brushing teeth and having meals are examples of non-negotiable activities. You need to do them to function and to get through the day. Similarly, you need marketing to make your business function, to get clients, and to make money. Marketing shouldn't be a "should I do it today?" kind of activity. It should be something that you do constantly, weaving it into your every day.

I recommend that you spend at least 50% of your time on marketing. That's what I do, and that's what every successful entrepreneur out there does as well. Unfortunately, many of us remember about marketing only when we suddenly realize that there are no more clients left in the pipeline.

263

Recently, I was attending a seminar at the Philadelphia Marketplace Design Center and started talking to a colleague during the networking session. I asked how things were going and she said, "Great, I've been really busy!" I was so excited for her, but then she said something that really dampened my spirits. She said, "I've been so busy, I don't remember the last time I did my newsletter; I just don't have the time."

Unfortunately, I see that happening quite frequently. Designers get busy with client work and let their marketing go by the wayside. They view it as no longer important, because they are busy for the time being. Or they realize that marketing is important, but they just don't make time for it during their busy periods.

When client work dries up, they scramble and feverishly start networking, calling on potential partners, posting on Facebook, and doing other random marketing activities to drum up the business and fill the pipeline. Of course, had they been doing these activities all along, the pipeline would have never dried up in the first place. That's the power of consistent marketing.

Action Is the Best Prescription for Success

Now that I've convinced you that marketing is your most important job, I'd like to encourage you to take action on everything you've learned in this book. Here, you have everything you need to get more clients (or fewer, but better ones), go on more appointments (or fewer, but better ones), and make more money.

> ## Important!
>
> Taking action is the difference between high-achievers and everybody else.

Taking action is the difference between high-achievers and everybody else. Taking action is what gets you from where you are right now to where you want to be. Taking action is THE ingredient to a successful design business.

As a productivity expert, I always encourage my clients to start taking action immediately – no matter how scared they are, no matter how unfamiliar the situation is, no matter how imperfect the circumstances are. I believe that action is the prescription for overcoming our fears. It is action that builds our experience and confidence.

Looking back at my business and the times when I had to make myself

264

take action, I can't help but recall my very first appointment. I was scared and shaking like a leaf. I still remember my very first customer (Mrs. Riley), the first product (woven woods), and the very first sale amount – a whopping $277.77!

Before meeting her, I found out that she wanted shutters. Of course I brushed up on everything I possibly could about shutters. As many of us know, though, customers say one thing, but the reality often turns out to be completely different – and at the end, we decided to go with woven woods.

The challenge was that at that point (just starting out and not knowing my products that well yet), I didn't know anything about woven woods (and very little about shutters, for that matter). So what were my choices? I could have shriveled up and declined the appointment altogether. I could have gotten scared of the change in product and asked for another meeting. I could have stayed in my office and tried to study and memorize every line of every product binder. I could have done many things, but not grab the opportunity.

> ## Action Item!
>
> Take action because your desire to succeed is just a little bit greater than the fear that holds you back.

I was scared to appear unknowledgeable, to make mistakes, to say the wrong thing, to not get the order, to mess up the measurements…and the list can go on. But I took action, in spite of my fear.

I took action because my desire to succeed was just a little bit greater than the fear that was holding me back. I took action because I believed in my core that after this first experience will come the second one, and it will be just a little less scary.

Looking at my business for the past 5 years, and my whole working experience for the past 15 years, I can confidently say that it is through taking action that I built up the needed confidence to take the next step – whether that next step was the next appointment, a networking event, a big client, or an international telesummit. We can try to study, learn, and read, but it is only through action that we experience the exhilaration of achieving results.

I want you to experience the exhilaration of achieving results, too! I want you to use what you've learned in this book and feel like you've spent your time in the most productive way possible. This productive way is to take action. So here's how to take action based on what you've read here.

2 Steps for Immediate Action

Step 1: Make a comprehensive action list.

If you followed my advice from the "How to Use This Book" section in the beginning, your job of making a comprehensive action list is easy. Just go through your red arrows in the margins and, on a separate sheet, write or type out everything that you deemed actionable while reading.

Action Item!

Make a comprehensive action list – today!

If you skipped my advice in the beginning, here's what I encourage you to do. Get a red pen, and as you read each chapter of the book, put a red arrow in the margin next to a point that you can implement in your business.

Here are some examples of the action points (in no particular order):

- Find a partner with a location where you can make a presentation;
- Create a fan page;
- Create an email signature;
- Host a trunk show;
- Create a real estate program;
- Call your past customers;
- Develop an e-zine;
- Find one upscale neighborhood in which you will consistently and persistently market;
- Decide which groups have the most of your ideal client, and
- calendar all of their networking meetings;
- Create a system of how you will be asking for referrals from every customer;
- Pick one project from the past year and photograph it (even if you're afraid it may not be worthy enough);
- Make a list of your local home and garden magazines;
- Survey your family, friends, and customers about your personal attributes;
- Decide whether a partnership is right for you.

Please know these are just examples of the items that will go onto your comprehensive action list. It's not sorted yet. It's not prioritized. It's not

266

pared down to small chunks. It doesn't have deadlines. It doesn't know whether you're scared. It doesn't care if you don't know how to do it. But it is comprehensive. It is everything you want to accomplish in marketing your business.

By making this comprehensive list, you've taken all the thoughts and ideas out of the book and out of your head, and put them in one central place where you can see them all together. Putting them into a central and tangible place sets you up for the next step.

Your next step is to prioritize the list. But before we move into the priority step, let me ask you. When, in the next two days, will you make your action list? I want you to look at your calendar right now, look for a window of opportunity of about 30 minutes, set that appointment with yourself, and do it. So let me ask you again: "When, in the next two days, will you create your action list?"

Are you feeling the pressure? Maybe a little bit? It's a good thing. Without the sense of urgency, nothing will ever get done. Without a dealine, no project will be finished. When I mentor my clients as part of my GET IT DONE Mentoring Program, I make it a habit to ask them to commit to a specific day for when they'll complete a task. This way they know exactly what they have to do and when they have to do it, and they feel accountable to me for doing it.

Step 2: Prioritize your list.
Now that we have the comprehensive, maybe even scary, action list – now what?

Now we prioritize it. My suggested priority categories for you are these: immediate term, short term, and long term.

A. Immediate priority action items. They are easy. They are fast. You know how to do them. They may be personally interesting and exciting for you. They are no-brainers.

An example of an immediate priority action item would be to create your email signature. You know you should have one, you know it's important, you know it will take you only a few minutes, but you just haven't made time for it because other things got in the way.

Another example of an immediate priority item is calendaring. All of

267

your known commitments, personal or business, should be included in your calendar. I live and die by my calendar and I carry it with me at all times. Everything goes into the calendar, whether it's personal or business: all the client appointments, networking events, seminars, meeting, gym, hair appointments – everything. The calendar keeps me in check, so that I not only know where I'm supposed to be and do, but feel accountable for doing those things that may tend to get forgotten or put off, like going to the gym. For more information on calendaring techniques, check out this great post on my blog at www.vitaliainc. com/blog/2010/02/secret-to-managing-your-calendar-productively/.

Did You Know?

Effective calendaring is one of the keys to success for any designer.

The timing of an immediate priority action item is about one week. So within a week, all your immediate to-do's should be completed. If it seems short, it is! But setting short timelines and aggressive deadlines is what will make you accomplish more in less time.

So your next step is to go through your comprehensive action list, and put an "I" next to the immediate priorities. Sort your total list so that all "I's" are grouped together – this becomes your sub-list. Pick a time in the next week, and tackle each item, one at a time, one after another.

Again, I want to ask you: "When, during the next week, will you embark on your immediate to-do list?" Take a look at your calendar for next week right now, find a window of opportunity, and schedule this appointment with yourself. Now. You'll see how great it feels to get so much done in one sitting!

B. Short-term priority action items. Your short-term priorities take a bit longer to accomplish, they may be more complex, and they may require planning and research.

How do you decide which items are more important than others? In other words, within this group of priority, how do you prioritize it even further? Here are the criteria I use and advise my clients, as part of my mentoring program.

I. Which activity will cost the least and bring the biggest result?
II. Which one have I been wanting to do for a long time?
III. Which one can I execute consistently?

A great example of a short-term priority is doing your email newsletter (e-zine). You know you must have one, because it is one of the most effective follow-up systems you can have in place for your business. It will cost you very little, and the payback is enormous. You've been wanting to do it, but again life got in the way, and it's been on the back burner for some time now. This is your perfect candidate as the short-term priority action item.

Your next step is to go through your comprehensive list and mark your short-term priorities with an "S". This sub-list should take you about 30 to 60 days to accomplish. The best way to make sure that you actually do it is to follow this simple plan.

a. Set an appointment in your calendar. You can see that I'm really big on setting these business appointments with yourself. I believe that unless a task gets into your calendar and you dedicate time to it, it will keep getting postponed and ultimately get done much later than needed. b. Create a plan of action. Your plan is nothing more than a sequence of steps with time assigned to each step. So for our example of an e-zine, your plan may look like this:
- Research an e-zine service. I use and recommend www.ConstantContact.com. 15 minutes.
- Review and decide on the template. 15 minutes.
- Decide on the type of sections you will have. 10 minutes.
- Rework the template to fit your colors, design elements, and overall feel. 60 minutes.
- Write copy for each section. 60–120 minutes.
- Find images to use (if any). 10 minutes.
- Import copy and images into the template. 30 minutes.
- Check it over again and publish. 10 minutes.
- Your first issue is done!

c. Work your plan. Resist interruptions and commit to finishing it. This means switching off your phone, turning off your email, not thinking about "what to make for dinner," not doing laundry, etc. Focus on your task at hand.

One of the well-known techniques to work faster is to use an egg timer – there is just something about that clicking sound that makes us focus, speed up, and get things done. The feeling that you're going for is the same one that you get before going on vacation – you know that feeling of controlled intensity, in which you get more done in a short time than you did the entire prior week.

269

For me, a big productivity lesson came after I had my baby. Anyone who has kids remembers that you get 60–90 minutes of "free" time during their naps. My baby's nap was my start and finish time – and there were no but's or if's about it. I had a very finite amount of time to finish my project, or it wasn't getting done. And not getting done just wasn't an option.

> **Great Tip!**
>
> When not getting it done is not an option, you have to let go of perfectionism.

d. It doesn't have to be perfect! But it has to be done. You've read it in this book before, but it begs repeating: Don't go for perfection, or you'll never finish it. Go for about 75–80% and consider it done for the time being.

C. Long-term priority action items. Everything that didn't make it into the immediate and short-term priority lists falls in this list. But long-term doesn't mean never, or someday. It still needs a date. I recommend that you strive to accomplish your long-term list within 90 to 120 days.

A good example of a long-term priority action item may be booking a speaking engagement. So while during the first 60 days you will primarily concentrate on quicker things like your email signature and e-zine (just using these two things as examples – you will of course have much more on your list), you can still start thinking about a speaking engagement.

You can start weaving the idea of speaking engagements into your conversations, using opportunities to make contacts, making notes of possible topics, asking questions, noticing attractive marketing materials, and creating loose plans for making it happen. When you open yourself up to a possibility, your level of awareness rises (much like when you buy a red car, you start noticing all red cars on the road) and the universe starts bringing you clues and answers.

When the time comes to move this task onto your short-term priority list, you won't be starting completely from ground zero, because you will have thought through a lot already.

Those were your three priority categories: immediate, short-term, and long-term. Regardless of when you'll tackle your priorities, they all fall within the marketing pie. It doesn't matter whether you are a seasoned designer or just starting out, the marketing pie doesn't change – what does change is your knowledge and experience with each "slice of the pie." Every designer still needs a plan of action that spans each "slice." When I work with my clients one-on-one, in my GET IT DONE Mentoring Program, that's exactly what we do – together we create their very own personalized action plan, prioritized based on exactly where they are in their business and tailored to their level of experience.

Your prioritized action list is your marketing plan for the next 120 days that will bring more visibility to your business, more clients, and more income.

How to Excel at Executing the Marketing Plan

Now that you have your prioritized marketing plan of action and you know how to chip away at each priority, next question is "How do you become good at it?" One of the ways to be good in marketing is to execute your marketing plan repeatedly, persistently, and consistently.

And three absolute best way to execute your plan repeatedly, persistently, and consistently is to set up systems and processes that support you. Only with systems and processes does your marketing go on autopilot, so that you don't have to reinvent and rethink it every time.

> ### ⦿ Action Item!
>
> Make sure that every activity on your marketing plan has a corresponding process or system to accompany it.

Let's go back to the example of your email newsletter. There are several processes that you can have in place. Process number one is that you can simply outsource the entire task. This book gave you several services that can take care of it for you. Process number two is that you can outsource just the article writing. If you go on www.VitaliaInc.com/resources, you'll find the Done4U pre-written articles that you can start using immediately.

Process number three is that you can take a DYI approach. That's what I do and here is how I do it. I've taken the time to set up the template, where my logo, colors, and sections have been established. I have decided to publish my e-zine on the first Tuesday of every month. So Monday prior, I make sure that I write my personal note and my article. This is my marketing activity that's non-negotiable, it's in the calendar, and it doesn't get derailed by something that might have popped up in the course of the day.

271

Once the content is written, I then send it off to my assistant Michelle, who imports it into the template, adds appropriate images, and makes sure everything lines up correctly. She sends me a test version, I approve, and off it goes. Done. There is no additional thinking involved. No "when should I do it?" and "what am I supposed to do" kind of questions. I know exactly when to do it, how to do it, and who on my team is responsible for doing it. It gets done. That's the power of systems.

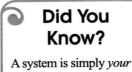

Did You Know?

A system is simply *your* sequence of steps that you always take that gets you from "to do" to "done."

Having a marketing system makes it faster and easier to do things, which leads to quicker results and more fun. When things are easy and fun, it makes you want to do them again and again. And doing a marketing activity repeatedly will make you better at it with every time you do it.

What does a system look like? A system is simply your way of doing a marketing activity (or any activity, for that matter). It is your sequence of steps that you always take that gets you from "to do" to "done." So my example above about my way of getting my e-zine published is my system for getting it done. In my business I have a system for almost everything I do – so I easily have 30 to 40 systems. Here's just a short excerpt from my total list:

- First phone call with a customer
- What happens before I even go see a customer
- During a client appointment
- Measuring
- Taking notes
- What happens after the appointment
- Order processing, tracking, receiving
- Production order with the workroom
- Pick-up process
- How I calendar my appointments
- Organize desk
- Organize car
- Organize fabrics books, trims, samples
- Marketing process
- Process for dealing with mistakes
- Process for checking mail
- Checking email

272

Everything that you do more than once must receive a system. If you've tackled a task already and figured out the best way of accomplishing it, there is no reason to reinvent the wheel all over again. There is no reason to think of the best way to do it again, because you've done it before. It's inefficient to do the same thing twice. It is much more productive to document what you've done originally and simply follow those steps without thinking much about them.

Action Item!

Document your systems. They should be written out for you and everyone else on your team to see and follow.

This brings us to the next very important point. In order to view your systems in a more tangible way, it's important to get them out of your head and onto paper or computer. Your systems should be documented. They should be written out for you and everyone else on your team to see, follow, and simply be on the same page about. You'll also find that if you document your way of doing things, you can easily delegate it to an assistant later or teach someone else how to do it!

A final note about systems. Any system makes you less crazy and overwhelmed. A *good system* makes you really productive. Because a *good system* makes sure that *your way* is the most effective, meaning that it produces highest results in the shortest amount of time. In other words it's not enough to just do something because it's the same way you've always done it. It's important to do it in the best way known.

This is something I concentrate heavily in my work with designer mentoring clients, as part of the GET IT DONE Mentoring Program. Recently, one of my clients complained that her networking efforts where falling flat, even though she dedicated a significant amount of time to it. She did have a system for which networking events she went to and how she followed up afterwards.

After spending some time with her on this topic, it was very evident that her system, although it was great she had one, didn't work as well as it should have. So we devised a plan of action and she became very clear on which events to attend, how many a week to go on, what to do at them, how to reach out to the people she met, how to meet with them again, and how to monetize her efforts. Her system is now solid and effective: She knows exactly what to do without thinking about it. And the best part is that she feels great about it!

I encourage you to look at everything that you do on a daily basis and question whether you're being the most productive. In other words, does *your way* bring you the best results for the amount of time you're spending on it? Do you know what *your way* is? If you don't, dedicate time to think it through. If you are not sure how to do it, enlist help – it's that important. Because once you start operating at the top of your productivity, you will get more done in less time, while working less and enjoying what you do much more.

The 2 Main Ingredients to Getting More Done in Half the Time

As I look back at my business, I believe there are two main things I've implemented that made me more successful than anything else I've done.

Delegating

The number one ingredient is the realization that I can't do it all myself. This one was very difficult for me, as I imagine it is for a lot of designers. Probably much like many others, I've been brought up with the idea that hard work leads to success. I translated it to mean working all the time: in the evenings, on the weekends, during holidays, you name it. If I didn't work, I thought of myself as lazy. The more I worked, the more successful I felt I was being.

Beware!

If you're still holding on to the belief that you can do it all yourself, you will not achieve your highest levels of success possible for you. Accept help, delegate – and watch your results soar.

Of course, one can only sustain that kind of life-style for so long. Eventually you either burn out or realize that it's not the way to a fulfilling life. For me, it was a combination of both, and the realization was a tumultuous soul-searching process.

And while my soul-searching process was a complicated one, in the end, it was simple mathematics that made it very obvious. Even if you worked 24 hours a day, you could only get 24 hours' worth of work done. However, if you brought in an assistant for, say, 10 hours a day, suddenly, you could get 34 hours worth of work done in the same time-frame. Same way that two heads are better than one, two pairs of eyes

274

are better than one, etc. See, simple mathematics!

So the next question is: "What's the best way to find an assistant?" For me, and for hundreds of other entrepreneurs, the answer is Virtual Assistant. A virtual assistant is someone who is located anywhere in world, works out of her own office, and helps you run and manage the business using virtual tools like email, phone, and fax.

My virtual assistant (VA) Michelle has been with me for close to three years. We started very small, with just a few hours a week, and now we are up to almost full-time, depending on the season. She runs my world (business and sometimes personal), and I don't know what I would have done without her.

There are many resources for VA's, and you can see for yourself how vast this world is simply by doing a quick internet search. The two resources that I personally recommend are www.teamdouble-click.com and www.assistU.com.

Here are the criteria to use when deciding what to delegate out.

> ### Did You Know?
> A virtual assistant is someone who is located anywhere inworld, works out of her own office, and helps you run and manage the business using virtual tools like email, phone, and fax.

What doesn't make you money.
Look around your office and ask yourself, "What doesn't bring me money?" An excellent example of this is QuickBooks. Is it important for your business – yes! Is it necessary to make sure it's done – of course! Does it bring you additional business – no!

From personal experience, I know how much time, and most importantly, energy it takes to do your own QuickBooks. I remember when I first started my business, I had great intentions of devoting at least one day a month to making sure all my receipts were entered and invoices were done. Well, this great intention lasted about 2 months. Then I got too busy and the whole thing fell by the wayside. Receipts kept piling up, statements went unreconciled, and my energy level plummeted every time I looked at the heaps of paper I had to process.

You see, I didn't want to do my own quickbooks. I didn't look forward to sitting in front of the computer and entering every little piece of receipt I collected. But most importantly, I understood that for every minute that did it, I didn't get to do my genius work, which in our field is marketing and design work.

So I highly encourage you to find a service who can do your quick-books for you, freeing you up to do what you love to do, from which you draw your energy, and what ultimately brings you your income. This service can be in the form of a VA, and accountant, or special-ized QuickBooks help. Someone who is highly skilled in this area and knowledgeable in our industry is LeeAnn Reed of www.LReedConsult-ing.com – look her up and be sure to tell her that I sent you.

Action Item!

When trying to delegate, ask yourself: "Does it have to be done by me?" And be brutally honest with your answer. It will surprise you.

What doesn't get you new business. As all of us know, administering orders is a highly time-consuming, detailed, and often frustrating part of our business. You know what I'm talking about – it's all the purchase orders that need to be placed after the client has signed the contract.

The business has been consummated. You got the order. Now it has to be managed. PO's need to be placed. Reference numbers recorded. Questions from the vendors answered. Orders followed up on. Tracking numbers checked. This list can go on and on. This is a highly necessary part of our job, because it speaks to the customer service and overall experience that we provide to our clients.

But ask yourself, does it have to be done by you? Does it bring you any additional business? The answers to these questions, if you're really honest with yourself, are "no, it doesn't." So what this means is that it can be delegated to your trusted assistant so that you can spend your time on your genius work again, which, you remember, is marketing and design work.

What can be systematized. You'll remember how we said earlier that anything that you do more than once deserves a system. It's a good idea to document your systems so that you can easily and quickly teach someone else to do it and delegate it to them for the future.

Many of my marketing activities run on a system that's been tested, proven, and ingrained into the interworkings of my company. One such system is the "staying in touch" vehicles that I use with my clients, such as postcards.

276

In the earlier days of my business, I remember gathering the whole family around the kitchen table, pulling out stacks of customer files, manually hand-writing each card, addressing and stamping each envelope, and schlepping hundreds of cards to the post office. It sure was a system and it served its purpose, and we had fun. But as my business grew, it obviously became ineffective.

So nowadays I use a service called www.sendoutcards.com to design, print, and mail my cards. My system works so that I only approve the card, write the message, and supply the inside image – everything else is done by my VA Michelle. She searches the database for appropriate cards, suggests suitable verbiage, imports all graphics and text into the software, exports the database, places the order, and deals with issues. You see, there is a sequence of steps, and I could easily do it myself, but I choose not to. Not because I can't. But because it's been systematized to the point where Michelle can easily handle it, freeing me to concentrate on my genius work: marketing and design work.

For my GET IT DONE Mentoring Program, my system works so that I review each application that is submitted. Once it's approved, Michelle takes over the process where the mentee is notified of being accepted into the program, sends them their action binder, sets up their call-in times, and answers their administrative questions. What it does for me is frees me up for my genius work – in this case my capacity to be present, supportive, and knowledgeable for my mentees.

And since we are on the topic of a mentoring program, it actually serves as a great segue to the next ingredient, getting more done in half the time.

Getting a Mentor

> ## ◉ Action Item!
>
> Get a mentor! Having a good mentor is your ticket to getting more done in half the time.

Ingredient number two is a good mentor. When I first started my business, I didn't have anyone to look up to or guide me in the entrepreneurial world. Truthfully, I didn't think I needed anyone. I came from the corporate world, and thought that if I could make it there, I could make it anywhere.

As you can imagine, I quickly realized that owning your own business, especially a decorating business, is much different than having a traditional job. So many times it felt very lonely, frustrating, and exhausting.

After working 70-hour weeks almost every week during the first year, I realized that something needed to change. One of the first changes that I made was I got mentors.

Fast-forward to today. I continually read self-improvement books, go to conferences, and listen to marketing and inspirational CD's in my car. I also currently work with a personal mentor, who kicks my butt, holds me accountable, and steers me in the right direction.

A good mentor sees your blind sides. She "fills in" where you are weak. She pushes you forward, especially when times get tough. She sees your potential, even if you're not able to see it yet. She celebrates your successes with you!

What can the right mentor do for you?

> **◉ Important!**
>
> Just like you are a mentor to your clients, moving them along their decorating project, you need a mentor who can move you along your own business path.

Think about your own client work. In a way, you're a mentor for your clients. You see design solutions that they are not able to see for themselves. You push them to take design risks because you know those will pay off and because the clients will never take them on their own. You see the potential of their rooms, way before they'll ever recognize it.

You believe in yourself as the right mentor for your clients. You believe you're worth the price and encourage your customers to invest in themselves. So I encourage you to "walk your own talk" and invest in your own mentor.

You can't afford NOT to. You know it first-hand, that only with someone else's help can one truly achieve what's really possible. Doing it on your own will get you marginal results, but surely will not propel you forward to where you deserve to be.

My GET IT DONE Mentoring Program has three levels, and you can always check out which one is right for you at www.GetItDoneProgram.com. What you get with a good mentoring program is priceless, and here's my attempt to list some of the benefits.

1. Focus. No longer will you feel overwhelmed by the amount of information. No longer will you wonder what you should and should not be doing. Laser-focus on your goals and results is what will move you forward. Laser-focus is what you will gain immediately in this program.

2. Clarity. Being clear on who you are, what your business is, what makes you unique, what your goals are, and how to achieve them will position you perfectly for massive action. Confusion about those things will paralyze you. A good mentoring program helps you get crystal clear on your USP (unique selling proposition) and your marketing plan of action for maximum results. No longer lost and wandering, you will have the exact course of action to follow and execute.

3. Priority. Without priorities, everything comes crashing down on us. Knowing your priorities makes your plans peaceful, composed, professional, and most importantly, possible. When you know what one thing will bring you the best results, your life gains a new meaning. A good mentor is there by your side every step of the way to coach "that one thing out of you."

> ## Did You Know?
> Among many benefits of having a mentor, accountability is perhaps the most important one!

4. Accountability. You are accountable to your mentor. She holds you responsible for your promises and actions. She is there by your side, working through your challenges, asking tough questions, "holding your feet to the fire," and pushing you to stretch yourself, even in uncomfortable situations. She is your loving but firm friend eho pulls the best out of you so that you experience rapid financial growth doing what you love. Much like you do this very thing for your clients in the design realm, I will do it for you in the business realm.

5. Knowledge and expertise. When you're unsure what to do and how to do it, your mentor is there to walk you through it. As someone who has been in your shoes and has grown her business from ground zero, and as an MBA, a corporate marketing fugitive, and a highly successful entrepreneur and decorator, I personally answer my mentees' marketing questions and walk them through the marketing maze.

6. Thoughts, Action, Results. Positive thoughts lead to strong actions, which lead to powerful results. I want to see you take action, immediate action, so you can celebrate fast results. That's my focus and my goal for you.

279

7. **Power and Control.** You will start feeling differently about yourself and your business. Springing into action unleashes a powerful state of being that's unparallel to anything else. It quite an experience. And it's amazing! You will finally be in control. You will finally feel in charge of your life and your business.

Whether you mentor with me through my www.GetItDoneProgram. com or with someone else, one thing I know for sure: Getting a mentor accelerated my business growth, and it will do the same for you!

In Summary: 3 Action Steps

1. Schedule time in the next two days to make an action list and prioritize it.
2. Get a virtual assistant (VA) – start with a few hours and grow from there. You'll see how empowering and addictive delegating really is.
3. Get a mentor – and really propel yourself forward.

ABOUT THE AUTHOR

Vita Vygovska is the owner of Vitalia Inc, an MBA, and a window treatment and productivity expert. She is known for her no-excuses attitude to running a design business and getting things done, fast. A very successful entrepreneur, she's worked with countless clients, who are amazed at her organization, discipline, professionalism, creative marketing, and the ability to accomplish great results in a short amount of time. Vita's resources for designers include special reports, CD's, articles, and 1-on-1 coaching programs.

Vita is a high-energy speaker and mentor who bases her content on knowledge, experience, and proven systems. She delivers specific and actionable advice that designers can implement immediately. Even more, she empowers them to take action by showing practical marketing solutions to grow their business. To check out her programs, products, and free resources, including the free CD "101 Design Ideas for Beautiful Windows," visit www.VitaliaInc.com.

280

SPECIAL OFFER!
FREE CD Order Form

As my way of saying Thank You for reading this book, I am delighted to send you a special audio CD: "7 Habits of Highly Successful Designers." Worth $29.90, it is yours FREE (just a small S&H fee of $4.90 per CD).

On this valuable CD, you'll learn:
- #1 limiting belief that's holding you back and how to overcome it starting today
- 3 simple secrets to achieve maximum success, and stay on track every day
- The most important thing you must do today, to achieve a different result tomorrow

3 ways to order:
On the web: www.VitaliaInc.com/7Habits.html
By fax: 866-572-3285
By phone: 267.234.7174
By mail: Vitalia Inc., 44 Parkview Way, Newtown, PA 18940

Please print clearly

- -

ORDER FORM
Name _____
Address _____
_____
Phone _____
Email _____
Fax _____
Payment Type: **Check** _____ **Credit Card: Visa/MC** _____
Cc# _ _ _ _ - _ _ _ _ - _ _ _ _ - _ _ _ _
Exp. Date _____ **Qty.** _____ **Amount $** _____
Signature_____

- -

Please note: You will also receive Curtain Call for Designers – my monthly e-mail newsletter filled with tips, hints, news, and notes for stress free and productive design business. If you loved reading this book, you will love additional tips that will help you run a profitable and productive business. We never rent or sell our mailing list. If you decide that it is not for you, feel free to unsubscribe any time.

Breinigsville, PA USA
03 February 2011
254796BV00005B/1/P